12.50

This title is essential t   Reform
Jewish collection. Re
a replacement can be

D0000230

Choices in Modern Jewish Thought

A PARTISAN GUIDE

Eugene B. Borowitz

Behrman House, Inc., New York

© Copyright 1983 by Eugene B. Borowitz
Published by Behrman House, Inc.,
1261 Broadway, New York, N.Y. 10001

Library of Congress Cataloging in Publication Data

Borowitz, Eugene B.
  Modern varieties of Jewish thought.

  1. Judaism—20th century—Addresses, essays, lectures. I. Title.
BM565.B67   296.3'09'04   82-4443
ISBN 0-87441-343-5   AACR2

MANUFACTURED IN THE UNITED STATES OF AMERICA

As we celebrate
the Bar/Bat Mitzvah year of
Sh'ma,
a journal of Jewish responsibility

I wish to pay tribute to three friends, without whom it could not have been founded or maintained in its devotion to the virtues of Jewish pluralism despite our serious differences of opinion on political, social and religious issues.

SEYMOUR SIEGEL,   MICHAEL WYSCHOGROD
and, in particular, to
ARNOLD JACOB WOLF

Contents

PREFACE

PART I *Setting the Context*   1

1 The Challenge of Modernity to Judaism   3

PART II *The Six Systematized Positions:*
Rationalistic Models   27

2 Neo-Kantianism: HERMANN COHEN   29
3 Religious Consciousness: LEO BAECK   53
4 Nationalism: the Zionist Interpretation
of Judaism   75
5 Naturalism: MORDECAI KAPLAN   98

PART III *The Six Systematized Positions:*
Non-rational Models   121

6 The Pioneer Existentialist: FRANZ ROSENZWEIG   123
7 Religious Existentialism: MARTIN BUBER   141
8 Neo-Traditionalism: ABRAHAM HESCHEL   165

PART IV   *The Contemporary Agenda*   185
9 Confronting the Holocaust   185
10 A Theology of Modern Orthodoxy:
    RABBI JOSEPH B. SOLOVEITCHIK   218
11 The Crux of Liberal Jewish Thought:
    Personal Autonomy   243

PART V   *A Concluding Reflection*   273
12 Facing up to the Options in Modern Jewish
    Thought   275

A BASIC READING LIST   291
INDEX   297

Preface

In few other periods have so many important, divergent theories of Judaism been proposed as in the twentieth century. This book celebrates the achievement of the thinkers who responded to the unprecedented challenge modernity issued to Jewish faith. Other ages have, without doubt, been intellectually troubled; few have known the depth and range of the difficulties modern Jews confront. Large numbers in our community doubt God's existence, are skeptical about the revelation of the Torah, and cannot believe that the Jewish people has a unique role in human history. Not since rabbinic Judaism became the accepted standard for Jewish living has so great a proportion of our community been unobservant of the law, ignorant of our heritage, and only mildly discontented with such minimal Jewishness.

Many practical efforts have been made to rectify this situation: better education, the beautification of religious services, group involvement, community organization and political activism. These set the positive patterns of everyday Jewish life. They produce the facts which we hope will one day be the basis of our place in Jewish history. As the stuff of our Jewish existence, they are reasonably well known, carefully observed and often commented upon.

The intellectual efforts to respond to our troubling situation, being abstract and academic, remain in the background of Jewish self-consciousness if they are present at all. To many, the last significant Jewish philosophy or theology—I shall use the terms loosely and interchangeably—was produced by Maimonides and his contemporaries. People who hold this view assume that knowing the Jewish intellectual classics of the Middle Ages or the Talmud (from an earlier period) equips one to fashion a philosophy of Judaism that will speak to our situation. They do not appreciate the unique difficulties which modern science and culture raise for all religions and particularly for a minority faith. Yet Philo mastered Hellenistic thought to expound Judaism to his first-century contemporaries in Alexandria,

ix

Saadiah Gaon in the ninth century reacted to the Kalam philosophy
of Islam, and Maimonides later utlized the newly rediscovered ideas
of Aristotle. These efforts were undertaken to make Judaism intelligible within the context of a particular time and place. Clearly, the
responsibility inherent in this chain of Jewish theological tradition
did not disappear some centuries ago.

Modern Jews have had an unusually creative group of philosophic
pioneers. Though their names are not well known to the masses of
Jews, their ideas provided the framework by which modern Jews have
thought about their Judaism and, often, the patterns by which they
have chosen to live it. To this day the sermons and lectures and
magazine articles and popular books which make up the bulk of
American Jewish intellectuality, derive from six main streams of
thought. The thinkers who created these generative systems deserve
to be better known. Their ideas deserve the compliment of being
directly confronted rather than communicated through the teaching
of disciples' disciples, who may no longer know the source of their
fervent proclamations. Besides, for those who enjoy good thinking,
the conceptual elegance of our great modern philosophers is itself a
source of much pleasure. Studying them, even when one disagrees
with what they propounded, stimulates one to think more keenly
about one's own Judaism. If we desire to transcend them, we must
first rise to their level of cultural sophistication and Jewish commitment.

Happily, I have been able to spend much of my life working in the
discipline of contemporary Jewish thought. I have had personal contact with five of the thinkers whose work has been significant enough
to be discussed at chapter length. I also continue to be involved in
the contemporary discussions described in the latter part of this book.
I make no claim to be writing here as an objective historian of ideas.
My own theological position has inevitably influenced my choice of
themes to be analyzed and determined the criticisms I level.
Nonetheless, as I was writing, I tried to distinguish carefully between
giving a fair hearing to each thinker and persuading you that my
evaluation of each is the proper one. Should you disagree with my
personal judgment of the continuing value of their thought, I trust
you will still find my description of their philosophies reasonably
accurate.

My position on a number of the issues treated here has not substantially changed over the years. Hence I have felt free to utilize for this book various of my previous writings, which are now out of print, always with careful revision. For permission to do so, I am grateful to the Westminster Press. I also appreciate permission of the Central Conference of American Rabbis to reproduce, in Chapter 12, a portion of my paper from their 1977 *Yearbook*.

Over the years my admiration for Seymour Rossel's editorial and publishing skills have grown, accompanied by a friendship which I prize. He was nice enough to propose that I undertake this project and his sure hand has improved it greatly. I joyfully acknowledge his helpfulness. I am grateful also to Louis Jacobs for his perceptive and generous reading of this manuscript, which enabled me to correct several errors in it. My thanks are also extended to John Simmons for the high sensitivity and fine hand he brought to the final editing of this work.

The process of bringing together the experience of three decades or so has made me freshly conscious of the passage of time and ever more thankful to God who has enabled me, once again, to see a long and demanding project through to completion.

בָּרוּךְ אַתָּה יְיָ. אֱלֹהֵינוּ מֶלֶךְ הָעוֹלָם. אוֹזֵר יִשְׂרָאֵל בִּגְבוּרָה:

"We bless You, *Adonai*, our God, ruler of the universe, who girds Israel with power."

EUGENE B. BOROWITZ
The New York School
Hebrew Union College/
Jewish Institute of Religion

PART I

Setting
the
Context

1

The Challenge
of Modernity
to Judaism

JEWISH belief is closely tied to Jewish history. From ancient times, even as the Bible makes plain, Jewish thought has largely emanated from reflection on the mixed personal and social experience of the Jewish people. Modern Jewish thought is the continuing reponse to the special problems posed by the emancipation of the Jews from their previously segregated social situation. Our proper point of departure, then, is the historical background which forms the context for modern Jewish thinking.

For purposes of condensation, the development of Jewish religious life before the modern era can be broken into four major stages.

First, the most fundamental phase, was the making of the Covenant. The one God of the universe made an eternal covenant with all humanity, as specified in the story of Noah, but the Bible recounts that humanity remained obdurate and disobedient. So God called one man, Abraham, to be specially loyal to God so that, through him and his descendants, all humankind might one day come to know—that is, to obey—God. In return, God promised to make Abraham's family a mighty nation, to give them a land and to protect them through history. Self, society, and responsibility are thus fundamental elements of Jewish faith. In the Exodus, the Hebrews saw God's Covenant promise spectacularly fulfilled; and at Sinai, they

3

received the Torah—the teachings and traditions—which would structure their lives in holiness, as individuals and as a nation settled in their own land. Judaism centers on that experience of election, promise, redemption, and mission. Jewish liturgy reviews it every day; the Jewish calendar follows it each year. Believing Jews live in the reality of the Covenant.

The second formative period for the Hebrew spirit occurred on the land. There was settlement, kingdom, the Temple, social division and decline, prophecy, the loss of ten tribes, the conquest of Judah and destruction of the Temple, exile, and, most startling, there was a return and the Temple was rebuilt. Hebrew saga and legend, law and history, prophecy and wisdom, apocalyptic and story, all found fixed verbal form in this period. The Covenant was amplified by this historic experience and climaxed in the dream of a messianic day when history would be fulfilled in the universal, free service of God.

Jews do not consider the so-called intertestamental literature sacred, yet the era in which it was written constitutes the beginning of the third formative period. Some centuries divide the time of the completion of most of the biblical books from the written teachings of the Rabbis. The Rabbis are the authorities cited in compiling the Mishnah traditions of the first two centuries of the Common Era and next three centuries of talmudic commentaries on them. The Rabbis, inheritors of the tradition of the Pharisees, framed the Jewish religion as we know it today. Modern Jews read the Bible through their eyes; celebrate and mourn and pray and study in the patterns they created. Thus, when the second Temple was destroyed, the Rabbis, responding to the event in terms of the Babylonian precedent, created the synagogue style that remembers the Temple but has no sacrifices and whose service any learned Jew may lead. Rabbinic law, *halachah*, intertwines with spiritual teaching, *aggadah*, and together they create an emphasis on democracy and education characteristic of all succeeding Judaism.

In this Rabbinic period, the Jewish people were already scattered across the civilized Western world. This Diaspora (from the Greek word for dispersal) existence of approximately the next 1,400 years

had major spiritual consequences, many of them negative. Islam and
Christianity debased and degraded Jews. After the First Crusade,
European Christians increasingly attacked, robbed, expelled, forci-
bly converted, and murdered Jews. Ghetto and *shtetl* are relatively
recent terms, and yet they testify to the duration of Jewish segregation. Jews came to see themselves as God's suffering servant in history; and knew that their defamers, by their very persecution of
others, could not be God's chosen. Positively, Jews learned from
those cultures that permitted their participation. They began to systematize Judaism in philosophic fashion and developed the speculative mysticism called *kabbalah*.

After more than a millenium of ostracism and persecution, Jews
were astounded when the French Revolution signalled a call for
political freedom in Europe, a freedom eventually extended even to
Jews. Thus began the modern period of Jewish history. To clarify the
nature of the challenges it posed, it is necessary to see the contrast
between pre- and post-Emancipation Jewry.

From Pariah to Citizen

The segregated pattern of medieval Jewish existence is justly symbolized by the ghetto. In its standard form, from about the year 1500,
the Jewish residential quarter of a city was walled in and its gates were
locked from sundown to sunrise. Many scholars think that the impo-
sition of the ghetto may be traced to the Jewish practice of voluntarily
living together in close community for protection from the Gentile
and for companionship in maintaining the Jewish way of life. Thus,
the *shtetl* of Eastern Europe was not created by an imposed physical
barrier and the *mellahs* of North Africa were often unwalled.
Nonetheless, these Jews too lived in isolated and relatively self-
contained communities. The image of the locked and guarded
ghetto gates of Western Europe poignantly sums up centuries of
legislated disabilities among Moslems and Christians alike: the busi-

nesses Jews might not enter, the social activities they might not
engage in, the hats or badges or other distinguishing marks of
Jewishness they were made to wear, the conversionist sermons they
were forced to attend, the riots and pogroms to which they were
subjected.

When modern Jews read of the conditions under which Jews lived
during this period, they visualize an extraordinarily trying existence
which makes it all the more surprising that, as far as we can tell, the
typical Jew then lived with great integrity of self. In Babylonia,
Franco-Germany or Poland, during the Moslem conquests, the
Crusades or the Cossack pogroms, Jews felt no conflict or ambiguity
about their identity. Society had a definite place for them as Jews,
negative though it was, and they had a countervailing inner certainty
which gave Jewishness great worth and deep significance. They knew
they were God's own people, chosen for a separate existence and
dispersed by God among the nations; God loved them and their
people and would ultimately vindicate their suffering for God's sake.
Believing Jews possessed an inalienable dignity and lived with high
human nobility.

With the European emancipation of the Jews, beginning about
the time of the French Revolution, the lengthy medieval era of the
Jews came to an end. Imposed segregation ceased and, to use the
symbol once again, the ghetto walls came down. The Jew was admitted into society as an equal and given full rights as a citizen. That, in
theory, was what the Emancipation meant.

Yet there are immediate and important qualifications. The Emancipation was not one dramatic event, but a long process, proceeding
by fits and starts, and with great regional variation. The United
States, having little tradition to defend, gave the Jews freedom almost
from the beginning. England, France, the German states, the
Austro-Hungarian Empire, were much more liberal than the prin-
cipalities and nations of Eastern Europe. In Eastern Europe the
Emancipation was tediously slow, to the extent, as some have argued, that it hardly took place at all. And in North Africa, it was only

where the French took over at the beginning of the twentieth century that there was any equality for the Jews. In more backward Moslem countries there was none. Moreover, one can hardly say the emancipatory process has ever, anywhere, been completed. Many Jews still find themselves facing social walls and psychic gates. And Jews in some countries, notably Russia, are less free today than before.

Individual Rights as a Jewish Problem

The revolution in the social status of Jews ended their degradation, but ironically also destroyed their sure sense of self. After the disastrous Catholic-Protestant religious wars, the question of belief was increasingly separated from the political realm and assigned to the area of private activity. The European state began to conceive of itself less as a Christian entity than as a secular one, neutral to the private religions of its citizens and tolerant of all faiths. That is why Jews could properly be allowed to participate in it. By contrast, Jews in feudal times had of necessity been outsiders, for they could not swear the Christian oaths which tied one level of society to another.

In the modern world the only interest that the state, as such, came to have in people's religion was whether it prevented or encouraged them to be loyal citizens. When in 1806, Napoleon, in full imperial grandeur, summoned the Grand Sanhedrin (a council of elders) to speak for the French Jewish community, he wanted assurance that Jewish religious faith, privately held, did not interfere with civic responsibility as publicly enacted. Three of the dozen questions Napoleon placed before the Jewish notables in March 1807 set forth this issue:

> No. 4. In the eyes of Jews, are Frenchmen not of the Jewish religion considered as brothers or strangers?
>
> No. 5. What conduct does Jewish law prescribe toward Frenchmen not of the Jewish religion? No. 6. Do the

> Jews born in France and treated by the law as French
> citizens acknowledge France as their country? Are they
> bound to defend it? Are they bound to obey the laws and
> follow the directions of the civil code?

The Sanhedrin had little difficulty (except in the case of one question regarding intermarriage) in giving Napoleon what he wanted. They said, in effect, that Judaism, like Protestantism or Catholicism, is a spur to good citizenship; and being Jewish is, like being Christian, only another way of being personally religious and therefore is a legitimate identity in a modern state.

This transformation of the Jewish position in society which seemed so natural was also the beginning of the divided Jewish self. In a secular nation, rights are given to individuals not groups. In the medieval world, Moslem or Christian, the Jews had a fixed place in society *as a community*. Individual Jews received their right to live in a given locale by virtue of being a member of the local Jewish community. If the Jewish community did not acknowledge them, the gentile society could treat them as outlaws.

Those rationalists who fought for Jewish equality in post-Revolutionary France had no doubt that the rights were to be granted on a personal not a communal basis. In 1789, Mirabeau denounced the idea that Jews or anyone else could be a nation within the French nation. Clermont Tonnere, another great defender of Jewish rights put the thesis in its classic form: "To the Jews as a nation we must deny everything. To the Jews as individuals we must grant everything." In the secular state, the Jew no longer had to be a member of the Jewish community in order to have a place in things. Rights came by virtue of being a citizen.

Society now taught the Jews that they were basically citizens. They might be Jewish in private, less extensive areas of everyday life if they so wished. The freedom granted was extraordinary but the conditions created a split in the Jewish soul. One had one's modern and one's Jewish lives. How to relate them intellectually emerged as the continuing problem of modern Jewish thought.

Appeal of Modernity; The Problems of Being Jewish

The modern Jew, having been emancipated, could not now easily justify Jewishness on the grounds of the gentiles' inhumanity. Rather as Jews took advantage of the opportunities offered by the Emancipation, as they wore the society's clothes, spoke its language, attended its schools, mastered its culture, benefited from its economy, they could not help but be impressed. The *goyim* were not so bad as they once had seemed.

Self-segregation no longer made sense. The emancipated life and Jewish values, it appeared, seemed to fit together very well. Only some such sense of basic affinity explains, on the intellectual level, why Jews everywhere avidly took advantage of the new freedom when it was offered, despite some pockets of resistance to modernity—the Hasidim, for example. Overwhelmingly, Jews sensed that there was something sufficiently worthy about western civilization to enable them to embrace it fully. Indeed, a new question was raised: If modern culture is so acceptable, why bother being Jewish?

The attractions of modernity were all the more glittering when contrasted to the realities involved in asserting one's Jewishness. It might be permitted, but it alienated one culturally and handicapped one personally. The Jewish religion seemed to smell of the ghetto. Christianity, however, was an active part of western civilization, endemic to its art, its music, its architecture.

In the early decades of the nineteenth century there was a steady movement of Jews converting to Christianity. It was the impetus of losing such Jews as Heinrich Heine that forced Jewish thinkers to action. Intuitively, they knew that modernity did not imply Christianity. Within a generation or two they made the basic reforms in Jewish education, worship, and general life style that showed how, on a practical level, one could accommodate Jewishness to modern culture. That initial spasm of self-transformation is mostly associated with the Reform Jews of Germany but Jewish modernity is not the product of any one movement or any single charismatic leader. It is the creative response of an entire community to a new social situation, and—as befits a people of such diversity and individuality—it has taken many forms.

The social adjustments Jews made as a result of their emancipation only exacerbated the basic dilemma of modern Jewish existence. Without these transformations, there would be great difficulty remaining both Jewish and modern. Yet the very act of adaptation acknowledges values in the general culture, thereby making being Jewish at all problematic. As it happened, an even more specialized historical situation appertained for the Jews in America.

Latecomers to Emancipation

For most of American Jewry, emancipation has come only in the last few generations. The great majority are descendants of immigrants from Eastern European countries which never permitted free Jewish integration into their societies. Leaving an essentially segregated, almost medieval, way of life, they came to one of the most technically advanced and democratically organized countries in the world. To be sure, the more emancipated Western Jews, largely from German communities, came by the tens of thousands to these shores in the period from 1840 to 1880. And a minority of the Eastern European Jews who arrived in the United States at the rate of a hundred thousand and more each year (the war years excepted) until 1924 had been educated in *gymnasia* or at universities, while others had made their way into the world of general literature or politics. Nonetheless, most of these families did not come from emancipated Europe but were, so to speak, fresh from the ghetto.

The immigrant generation before World War I arrived so bound up with Jewish values and emotional patterns that no matter how American their life style became, it was still quite patently Jewish at its roots. Today, looking back at the various forms of humanism or cosmopolitanism that they adopted, we see them less as modern universalists than as secularized Jewish types. Even in radical defiance of Jewish tradition, they somehow showed themselves to be authentically Jewish.

That did not carry over to the second generation, for whom, to be a Jew smacked of clinging to the immigrant status they were most eager to leave behind. Young American Jews in the generation before World War II carried out a cultural exodus, fleeing the memories of the ghetto and its mores in a passionate effort to be fully American. They responded to anti-semitism by seeking invisibility and protective camoflage. They gladly abandoned the Judaism and Jewish style that they felt stigmatized them.

A Community Accepted, Accepts Itself

After World War II, a highly positive attitude toward Jewishness characterized most Jews. Two stages may be seen in the emergence and development of this reversal. First, in the period from 1945 to 1967 expanded freedom made possible a joy in Jewishness that, at its heights, bordered on illusion. Second, in the period from the Israeli Six-Day War in 1967 to the Israeli-Egyptian peace treaty, a series of harsh realities radicalized the Jewish social situation and thus turned Jewish identity from a possible option into an appealing way to live. The earlier, postwar era was characterized by a new sense of Jewish at-homeness in America and a sense that the democracy World War II sought to preserve had begun to function properly. Thus, anti-semitism faded from the public scene, and such anti-semites as appeared remained on the fringes of society. Despite their noise, they attracted few followers. Through the mid-1960's, sociologists reported that many young American Jews had never had firsthand contact with anti-semitism, not even by word of mouth, much less by physical act. At the same time, educationally, economically, and culturally, postwar American welcomed the participation of Jews—and a small-scale miracle took place. The outcasts of a previous era achieved money, status, success, and power to an extent utterly unanticipated in the Jewish community in the late 1930's.

The disproportionate Jewish benefits from the general American economic boom had an ironic side. In the Depression years vocational experts regularly tried to get the Jewish community to abandon its abnormal economic concentration on white-collar and professional occupations. Twenty years later, the new economy demanded the sort of educated, risk-taking, entrepreneurial style that Jewish culture and experience had created. As a result, Jews became one of the wealthiest religio-ethnic groups in the United States. With that came the emergence of Jews in every area of cultural activity. Not only were there more Jewish writers, artists, and professors than ever before, but now they made no secret of their Jewishness—indeed, they often utilized it in their work. By the mid-1960's there was hardly a field where American Jews had not made major contributions and come to positions of leadership.

Being Jewish as an Attractive Life Option

The effect this had on the inner life of the Jew is difficult to overestimate. Despite Sartre's famous definition of Jewishness as merely a status imposed by society, American Jewry discovered that the non-Jew no longer served the role of keeping Jews Jewish. In America, one really had a right "even" to be a Jew. This acceptability caused American Jews to see themselves as the first truly free generation of Diaspora Jewry. Some American Jewish thinkers even began to discuss the new freedom as a special peril to Jewish existence. With little anti-semitism to stand in the way, Jews were free to drift away from the Jewish people. In America, with its pervasive secularity, it was even unnecessary to convert to Christianity to become fully identified with the majority. Already then the increasing rate of intermarriage made the new acceptance of Jews something of a mixed blessing.

The same freedom to give up their Jewishness also made it possible for Jews to choose consciously to be Jewish. That is, rather than a biological and cultural accident, being Jewish now became a matter of personal decision about how one wanted to live one's life. What began as a fact of birth became an act of existential self-determination. One unexpected result of the new social ease was that noticeable numbers of Jews were positive enough about the emerging American Jewish life style that they were consciously choosing it for themselves. There were not many such newly self-affirming Jews but they were so radical a contrast to the negativeness of Jewish life thirty years before that they were a significant communal phenomenon. And they were the vanguard of the larger number who in the succeeding period made their Jewishness an essential part of their lives.

This process of social acceptance and self-affirmation was so dynamic that it created a special variety of American-Jewish euphoria. Suddenly it seemed as if the community might be entering upon the Golden Age of American Jewry. Much of the shock of what followed and a good deal of the high fearfulness it engendered was the result of these exalted notions American Jews developed about themselves and their place in society.

Rise of Self-Conscious Jewish Ethnicity

Then the time of radicalization began, and the Six-Day War, in both positive and negative ways, dramatically heightened what was at stake in being a Jew. In June 1967, Jewish ethnicity surfaced in a way that no one had ever anticipated. That American Jews had some feeling for the State of Israel was never a question. But no one believed such emotions would prompt significant action or be felt by marginal members of the community. On both accounts, the spontaneous, emotional, activist, nearly universal response of American Jews proved the skeptics wrong. With the Six-Day War began a radical shift in American Jewish self-consciousness. This phenomenon has usually been explained in terms of the hold of the State of Israel on world Jewry and the needs of Jews to assuage their guilt over the Holocaust. After nearly twenty years of existence the State of Israel had come to mean far more to most Jews than they realized. These feelings were heightened by anxiety that the war might result in a second Holocaust. American Jews in particular were freshly conscious of their indifference to the suffering of European Jews during the 1940's, and the importance of the State of Israel as a positive response to human barbarity. The worldwide attention given to the trial of Adolf Eichmann (1960–1962) brought home the lesson that ordinary people, merely by doing what they are told and by not taking a stand against evil, do the demonic work that degrades humankind. Guilty and caring, American Jews were moved by the crisis of the Six-Day War to act as Jews with a directness and commitment they had never shown before. And in due course, this inestimably raised their Jewish self-consciousness.

The Six-Day War precipitated what two decades of sociological shift had brought to readiness. Significant was the new American attitude toward ethnicity. With blacks showing the way, various American groups had begun vigorously asserting their democratic right to maintain and enhance group identity. This disparagement of the melting-pot theory of cultural assimilation encouraged Jews to be "more Jewish." The Jewish community learned the legitimacy of using political pressure and public campaigns to protect their ethnic interests. Jews now found themselves, for the first time, marching and demonstrating on behalf of the State of Israel, Soviet Jewry, and other causes.

Anti-semitism Again Becomes a Factor in Identity

This shift in Jewish ethnic self-awareness was made more effective by two negative forces. The first of these was the American Jew's reawakened sense of anti-semitism. For most American Jews, anti-semitism has again become a possibility, perhaps even a threat— something that in the glow of the mid-1960's appeared unthinkable. In the critical period from the closing of the Strait of Tiran to the outbreak of the Six-Day War, the United States government did nothing to forestall the threat to Israel's existence—despite the assurances it had given that it would back freedom of passage through the

Strait. The State of Israel was left to its own fate; and American Jews felt that they had been abandoned by their own government.

Of course, such aloofness is not anti-semitism. The move was prompted not by any hatred of the Jews but by calculating American self-interest. Yet, in that reckoning, the fate of the Jews was not very important. If necessary, they would—as in the days of the Holocaust—be sacrificed. In the face of such a self-serving diplomacy, American Jews sensed that they, as Jews, were still outsiders to America. This was the more traumatic for it came hard upon a period in which American and Jewish interests seemed closely intertwined.

The reaction of the official Christian bodies in those critical days was similarly disheartening. Despite direct appeals, almost no Christian organization spoke out on behalf of the State of Israel. The hopes raised by a decade or more of Christian official pronouncements rejecting anti-semitism and by the joint work undertaken in many fields of social welfare, particularly civil rights, were shattered. And here one might suspect subterranean prejudice against Jews for stubbornly remaining Jews.

Those wounds could not easily heal in the atmosphere of confrontation that characterized American politics well into the 1970's. With minority groups actively seeking their rights, particularly in the great urban areas, the Jewish middle class found itself increasingly threatened. Particularly as blacks pressured to get a responsive educational program, reparatory job opportunities, and a humane standard of housing, it was often the Jews who stood in the place they were determined to occupy. Worse, there seemed a good likelihood that the established Christian power groups would sacrifice Jewish interests as the cheapest way of keeping blacks from insurrection.

The urban crisis gradually became less frightening but the threats against the State of Israel did not. Until the signing of the Israeli-Egyptian peace treaty, American Jews lived with a constant sense of Jewish vulnerability. The cruelty of terrorism, the international isolation of the State of Israel, American pressures on the Israelis to sacrifice their understanding of their security, the bombings of synagogues in Europe and the swastika daubings in the United States—all these combined to give a powerful if negative reason for American Jews to think of themselves in terms of their people and its peculiar destiny.

Redressing the Balance Between Judaism and Modernity

As Jewish self-concern stayed high, the passionate modern Jewish concern with western culture substantially lessened. In this Jews were not alone. They shared the identity crisis which other Americans have undergone. For one, there was the widespread loss of morale, for which the Vietnam War has largely been held to blame; but there have been other causes as well: the dehumanizing effect of population growth and technology; the failure of character in the face of affluence and social permissiveness; the great expectations of American destiny and the fearful revelations of American venality and violence. In a time of extraordinary human stress there has been no moral force in the culture strong enough to find new insight or provide a sense of noble endurance, much less of human triumph. To the contrary, it is the undeniable reality of a pervasive amorality in individuals and collectives—economic and political alike—that has smashed the old reliable image of America as good and ethical, if often ineffectual; and it has left much of America cynical.

America's failure of national self-confidence had a special effect on Jews. The truth is that for most Jews the American way had become the real faith, the effective Torah, by which they lived. In their amalgam of being Jewish and American, Americanism had become dominant. Now, as American Jewry's operative "faith" collapsed, the possibility of a serious return to one's Jewish roots became more attractive. This rarely involved a total turn from one milieu to the other—it was no migration back to the ghetto. Instead it was the possibility of a new mix of the American and Jewish ways of life. Perhaps the subordination of one's Jewishness was wrong and being Jewish ought to play more of a role in one's life. Some suggested a reversal of the old priorities, making one's Jewishness the foundation of one's existence.

In the 1970's a minority of Jews began actively searching for a new sense of Jewish identity. The movement was largely inchoate but its characteristic social form was the *havurah*, the small face-to-face Jewish group, and its major document, *The Jewish Catalog*, a widely circulated series of volumes which give detailed instructions on how one might fill one's life with Jewish practice and spirit. In a community previously so dedicated to social integration this was a surprising development. An even more utterly unexpected aspect of it was the effort of some of these Jews to center their Jewishness on personal piety. Belief once more became a matter of Jewish concern. That led a number of searchers to Orthodoxy, while others sought a liberal if recognizably traditional way of living with their Jewish faith. This shift in consciousness is essential in understanding the consequences of the discussion of the Holocaust in Jewish thought.

Beyond Ideology to a Philosophy of Judaism

During the course of these two centuries of emancipation, Jews have responded more in a social than an intellectual fashion. There is a substantial difference between the ideological position of the various Jewish religious movements and what may loosely be called the fully developed philosophies of Judaism. Thus, one may be tempted to try to divide modern Jewish religious thought between Orthodox, Conservative, Reform, and other points of view. Most movements have an ideology, a platform of ideas on which they stand, thus giving their organization some intellectual content. On rare occasions, when a group originates in response to an intellectual plea, it may be highly ideological, as certain Marxist splinter groups or artistic circles have been. Most groups, however, are essentially programmatic in that they appeal to people because of what they suggest to do, or how to act, in a given situation. If they are to grow and thus extend their ranks, they must appeal to people of different temperaments and concerns. They therefore keep ideological definition to a minimum. In turn, this leads to continual identity crises of successful movements as they make desperate efforts to explain what they uniquely stand for while not losing too many adherents in the process. This has been a primary problem in the Zionist movement, but it affects Jewish religious organizations as well.

One intellectual matter does divide Orthodox Jews from non-Orthodox or liberal Jews: God's revelation of the Torah, particularly the revelation of the Oral Law and the belief that there is but one way of amplifying it as exemplified in the recognized Orthodox sages of our day. That is clearly a conceptual issue. Aside from that point, the Orthodox and non-Orthodox communities each split into a number of subgroups which often claim to have a distinctive "philosophy" but which seem to attract their adherents more by their social style than by their intellectual content. Most Jews cannot specify in any detail what their movements stand for theoretically but they are generally quite clear as to what sort of behavior is expected from them.

There is then a considerable gap between the sort of thought one finds in the writings of the ideological leaders of a movement and the sustained intellectual analyses we will be dealing with in this volume. Men like Abraham Geiger of the early Reform movement and Solomon Schechter of the Conservative movement wrote thoughtfully and out of great learning about the nature of Judaism. They did not, however, deal with it in very abstract fashion. In retrospect, they seem unaware of the intellectual problems hidden in their formulations. Perhaps they did not find it fruitful to pursue such questions as: How do we know there is a God? what is the human role in revelation? How is the people of Israel to be defined and its purpose set? When such issues arise in their work, they do not concentrate their intellectual energies on them and seek to give a systematic—that is, a detailed and coherent account—of what they believe and why. There have been Jews who have carried out such an advanced, academically sophisticated analysis of the meaning of Judaism today, and it is with their work that this book is concerned.

Can There be a Creative Tension Between Judaism and Modernity?

The central issue of modern Jewish thought is set by the situation of emancipation. Being freed brought forth the question, how can one be modern and Jewish? The great movements in modern Jewish life give *practical* answers—that Jews should modernize religious life or revive nationhood. In the one case Jewish observance and in the other Jewish peoplehood are recast in the mold of contemporary social patterns. By contrast, the thinker is concerned with modernity in its *intellectual* manifestations. How can what it means to be a Jew be understood and explained in a convincing fashion, that is, in terms of ideas which carry weight with people today? In America, the challenge may be put more specifically: it is the university. The overwhelming majority of American Jews have had a higher education and their mentality has been shaped by that experience. How does one discuss Judaism with their most thoughtful representatives? The critical issue here is truth, not organizational effectiveness. The presentation of Judaism will be judged by the adequacy of the statement establishing its truth, not by its use in uniting groups for joint action, though a statement of Jewish belief will inevitably have practical consequence for the Jewish people's self-perception and its way of life.

For a thinker, to be modern means to have a system of ideas which have currency in contemporary culture. Finding such a modern way of thinking and determining the way it and Jewish tradition can best be brought into harmony, constitute the basic task of the discipline we are examining. Because modern intellectual life in general has been unusually dynamic and many shifts have taken place in it, there have been correspondingly diverse patterns of thought developed among Jewish thinkers. Five substantially different ways of explaining Jewish religious belief have emerged in the past century and a sixth arises from the intellectual issues raised by the Zionist movement and the establishment of the State of Israel. Zionism has seldom advanced beyond the ideological level but the impact of its historical accomplishments and the questions implicit in them have affected all serious Jewish thinkers. Within these six major intellectual options, as might be expected, certain themes recur. A short analysis of these may help to set the varieties of modern Jewish thinking into perspective.

What Should Jews Make of Science, History, Democracy and Culture?

The first of these is empirical science. The Emancipation brought the Jews from a world of talmudic or medieval Aristotelain assumptions into an era rapidly building on the science of Galileo and Newton. It contradicted classic Judaism on matters of fact, like the age of the earth, or in the likely understanding of nature, like the evolution of humankind, and made the demonstration of God's power by miracle seem mythological. It provided a simpler more integrated view of the world than Judaism knew, one where mathematically describable patterns, not God's immediate rule, were to be found. Its precision made possible control of much of nature and its knowledge opened up the possibilities of creating better ways to live than had ever been imagined. Any modern Jew would have to come to terms with science.

History, in its contemporary critical, inclusive sense was a particular challenge to emancipated Jews. Their tradition had implied, and most Jews believed, that Jewish life had changed little since biblical times. It seemed natural that an eleventh-century French Jew, Rashi, living in a Christian setting, should be the authoritative commentator on the talmudic discussions edited in a Parthian, Zoroastrian setting (early in the sixth century) of the Mishnah which was compiled at the end of the second century by Judah the Prince, who lived under Roman rule in a country many of whose inhabitants were idolaters. By contrast, modern history was determinedly chronological and contextual. It took change to be the basic law of history. It was skeptical, critical of all claims to authority, even in sacred books, unless these could otherwise be substantiated.

As applied to classic Judaism, the results were devastating. When examined like any other text of its time, the Torah appears to be a compilation and harmonization of a number of different traditions about Israelite religion and origins. Modern historical analysis shows that Jewish law has changed radically under the impact of economic reality and social situation. Jewish practice also is often seen not to have been as old as most Jews imagined it to be. When set in the context of human history generally, the development of the Jewish people, its religion and institutions, is similar to that of other peoples. For all the problems it creates, this view includes the Jews as part of humankind, a matter of great concern to emancipated Jews. How can today's Judaism not reflect something of that universal sense of history?

Democracy, as it became increasingly effective, held out new opportunities for Jews to determine the social order in which they lived. The ghetto mentality considered the communal arrangements of previous generations fixed almost by divine sanction. The modern political sensibility considers them capable of improvement and invites each citizen to share in bringing about greater common happiness. The Jews had themselves benefited from the new political activism for they were being emancipated. They were challenged to effectuate their social ideals and their messianic hopes more directly than by performing commandments and waiting for God's saving action. Through politics they might take greater responsibility for achieving their destiny. Any modern description of Judaism would have to deal with the role human beings play in determining and realizing their goals.

Less precisely but often with greater effect, the notion of culture itself challenged the old Jewish sense of the proper dimensions of human existence. Thinkers and writers in general society were concerned with a breadth of human issues that extended far beyond even the vaunted comprehensiveness of rabbinic literature. The social sciences radically changed the common perception of humanhood and social criticism explored every aspect of contemporary existence. Aesthetically, human creativity was celebrated in ways that went far beyond anything the Jewish community had known. Jews have spent much of the past century catching up with modern standards in fiction, painting, sculpture, musical composition and the like. The culture also encouraged recreation, play and enjoying oneself, for it had an intuition of human fulfillment substantially different from that found in the preemancipation Jewish community. Can a modern explication of Judaism avoid this inclusive sense of what it is to be a full human being?

Modernity Implies More Confidence in Humankind, Less in God's Revelation

Above all, the nineteenth-century civilization into which the liberated Jew came centered about the idea of progress, especially that which might be achieved through the use of human reason. Instead of relying on God to save them in this world or compensate them in one yet to come, people felt that they themselves could radically improve things. The impediments were generally either ignorance or thoughtless tradition. Both would be swept away by education and knowledge. What was unknown now would likely soon be discovered through research and analysis. Discoveries concerning disease not only affected people's longevity but gave them added self-confidence that human beings would master the world. The economic expansion of the western world through much of this period likewise made belief in human creativity the cornerstone of contemporary existence.

Seeing these five strands as major components of what most Jews would take modernity to be, it is clear why Orthodox Judaism has no representative among the creators of major models of modern Jewish thought. By definition, being modern means adopting stands in opposition to the God-given truths of traditional Judaism and the way of life which enshrines them. The Hasidim and the so-called *"yeshivah* world" reject all such modernity. But another view is taken by the self-consciously modern Orthodox. They may be said to follow the general approach of the great ideologue of nineteenth century German Orthodoxy, Samson Raphael Hirsch (1808–1888). He interpreted the rabbinic praise of *torah im derekh eretz*, having a worldly occupation while studying Torah, to mean that one can be true to the Torah while adopting the forms of the modern world, those at least which did not contradict Jewish law. The spokesmen of modern Orthodoxy have participated in various contemporary intellectual discussions but have thus far (the works of Joseph Baer Soloveitchik remaining largely unpublished) given us no comprehensive intellectual account of what an Orthodox modern Jewish philosophy might be.

What Liberal Jews Learned from Moses Mendelssohn

For non-Orthodox Jews, the challenge of modernity came to be symbolized by what was seen as the critical failing in the thought of the first notable modern Jew, Moses Mendelssohn (1729–1786). By the middle of the eighteenth century, this slight, ungainly man had made himself one of the most admired thinkers in Germany through his writings on the newly fashionable topic of aesthetics. A self-taught intellectual, he was a follower of the renowned philosopher Leibnitz, but his own restatement of the rationalist position was highly regarded in the pre-Kantian era. His development of a defense of the immortality of the soul, based on that position, was published under the title *Phaedon* and became an international bestseller. Thus, some years before the emancipation process was generally under way Moses Mendelssohn had found a path out of the ghetto and into modern culture.

The anomaly of a Jew being a full participant in the general civilization prompted one of Mendelssohn's critics to address an open letter asking why Mendelssohn had not yet become a Christian. Mendelssohn's response took the form of a small book, *Jerusalem*, in which he expounded his theory of Judaism. He argues that being a Jew is a matter of religion and that the Jewish faith has an unusual character to it. When it comes to beliefs, Judaism is entirely free. It has no dogmas but allows the human mind to search without hindrance for the most comprehensive truth. A Jew has no difficulty in being modern in religious faith and if the state would only give the Jews true civil freedom, it would find them willing, on their part, to participate fully in society. What keeps the Jews distinctive is the law which God had given them to regulate their behavior. In that respect, Jews are not free to change or modify anything other than in the way their revealed law allows. For Mendelssohn—whose thought is far more subtle and rewarding than these few sentences can indicate—a Jew should be modern in ideas and culture while being observant of the law revealed at Mount Sinai and interpreted by the sages.

Since Mendelssohn was a Leibnitzian rationalist and revelation was still widely accepted in the strongly Lutheran atmosphere of Germany, his answer met the immediate needs which generated modern Jewish thought. In the process, he violated a condition which liberals now find critical. Mendelssohn's system found few intellectual followers, for his position seemed to advocate maintaining two sections in one's mind—one which adhered rigidly to the requirements of Jewish law while the other was free to adopt the ideas of modernity. Most of Mendelssohn's contemporaries soon came to believe that his two compartments cannot be so rigidly separated from one another. There are conceptual implications in Jewish practice which clash with the results of free intellectual inquiry. The very notion of a mind divided is even more troublesome for it seems a direct contravention of that sense of unity which is the foundation of religion and rationality alike.

This matter of personal integrity became critical to the liberals. They did not want to be freely human in one part of themselves and constrainedly Jewish in another realm of their existence. They wanted no dividing line between what constituted the modern and the Jewish in the answer they were seeking. It had to be a system, a coherent, interrelated, single pattern of thought. Judaism might be reinterpreted by being seen in a different intellectual light. That would be as legitimate today as it was when the medieval philosophers interpreted Judiasm in terms of Neo-Platonism or Aristotelianism. In turn, Judaism was entitled to make its own criticisms of modern thought and resist those elements which were found unacceptable. The precise balance between adjustment and conservation was a problem for each thinker to tackle, although, as will become evident, modern ideas proved so attractive that most of the concessions were made on the Jewish side.

Precursors of Contemporary Discussion

Four thinkers are generally regarded as having made major efforts in the mid-nineteenth century to provide an adequate modern explication of Judaism. Salomon Formstecher (1808–1889) utilized the metaphysics of the spirit developed by Schelling as the basis for his book of 1841, *The Religion of the Spirit*. Samuel Hirsch (1815–1889) did the same with Hegel's thought in his volume of 1842, *The Religious Philosophy of the Spirit*. A thoroughgoing argument against reason in the name of faith was formulated by Solomon Steinheim (1789–1866) in his four-volume work, *Revelation in the Religious System of the Synagogue*. This might on the surface seem an unmodern work but, somewhat like Yehudah Halevi in the Middle Ages, Steinheim used the conceptual apparatus of his time to attack the authority of philosophic rationality and to defend the truths given by revelation. In the end, however, his statement of the major truths of Judaism turns out to be reasonably close to the fundamental liberal assertions of his two more philosophic colleagues. Nachman Krochmal (1785–1840) is the only non-German of the group. The more comprehensive contours of his conception of Judaism have often been attributed to his being a product of the Galician *Haskalah*, the Hebrew language movement for cultural enlightenment. Krochmal's book, *A Guide for the Perplexed of Our Time*, was published in incomplete form only in 1851, some time after his death. Krochmal's thought is remarkable for seeing the intellectual problem not merely as one of Jewish belief but of the nature of the Jewish people. He interpreted Jewish peoplehood in Hegelian fashion, contending that the Jews are an eternal people because of their identification with the Absolute Spirit that undergirds history. To investigate the spiritual meaning of the different periods of Jewish history, Krochmal undertook a number of pathbreaking investigations into the development of Jewish literature.

None of these works significantly framed the problems or suggested answers which remain on the agenda of contemporary Jewish discussion. For that we must turn to the intellectual system of Hermann Cohen which, as the last quarter of the nineteenth century began, effectively established the discipline of modern Jewish thought.

PART II

The Six
Systematized Positions:

Rationalistic Models

2

Neo-Kantianism: Hermann Cohen

EXTENDED abstract thought is not native to Judaism. The centuries of biblical and talmudic development are essentially free of it. There are traces of argument in the Bible, occasionally even an extended discussion, and the Rabbis use logic to expound the Torah. Nonetheless, these are not the sort of generalization and probing that characterize Greek philosophy or Christian theology. Not until first-century Judiasm confronts Hellenistic Greek thought in Alexandria does the first full-scale Jewish philosophy appear—only to be ignored by the normative Jewish community. Were it not for the church's preservation of Philo, there would be no record of Jewish theological reflection until the ninth century, when interaction with Moslem civilization, in which philosophy flourished, produced a steady stream of Jewish philosophical works extending through six centuries. Thus, for over two thousand years, from Moses to Isaac Israeli, Judaism, despite contact with Greek civilization, had little need for philosophic analysis of its faith. Only in the past thousand years, and then only in periods of open cultural intercourse (e.g., in Spain but not in Turkey or Poland) does a self-conscious concern with the intellectual content and character of Jewish assert itself.

The emancipation of European Jewry creates that sort of social hybridization more radically than did Alexandria or Spain, for the modern Jew is far more accepted in society today than ever before.

The Alexandrian Jew was a monotheist among pagans. The Spanish Jew was tolerated but inferior. The modern Jew is in theory and often in practice a person fully equal to all other persons.

Modern Jewish thought is substantially the product of the involvement of Jews with German philosophy. This has something to do with the relative freedom of the Jews of Germany and their sense of self-image in that culture. Then too, German philosophy in the thought of two of its great figures, Immanuel Kant and Georg Friedrich Hegel, set the agenda for much of western philosophic thinking until well into the twentieth century. The tones of German idealistic philosophy still remain in contemporary Jewish thought in a way that belies the relative marginality of idealism in academic philosophical discussion. Of course, the great Jewish system makers who set the problems and patterns for Jewish religious thought were either German or educated in Germany, the notable exception being Mordecai Kaplan. And, apparently, German idealism appealed to Jews seeking intellectual understanding of their situation in modern society. There is no better way to confront this German-Jewish philosophical synthesis than through the work of Hermann Cohen.

Neo-Kantian Philosopher as Jewish Teacher

The nineteenth century had other distinguished Jewish thinkers, but in Cohen the level of intellectual sophistication and the quality of its application to Judaism reached new and exemplary heights. His work spans the period of Germany's emergence from the Franco-Prussian War of 1870 to World War I, when his definitive book on Judaism appeared posthumously in 1919. In Cohen the era of rationality and social adjustment reached a climax; after him, as much the result of his accomplishment as of a sharp historical turn, a somewhat different set of problems increasingly preoccupies Jewish thinkers.

Born in 1842 and receiving his doctorate in 1865, Cohen was eventually invited to the University of Marburg to teach philosophy, which he did from 1876–1912. After only three years as a lecturer and despite his Jewishness, he was appointed full professor, a status far more difficult to attain in the German university system than in its American counterpart. Cohen's extraordinary rise to academic eminence was due to his brilliant reconstruction of the Kantian system which, after some decades of eclipse by various forms of Hegelianism, he and other philosophers now returned to prominence. Cohen's own solution to the problems of the Kantian philosophy was so telling it became one of the three great patterns of neo-Kantianism that now emerged, the so-called Marburg school version, and it brought him and his university international renown.

This work was purely secular and academic. It had no inner relationship to the fact of Cohen's Jewish birth or to his early Jewish education. (His father was a cantor and his good Jewish background was extended by his spending some time at the Jewish Theological Seminary in Breslau.) His unique interpretation of Judaism cannot be understood except in terms of his general philosophic system. Moreover, had Cohen not succeeded in the general culture, his exposition of Judaism might never have received the Jewish acceptance it did.

Cohen's technical work, resolving the paradoxes inherent in Kantianism, is not directly relevant here. Yet a word must be said about it insofar as it made possible his new philosophy of Judaism.

The Philosophical World Cohen Inherited

The Kantian revolution in philosophy may be described, with gross oversimplification, as a response to the skeptical questions raised by the thought of David Hume. This Scottish thinker had inquired about how we truly know what we claim to know about nature and reality. For example, scientists regularly speak in terms of cause and effect but one never actually sees a cause or hears an effect; one sees only a sequence of events. Our senses tell us that one thing follows another with regularity; our conclusion that this effect was produced by that cause is our mental way of describing what occurred. Since it isn't a conclusion produced by the senses themselves, it cannot claim comparable certainty. Why, then, do we rely so steadfastly on what our minds tell us?

Kant said that Hume's skeptical questions awakened him from "dogmatic slumber" about how we know what we know. Kant accepted Hume's problem as legitimate and, in responding to it, he rethought all the major problems of philosophy in a way that has affected almost all subsequent philosophers.

Kant proposed resolving the issue of the certainty of our knowledge, particularly that of science, by conceding that we cannot know what the world-itself really is like*. All we can know is how rational people would properly think about it. We best learn this by analyzing the necessary patterns a mature human mind utilizes. Kant thus shifted the focus of philosophy. Previous thinkers had assumed that what the mind had said about reality was, in fact, true of reality-itself. Kant agreed with Hume that we could no longer identify our thoughts with reality-itself. But since we could know what proper thinking would now be and therefore what true ideas are, Kant concentrated his philosophic efforts on how the mind would reason about the world-itself.

For Kant, the sophisticated intellect operated in three related but disparate realms: science, ethics and aesthetics. These are all characterized by our applying a rational structure to them. For example, in the realm of science our efforts are directed not just to the collection of facts but to their interpretation. We want to move beyond the data to an abstraction about the data. Scientific thinking is most fully carried out when we can speak of a given area in terms of a broad generalization, that is, in terms of a universal law. The best human reason is characterized by that sort of thinking and it was Kant's genius to show how such rational patterning operated not only in science but in ethics and aesthetics as well.

---

*World-itself, reality-itself, and other similar terms are used here to indicate the Kantian effort to analyze the faculties of reason and perception while acknowledging that apprehension of things-in-themselves (*noumena*) is impossible. By these *ersatz* terms, I am trying to avoid the intricacies of technical philosophy, while providing the reader with some critically needed orientation.

The skeptical concession which grounded Kant's philosophy destroyed the possibility of proofs for the existence of God which had characterized the philosophy of religion since medieval times. Kant forthrightly acknowledged this, insisting that the arguments of the human mind say only what people correctly *think*, not what is actually "out there" in reality-itself. Kant also went on to create a new way of intellectually validating religion. He argued that ethical experience gives us unique insight into the reality which transcends humankind, and reasonable people, based on the certainty of rational ethics, would believe in God, freedom of the will, immortality of the soul and such classic religious doctrines. This way of thinking about religion which starts from human experience and *then* seeks to establish God's reality is the opposite of traditional religion which was based on the idea of God giving people knowledge or revelation. The liberal approach to religion is based on this procedure.

Reconstructing Kantian Philosophy

Kant's philosophy did not vigorously survive the early decades of the nineteenth century. Kant had overlooked a basic problem: *If all we can truly know is how the mind operates, how can we assert that there is a world-itself to which our ideas reasonably correspond? All we know for certain is how we think.* That problem, in various forms, produced many systems of German idealism, that is, many intellectual structures of thought which tried to show how the ideas of the human mind produce our sense of reality. The absolute idealism of Georg Friedrich Hegel ingeniously equated fundamental reality with mind. But as the second half of the nineteenth century moved on, the suggestion was made, most notably in the work of Friedrich Nietzsche, that the old enterprise of rational philosophy had now come to an end and a radically new beginning to human thought, with perhaps wildly different contents, was now in order. The call to revive Kant came about in this situation and was soon successfully answered by Hermann Cohen, who had begun his philosophic work with studies of Plato.

Cohen argued that Kant had not been sufficiently rational in explaining even how the scientific mind operated. Kant had distinguished between raw sense data and the necessary categories of human thought like cause and effect or space and time, which give structure to sense perceptions. Cohen argued that even our sense data itself is the process of the mind's creative, structuring power. There is no "raw" data for by its being "data" it has already been shaped by our minds. For Cohen, reason, in this activist sense, is the basis of all knowing. We therefore need to understand the process by which science operates as a continual creative effort by the mind to construct a rational reality out of what confronts it. The realm of "what confronts it" cannot be defined or explained. In-itself, it is simply not within the reach of "knowledge." But we may accurately describe it as "the problem-over-against-us." Using our minds, we create problems to solve and work out patterns of understanding what we have encountered. We resolve some of our questions in new and more comprehensive rational structures. This increases our knowledge but, also, as it turns out, our sense of what remains unknown. Cohen's model for this sort of thinking is mathematical, the differential calculus, in which, by continual finite operations, extended to infinity, we come to know a technically limitless sum. Human knowing, then, is a process, going on endlessly, ever enlarging its scope and, as new concepts fit into the growing system, demonstrating its validity. Cohen's philosophy analyzes the patterns which the mind necessarily uses in this dynamic process.

Cohen maintained the Kantian distinction separating the three different areas in which the human mind operated: science (which Cohen identified with mathematics and thus often called, in his special sense, "logic"), ethics and aesthetics. He presented his own constructive statement concerning each area. In his last years, after his retirement from Marburg in 1912 and a move to Berlin where he taught at the *Lehranstalt für die Wissenschaft des Judentums*, the seminary for liberal rabbis, he paid special attention to the place of religion in his system.

Cohen's Emphases in Philosophical Ethics

To a great extent Cohen's view of religion grew out of his passionate concern with ethics. Cohen continues the Kantian description of the rational character of ethics, that is, that an ethic must be universal and take the form of law. Any imperative to act which is limited to given classes or races could not be ethical and nothing could be a moral imperative unless one's sense of what is right could make it a rule for all people in a similar situation.

Cohen extended this line of thought in a social direction. Face to face relations might lead on to social responsibility but a properly universal ethics, in Cohen's view, must be essentially social and take into its purview the whole of humankind. Every ethical act ultimately aims at the moral interrelationship of all people. We may begin with our own society but we cannot be content until there is global justice and understanding. Ethics, like science, is a dynamic, infinite enterprise. Each opportunity to act awakens a new moral challenge, one we cannot be relieved of because we were ethical in our last few deeds. And each act of goodness can be fulfilled only when we reach out and embrace all people in it. As is the case with scientific knowledge, our efforts to realize the good never accomplish the ideal, which, with each achievement, still seems to be as far away. Being ethical, like striving to know, is a permanent activity of the rational person.

While Cohen's conscience is directed to all humankind, he sees a special ethical role for governments in the accomplishment of a united humanity. States properly come into being when they express the will of their citizens. Since action on the basis of one's free choice is the heart of ethics, democracy is a major means of realizing

our social ethical responsibility. Cohen did not mean his ideal of the
state to be identified with any real state for that would mean it was
fully ethical and beyond improvement. Like individuals, nations
must continuously seek to improve themselves.

Cohen himself had no difficulty applying his philosophical
standard to the political situation of his day. He accepted that aspect
of the Marxist analysis of society which showed the many ways in
which the powerful exploited those dependent on them and then
trained them to accept their degraded status as right for them. He
considered democratic socialism the logical outcome of his ethical
theory and publicly espoused that position despite its unpopularity
and the special difficulties it caused for a Jew.

A *Rational Argument for God*

Cohen's ethical position led him, in a way different from that of
Kant, to the need of an idea of God. Two forms of this argument
have been noted in his work which may, in the end, be one. Initially,
Cohen's system as it develops from science to ethics suddenly manifests a basic incoherence. One cannot claim to be ethical because
one has been thinking about ethical problems or mentally analyzing
the nature of moral decisions. The imperatives of ethics need to be
acted out in the real world. But the world science discloses to us
seems alien to ethical striving. Nature is ruled by laws which determine what will happen. In ethics, the moral law confronts one with
a duty which one is free to do or not do—and the ethical decision is
found in the consequent response of the free will. The world science
discloses is indifferent to values like good and evil but goes its unconcerned, relentless way. Ethics is, by definition, the realm of what we
know to be good and of what ought to be done even, if necessary, in
the face of whatever contrary forces confront us. For a thoroughgoing rationalist like Cohen, this contradiction between the natural
and ethical realms is philosophically intolerable.

In order to maintain its rationality, the system now requires an idea which will allow the two modes of rationality their distinctive-ness yet bring them into relation with one another. Turning science into a free realm like ethics, or ethics into a determined order like science, would destroy the form of rational thinking characterizing each area. Hence the new idea cannot be identical with either the basic idea of science or ethics. It must be the ground of each realm so as to be fully related to it but it must not be limited to it. It must also transcend them both so as not to be the same as either of them. It must be more comprehensive than either of them so that it may bind them into a greater unity. That will give us an integrated world which we may be confident will permit ethics being lived out in the realm of nature. The classic term for such a grounding, tran-scendent, comprehensive, integrating idea is God. As Cohen sees things, a rational person requires an idea of God to harmonize a properly embracing world view.

Cohen, of course, is not talking about the world-itself for he does not see how any rational person can hope to do that. His God is not a being or an existent reality of some sort. Things, for Cohen, are far less important and, so to speak, less real than are true ideas, that is, ones which are required by a rationally elaborated system. God is the most significant "thing" Cohen can imagine, for God is precisely the idea which is at the basis of his entire intellectual system, integrating it into the unity which makes it properly rational.

Realizing the Ethical Task

The other line to Cohen's affirmation of God may be traced by way of the infinity of the ethical task. If people believed morality could never reach its goal, that might generate despair and abandonment of ethical striving. There is something about the imperative to do the good which makes people believe it will eventually be accomplished. But that again involves us with nature. For the ethical task to con-tinue infinitely to its ideal completion, there must be some guarantee that nature and humankind continue without an end. Yet the scientific view of the world includes the law of entropy, which states that the world is running down to randomness. This contradiction in the system is again resolved by the idea of God, which now is understood to guarantee the infinite duration of nature and humanity thus making possible the continuity of ethical striving.

The Kantian pattern of beginning with the certainty of ethics and then building on that to explain belief in God is evident in both these lines of reasoning. Cohen extended this liberal approach to religion in a consistent manner and suggested that all modern thought about God should follow a method he called "correlation." One should not make statements about God which are not correlated with some assertion about humankind. As against traditional religion, which knew about God from God's own revealed words, or traditional philosophy, which taught that human ideas could give one understanding of Divinity-in-itself, liberals know that human thinking is at the root of every assertion about God. At the same time, one cannot properly speak about human beings without also saying something parallel about God, for humankind is situated in an integrated world-view of which God is the most fundamental idea. Cohen's sense of God is humanistic, or, equally, his humanism is religious. And of course, with ethics the critical aspect of being human, the theory of correlation lends additional activism to Cohen's philosophy.

The ethical task will be accomplished only in that ideal time religion has called the coming of the Messiah. In Cohen's construction the Messiah cannot be one person who rather miraculously creates the peaceful and just world order. For him, such thinking remains mythological. He rather sees humankind gradually becoming more ethical and extending the range and depth of moral relationships through its own natural efforts. The messianic time itself, as a reality, never actually occurs. If it did, instead of being the fulfillment of human existence, it would be its negation for it would bring to an end our singular human task—that is, being ethical. Messianism remains our most exalted human ideal, one that we are continually approaching by our good deeds but which remains infinitely distant.

Though specifically biblical terminology has been used to describe Cohen's vision of human destiny, it must be emphasized that all this is part of his academic philosophy, not the explication of a sectarian religious doctrine. As a secular thinker dealing with purely intellectual matters, Cohen found a rational need for concepts like God and messianism.

Is Religion of Reason Philosophical or Religious?

Cohen termed his understanding of science, ethics and aesthetics integrated by an overarching concept of God, *religion of reason*. He meant that any rational person needs a God-idea to bring together a coherent world-view and thus would be involved in its ethical and religious consequences. Cohen originally meant the term *religion of reason* as another of the ideals which are so significant a feature of his system (and which make him part of the idealist stream of philosophy). In that case, no actual religion will be the same as the philosophically defined religion of reason but the latter serves as a criterion and a goal for the former. In Cohen's later years, when he gave special attention to religion and then to Judaism, there seems to have been some wavering on the issue of identifying religion of reason with a historic religion.

The beginnings of this problem are to be found in his book of 1915, *The Concept of Religion in the System of Philosophy*. The title might be read to say that Cohen, having expounded his philosophy in previous years now intended to show how religion fit into it. If so, religion is thoroughly subordinate to a philosophic idea of God and to ethics. It has no independent intellectual status and thereby could require only what philosophic reason mandated. One might say that for the fully rational person religion had been superseded by God-grounded ethics (an implication quickly picked up by later generations of Jews who heard of Cohen's teachings at second or third hand). Cohen himself had long insisted that religions were still a practical necessity. Most people were far from fully rational and the great faiths communicated religion of reason to them in a form in which they could accept it. It also was valuable for motivating them to live the ethical life. The fervor it generated was a major factor in helping people overcome the many lesser impulses in their lives and the many social and natural difficulties that hindered their moral growth.

These instrumental justifications of religion were supplemented in the 1915 volume by an argument that religion has a unique sphere of competence. Philosophy, by dealing with universals, necessarily slights the individual. Religion, despite proper concern with its community, is based on the single self. It speaks to one's particular situation in a way that no general philosophical system can. Specifically, religion deals with the problem of sin and the rectification of sin in a way philosophy cannot. Reason can elaborate the need to do the good, or the failure to use reason which leads to doing evil, or the consequent importance of being rational in the next situation. Still, there is the actual history of moral failure, a serious concern to any sensitive human being. Religion speaks to this human situation by teaching of a God who forgives sin. It declares that God not only "wants" the good but equally "wants" people, once they have sinned, to atone. God is "ready" to be reconciled to all people who repent. This doctrine remains humanly active. God's forgiveness is not magically obtained but is the result of a free human return to God, in contrition and with the resolve to improve. Religion, not philosophy, by imparting the faith that human repentance is accepted, teaches us how to face guilt without lessening our moral responsibility.

Is Judaism "The" Religion of Reason?

This theory of religion seems an extension of Cohen's previous thought, not a break with it. There the matter might have rested had it not been for Cohen's next book, his extended interpretation of Judaism. In his earliest years as a university lecturer, Cohen wrote almost nothing about Judaism. In 1880, he published his first significant essay on a Jewish theme, responding to a vicious anti-semitic essay by Heinrich von Treitschke. That esteemed German historian alleged that the Jews were an utterly unassimilable tribe, being thoroughly alien to the spirit of the German nation. From then on, and most notably after 1890, Cohen wrote many papers on various aspects of Judaism, interpreted from his philosophic position. Not until his retirement to Berlin did he write a full-scale exposition of his understanding of Judaism.

The book began as a series of lectures to students at the Lehranstalt. Cohen died before having fully prepared them for publication but since, as was the custom, they were fully written out, this did not prove to be an unmanageable task. The work was entrusted to the brilliant young philosopher Franz Rosenzweig and it appeared in 1919. Rosenzweig and others seeking a new path in philosophy were impressed that Cohen's lectures showed a passionate identification of Judaism with religion of reason. They felt this demonstrated that Cohen had finally come to recognize the inadequacy of a strictly intellectual approach to existence. They argued that the shift from pure philosophy implicit in the 1915 study of religion had been as good as completed in the new book. Now religion, specifically Judaism, broke the domination of philosophy and came into its own. As a result Rosenzweig gave the book the title *The Religion of Reason Out of the Sources of Judaism*.

If that interpretation is correct—and it certainly indicates the direction Rosenzweig himself was taking—then the carefully integrated rationalism of the Cohenian system had been shattered. Once a non-rational factor is introduced into so tightly logical a system, it cannot assert its ideas to be required by reason. At any point one might refer to belief or some other such non-rational and non-discussable ground. And one might introduce almost any doctrine into a religion which was more than rational. Many of Cohen's students thought he was fully aware of that problem. In their reading, his last work does not justify the judgment that Cohen had now turned his interest from the *ideal* of religion of reason to *actual* religion. When the second edition of the book emerged, they removed the article "The" from the title so as to make certain the reference to "Religion of Reason" is not too specific. The English translation follows that version and calls the book only, *Religion of Reason Out of the Sources of Judaism*.

The Essence of Cohen's Judaism

Regardless of what historians may yet determine concerning the development of Cohen's thought, the major outlines of his interpretation of Judaism are unmistakable from his essays as well as his posthumous book. Cohen came to Judaism with a sure knowledge of the truth about the human situation, namely, religion of reason. The Jews of biblical times, like all human beings, had been in search of truth. In that pre-philosophic time they sought it and expressed what they found in ways that mixed reason with less dependable aspects of the human consciousness. In Jewish literature, most notably the Bible but also the rabbinic literature, one finds the expression of the Jewish national spirit. This is particularly significant because Cohen, stressing the universal quality of truth, believes that a group's spiritual search is more valuable than that of an individual. He therefore studies classic Jewish texts—more precisely, he selects and cites texts—which show the Jewish people's intuitive recognition of the Neo-Kantian truths about God and ethics. His general program is to indicate how religion of reason may be found in the sources of Judaism—exactly as announced in the title of the book.

This may be put in condensed form. The central thread of Jewish national consciousness is ethical monotheism, a concept of the unity of God grounding moral responsibility. When one looks for this theme in ancient Jewish writings, one cannot help but be astonished at its omnipresence. Prophetic literature brings it most clearly to the surface, and Cohen's exegesis, demonstrating that the prophets anticipated philosophic religion, is extended and impressive. Cohen identified prophetic Judaism with the highest spiritual insight of the Jewish people and with ethical monotheism.

Uncovering Religion of Reason in Judaism

Cohen and his numerous followers showed the hermeneutic riches which resulted from a search for ethical monotheism in Jewish sources. Thus, for Cohen the biblical fight against idolatry is not a mere rejection of inadequate, pagan forms of religion. It conceals a major Jewish intuition about the proper relation of Deity to the world. In idolatry, God can be identified with some aspect of nature. That destroys God's transcendence and robs the concept of God of its power to command. For if God can be identified with what is, we may deduce that it ought not be changed. A passivity to the world sets in as when one says, "What can you do? That's just the way things are."

The biblical polemic against idolatry is at its root a fight against making God so imminent that God cannot effectively command us, that is, ground the realm of ethics. When the Bible and the Talmud refer to God as king or high in the heavens, they are not making anthropomorphic or spatial comments. They are symbolically trying to give proper transcendence to our concept of God. When God is understood to stand logically on another level than humankind, God has a right to set its proper standards and serve as the ideal for its development.

Cohen considers it simplistic to think of monotheism as primarily a rejection of polytheism. Of course, having many gods would not allow for an integrated concept of nature and ethics. However, the unity of God is not asserted in religion of reason as a mere mathematical statement about God but as a qualitative one. Monotheism fundamentally proclaims God's uniqueness. God is not to be identified with nature for that would destroy ethics, or with ethics for that would destroy science. God's oneness says that God is, logically, on a level where nothing else is. God is unique in being prior to all else. Thus what follows in the system is subordinate to God ("commanded").

As a result, Cohen, is as antagonistic to pantheism as he is to polytheism because pantheism's identification of God with the world similarly negates Cohen's sort of ethics. Spinoza is his chief target here and he considers that philosopher's famous usage, "God or nature," a contradiction of reason and a rejection of Judaism. Spinoza did write about ethics, but the passivity and resignation which he necessarily considers to be the highest good contrast radically with Cohen's activism and messianic aspiration.

Cohen's Justification of Jewish Observance

Similarly enlightening results come from searching for religion of reason in Jewish practice. In the popular mind Yom Kippur may be considered a day of fasting and prayer undertaken to persuade God to forgive people as the new year begins. Under Cohen's probing it turns into the great reaffirmation of human moral freedom. The heart of the liturgy that day is a call for repentance, an act whose great power is celebrated in the afternoon reading of the book of Jonah. That is not a story about a whale but the astonishing tale in which the honest return to God of the evil citizens of Nineveh, hated enemies of the Jews, is accepted, thus averting their punishment. Yom Kippur is not a series of magical rites which bring God to cleanse humankind from its sins. Rather, it calls people to use their freedom to improve themselves. For sins against others, the law mandates an effort at restitution as the prerequisite to repentance being accepted. Even for sins against God, people begin their return by gaining insight into the evil they have done, feeling sorry for it and confessing that to God. But it is the resolution not to commit the sin again, a return to one's self as a moral agent, that completes our responsibility. What the holy day comes to proclaim is that if we accept our ethical responsibilities—the day's confessions do not include ritual matters—God will find us acceptable despite what we may have done in the past. Without some such assurance we might be so weighed down with guilt we could not face each moment's new obligations. Our past would destroy our future. Repentance comes to restore the future to us and thus Yom Kippur makes the coming year literally new in possibility for us. As the book of Deuteronomy says, God sets before us life and death and asks us to choose life.

Similarly Cohen sees the Sabbath as an ethical institution unique in human creativity. As contrasted with Babylonian days on which no work was done for fear of the gods, the Sabbath is devoted to rest, worship and study. It testifies to the uniqueness of human rationality for it occurs not as a result of any natural phenomenon but in response to the human ability to count the days. It also exemplifies human freedom. People, by an act of will, cease work and devote themselves to other activities. Nothing else in nature could carry out so creative an act. The required activities of the day direct people to their rational capacities through devotion to God, to study and to personal refreshment. The crown of this observance is the insistence that the day of rest be extended not only to one's family but also to one's slaves and the aliens resident in the community. Not even the powerless and the outsider are excluded from the class of the truly human, but the concept of a universal human community is given nuclear recognition.

The Appeal of the Cohenian Approach to Judaism

Since Cohen believes religion has a significant function in human life, he argues that we ought to keep all the observances of our faith which sensitize and empower us to be ethical. By this standard he provides modern Jewry with an answer to one of its most important questions: which acts must we still do and which may we change and remain authentic Jews in the modern world?

For Cohen, ethical monotheism, as the truth about our world, is permanent. All the practices which inculcate or express it may not be given up. The many activities in which the Jewish religion indirectly substantiates that truth are also desirable and should be retained. But any law or custom which violates our understanding of religion of reason must be revised for it represents a faulty sense of truth.

This line of reasoning was well known in early nineteenth-century liberal thought. Cohen gave it much more compelling utterance and thereby made his understanding of Judaism highly attractive to many Jews. Seeking to modernize themselves, they sought the assurance that in avidly devoting themselves to the general culture they were not denying Judaism. Cohen's understanding of ethical responsibility, particulary in its social ramifications, gave rational justification to their dimly sensed judgment. Cohen's philosophy turned the focus of Judaism from the Jewish people itself, particularly as developed in the ghetto period, to humankind as a whole. His teaching encouraged the integration of Jews into their society as a primary religious duty.

Cohen's theory also performed another major intellectual service. It clarified why Jews who sought to be modern should not become Christians, an enticing option for many in those days. If religion of reason is the criterion by which actual faiths are to be evaluated, Judaism is superior to Christianity. It does not center on miracles like the virgin birth, the incarnation, the resurrection and the ascension, and its religious practice does not contain sacraments, human acts in which God is actually involved. Judaism is also more consistently monotheistic for it has no notion of a man being God or God's unity simultaneously being a trinity. It is far more directly ethical for it places its stress on acts, not on faith, and it directs them by law, not by appealing to an amorphous sentiment like love. Cohen did not invent these themes. They were common to previous Jewish writers, but in Cohen's towering exposition of religion of reason they seemed to many Jews particularly persuasive.

The Place of Cohen in Subsequent Jewish Thought

Directly or indirectly, Cohen's influence has dominated American Jewish thinking through most of the twentieth century. Practically speaking, it has shaped the way most Jews understand Judaism. They have largely received their ideas about it from their rabbis, who in turn received it from their teachers at rabbinical school. Until relatively recently, almost all scholars who wanted a doctorate in Judaica went to Germany, which meant studying in a milieu in which Cohen's understanding of Judaism was the common way of discussing it. Generations of rabbis were taught to think of Judaism in terms of its rationality and ethics. However, Cohen himself was rarely studied. Only in 1971 did the first translation of some of Cohen's Jewish essays appear. An English rendering of *Religion of Reason* was published a year later. Thus, though Judaism as ethical monotheism is probably the standard religious ideology of American Jews, the powerful intellectual structure which stood behind it has been largely forgotten.

Cohen's influence remains in the model he set for succeeding Jewish thinkers. He did not justify Judaism on a parochial basis, demonstrating only to the faithful what they were already fairly well convinced of. He clarified a standard of truth which any person of intellect might debate and challenge. He spoke in terms of a full range of humanistic knowledge and on a high academic level. He was fully conscious of the intellectual problems of his time and gave them a bold solution. He was a learned, loyal Jew but he did not hesitate to think fearlessly about how Judaism in the modern age needed to change in belief and practice. He gave leadership to his people and defended them against their maligners. Since Cohen, serious Jewish thinkers have been measured by his standard.

Criticizing Cohen's Views of God and Practice

The great success of Cohen highlighted what succeeding thinkers have also seen as his major failings. On every level of Jewish affirmation—God, Torah and Israel—critics have found fault with his teachings, often claiming that history itself has validated their objections.

Cohen's God is an idea. In the way that philosophical idealists might use the term, God is therefore "real." But most Jews are not philosophers and even fewer are so rigidly idealistic as to think that

the most real thing there could be is a true thought. The abyss
between the committed philosopher and the rest of us yawns wide at
this point. Cohen was devoted to ideas and they often roused his
passions to the heights we see reflected in his writings. In response to
critics who chided him for suggesting that people might actually love
an idea of God, Cohen wrote, "How can one love anything save an
idea? For even in the love of the senses one loves only the idealized
person, only the idea of the person."

The matter should also be considered on a practical level. Many
Jews accepted the watered down version of Cohen's ethical monotheism which they were taught because it required them only
to have an *idea* of God. That freed them from establishing a personal
relationship with God. All they needed to do was to utilize a God-
concept as the organizing principle of their view of the world. That
done, the idea-God could be respectfully ignored as one turned to
the ethical tasks of human existence. Subsequent thinkers who
agreed with Cohen in most other matters often felt compelled to
revise Cohen's God-idea. Leo Baeck is the outstanding example of a
thinker who sought to make a rational God-idea "more real."
Mordecai Kaplan's rationalism results from describing God in a different philosophic mode.

Cohen's justification of Jewish practice evoked a more ambivalent
response. In claiming that universal ethics is the core of Jewish duty,
Cohen elucidated a theme which was not often explicit in classic
Jewish texts but which spoke to the conscience of modern Jews and
legitimized their participation in an emancipated society. Cohen's
high estimate of ethics in Judaism remains the conviction of most
modern Jews. But the implications of Cohen's theory for the rest of
Jewish observance caused major difficulties.

Cohen knows ethics to be commanded as a simple rational matter.
No other Jewish duty has such compelling power, though study
might come close. All other religious activities are not required, only
desirable. Cohen can authorize them only on an instrumental basis.
That is, though they are not *necessary*, rituals, celebrations and such
are often *helpful* in bringing us to a proper ethical level. Most
human beings do not live by their ideas. They need religious activi-

ties to bring them to a higher spiritual state than they could achieve on their own. This makes the other than directly ethical acts valuable—but does not make them mandatory or even very important. They are at best useful, but that also means they may be evaluated in terms of how effectively they carry out their function. Should daily prayer or observance of the Shavuot festival on a Wednesday not prove particularly conducive to ethical living, one may dispense with them. Many American Jews have used that as an excuse to give up much of Jewish duty except for ethics. To them traditional Jewish practice seems an inefficient means to the ethical life. Politics, therapy, the arts, recreation all suggest themselves as leading more directly to it—so they become the new "Jewish" commandments.

Cohen's Troublesome Attitude Toward the Jewish People

Perhaps Cohen might have redeemed this situation by a strong doctrine concerning the Jewish people and its place in Judaism but that was inconsistent with his ethical universalism. He rigidly interpretated Judaism as a religion. The Jewish people's only legitimacy derived from its devotion to its idea of God and its resulting messianic ethics. Cohen scorned duties based on membership in a racial or national group. That derived commandment from mere biology or history, thus irrationally confusing science or continuity with ethics. Cohen was therefore a vigorous anti-Zionist. He dismissed, as unworthy of rational beings with a universal outlook, the calls for a return to the land and a revival of the national tongue. Jewish nationalism particularly distressed him, for he believed the Jewish people had a mission to instruct humankind in the notion of ethical monotheism.

In his final book he had tried to explain why, though any rational mind should come to religion of reason, the Jewish people were still needed in history. He argued that the Jews were the first people to break through to this understanding of the relationship between God and humankind. Then, in an uncharacteristic shift of logic, he insisted that this primacy in time had given them a permanent and special status in history. The statement is so odd for Cohen that it deserves citation.

> I do not assert that Judaism alone is the religion of reason. I try to understand how other monotheistic religions also have their fruitful share in the religion of reason, although in regard to *primary origin* this share cannot be compared with that of Judaism. This primary origin constitutes the priority of Judaism, and this priority also holds for its share in the religion of reason. For the primary origin is the distinctive mark of creative reason . . . which produces a pure pattern. Primary origin bears the marks of purity. And *purity* in creativity is the characteristic of reason.

The argument has seemed to critical readers a shift from logical priority to historical precedence, a movement from idea to experience normally not allowed by Cohen.

Cohen believed the Jewish people now existed to keep the ideal of ethical monotheism alive in history and to disseminate it to all humankind. He could not grieve over the destruction of the Temple and the consequent dispersion of the Jews for they were the necessary means by which the people of Israel progressed from a particular national existence to universal human service. As an ethical, not an ethnic duty, it rightfully claimed the allegiance of all Jews to their people. Zionism, by contrast, rejected the universal ties of humankind by calling on Jews to leave the countries in which they found themselves, and move to the one land where the nation might fulfill itself. Nothing could be more antithetical to Cohen's position than classic nationalist Zionism.

Two painful, additional themes occur in Cohen's Jewish writings which must be mentioned. Cohen believes that suffering is the price Jews must pay to carry out their messianic role in history. He writes feelingly about the pain Jews have had to bear in the past and he does not advocate seeking out persecution. There is a nobility to his call to

Jews to be ready to face any hardship in order to bring the message of ethical monotheism to humanity. But it must be said that he seems fundamentally acquiescent and uncomplaining about the pain others bring to the Jews and his God-idea in no way mitigates this. Cohen obviously had an exalted sense of duty; he also died some decades before the Holocaust. The contemporary reader would almost certainly agree with Richard L. Rubenstein that if the chosen people doctrine requires us to accept the Holocaust as our Jewish due, an ethical person would give it up.

Even more disturbing is Cohen's judgment about the German nation. He identified its spirit with the highest ideals of humanity and argued that all Jews faithful to Judaism ought to be its admirers. During World War I he wrote two pamphlets equating the German and Jewish ideals and calling on world Jewry to support the German cause. In philosophy one ought not let a mistaken historical judgment invalidate an otherwise compelling system of thought. In this case the error is so blatant and the consequences so tragic that one can hardly help doubt the rigid universalism he so enthusiastically espoused.

Evaluating Cohen from an Altered Historical Context

Most of Cohen's attitudes toward the Jewish people seem problematic today. They seem to us utterly unrealistic, but we come to them with sixty years or so of experience which include the Holocaust, the founding of the State of Israel, and a general decline of confidence in the moral quality of western civilization. (Only with temerity should a scholar today assert that what the European or American academic mind considers rational is universally true for all humankind, on whatever continent or in any circumstance.) In Cohen's day, Jews were primarily concerned about achieving full human status, not in deepening their Jewishness. Many Jews were still observant and well educated. They often lived in communities whose traditions went back centuries. And there were always anti-semites to reinforce their

Jewish identity. Their primary Jewish question was the authenticity of general human activity. Cohen answered their need convincingly. But to a generation secure in its humanness but concerned about Jewish particularity, Cohen seems a problematic guide.

When, however, inquiring Jews ask about universal issues, Cohen's thought once again becomes relevant. He remains a challenge to anyone who would assert that Judaism is essentially particularistic and mandates only a grudging participation in the affairs of human-kind. Cohen made universal ethics the center of modern Judaism. Anyone who would make Jewish duty radically folk-oriented must contend with his sense of the Jew as primarily a person of broad ranging conscience.

Reviving his philosophic defense of this position would be difficult today. The Neo-Kantian understanding of reason has largely been rejected by contemporary philosophers, so one would need to do for Cohen what he did for Kant. A view which considers people to be fundamentally rational, and rationality inevitably ethical, seems intolerably optimistic. Yet Cohen's teaching about Jewish hu-manitarianism bespeaks a central religious intuition of modern Jewry. It knew leaving the ghetto was the right thing to do and, despite its disappointments in Emancipation, it is not going back there. If emotionalism and thoughtlessness continue to grow in the western world, if moral permissiveness continues to foster selfishness and violence, Cohen's plea for rationality and ethics will increasingly seem self-evident and necessary. And any interpretation of Judaism that concerns itself mainly with the Jewish people and its practices will show itself false to the lasting universal message which he disclosed was implicit in our tradition.

3

Religious Consciousness: Leo Baeck

ONE MIGHT fruitfully study twentieth-century Jewish religious thought by asking how its leaders sought to overcome the nineteenth-century identification of Judaism with ethics. The virtues of that stand were so great it could not readily be swept aside. By emphasizing a well accepted modern truth, the primacy of ethics, it simultaneously validated Jewish participation in general society, invigorated the practice of much of Jewish law and explained the superiority of Judaism to Christianity. Most Jews still consider Judaism a uniquely ethical religion. Even the traditionally minded largely retain the liberal notion that the first among many Jewish duties is moral behavior to all people. They are somehow personally offended when a Jew who is meticulous about ritual observance, is publicly demonstraated to have acted unethically.

As the twentieth century moved on, Jewish thinkers were increasingly troubled by the liberalism derived from Hermann Cohen. It led to the easy inference that everything in Judaism other than ethics—belief in God, devotion to the Jewish people, the rich way of life mandated by the Torah—might almost be eliminated, or, at least, considered secondary. The issue is not so much the primacy of ethics but their sufficiency. The premise may be put positively: an authentic Jewish existence is more than ethical though ethics are central to

53

it. But what constitutes the more-than-ethical aspects of being a Jew? How are they to be validated so that they speak of the modern Jew with something like the authority of the moral law? These and corollary questions continue to be at the heart of debates on the nature of Jewish identity and obligation. We begin our pursuit of this theme—Hermann Cohen being the classic case of the equation of Jewish faith and ethical existence—with Leo Baeck's effort to modify rather than break with the rationalist interpretation of Judaism.

Harnack's Antagonist and Emulator

Cohen had foreseen that the intellectual most likely to carry on his work was Leo Baeck. At the turn of the century Baeck won wide and almost instant recognition with the appearance of his book, *The Essence of Judaism*. The German Jewish community recognized that the previously unheralded young rabbi of the provincial town Oppeln, had a unique gift for epitomizing and justifying his faith. Though he drew heavily on the ideas current in German Jewry and particularly on the Jewish thought of Hermann Cohen, Baeck already showed originality in his philosophy of Judaism.

Baeck's work was stimulated by the extraordinary reception given Adolf von Harnack's volume of 1900, *The Essence of Christianity* (entitled in translation *What is Christianity?*) and has often been seen as a Jewish response to Harnack—which in part it is. Baeck never mentions Harnack in his work, yet the continual comparison of his Judaism to Harnack's Christianity are obvious. For Harnack, Christianity is centered around one man and his teaching. By contrast, Judaism knows no single, dominating figure but rather a continuous succession of teachers around whom Jewish history centers. Christianity, according to Harnack, suffered a major dislocation of its pristine faith. This dislocation was healed by the Protestant Reformation, a healing, now renewed in Protestant liberalism. Judaism, Baeck contended, demonstrates an essential continuity of teaching expressed in different forms over the ages but remaining essentially true to itself. While the fundamental message of the Church is a love for all people that stems from being loved by God, Judaism preaches a more stringent social ethical relationship to God in which the deed rather than the heart is central.

Baeck borrowed more than a title from Harnack when he called his book *The Essence of Judaism*. He took over Harnack's claim that the thinker could expose the underlying, permanent truth of a religion. As religious liberals, both men believed in religious change. They therefore had the responsibility of clarifying what remained true in their faith today as in the past, despite all the apparent reforms of ideas and practice. Harnack did this by applying to Christianity some of the ideas of the philosopher of history, Wilhelm Dilthey. That sage had suggested that one could understand a historical period or great work only if one brought to it a certain measure of empathy. Scholars were, of course, tied to their own time and place but, knowing this, they might imaginatively enter another moment in history. The subjectivity this might unleash was to be kept in check by a deep personal immersion in the primary sources of the era.

Harnack was the ideal German historian to carry out this project in relation to Christianity. He had an awesome mastery of the sources of Christianity. During his long life he published hundreds of detailed philological studies and a number of major books. In the lectures which were published as his *Essence* he put aside his historical researches momentarily to let the data speak through him. Having steeped himself so thoroughly in the history of Christianity, he could hope that its eternal truth would attain utterance in his description of it.

Baeck borrowed Harnack's method and applied it to Judaism. Unlike Cohen the philosopher, Baeck did not begin his work by establishing rational categories with which to explain Judaism. He spoke more as a historian, in that special sense of German, idealist history in which the researcher is less concerned with specifying just what happened or why it happened than what it meant as a manifestation of the human spirit. While Baeck served all his life as a community rabbi, he was uncommonly scholarly. His special competence was *midrash*, a discipline which allowed him to range freely through the history of Jewish ideas. By his interest in mystic texts, for example, Baeck was one of the precursors of Gershom Scholem.

Baeck was free not only of a philosophical system as he approached the texts, but also of the traditional theologian's insistence that they were God's revelation. For Baeck the validity of Judaism did not rest on a unique event at Sinai, but rather on the truth of the central ideas which the Jewish people had maintained over the ages. Baeck maintained this intuitive-historical stance toward the interpretation of Judaism in all his writings.

Rationalism Alone Cannot Adequately Explain Judaism

In terms of result there is not much to separate the rabbi-historian Leo Baeck from the philosopher of Judaism, Hermann Cohen, because Baeck found ethical monotheism to be the essence of Judaism. Baeck, however, departed from Cohen in basing his exposition of Judaism not only on our sense of the ethical but on religious consciousness as well. To some extent, that shift from rigorous rationalism may be found in the first edition of *The Essence of Judaism*, but it dominates the greatly expanded and revised second edition which appeared in 1922. By then the major supports of Baeck's intellectual structure were firmly set, and in the seven subsequent editions which followed there are only minor alterations.

For all his new premise, Baeck did not abandon or modify the Neo-Kantian insistence on the primacy of ethics. He wrote:

> From the very beginning of the real, the prophetic, religion of Israel, its cardinal factor was the moral law. Judaism is not merely ethical, but *ethics constitute its principle, its essence*. Monotheism came into being as a result of the realization of the absolute character of the moral law. [Italics in original.]

Much still sounds like Cohen. But Baeck adds a sentence that hints at the move to another dimension: "The moral consciousnesses teaches about God." The word "consciousness" is highly significant to Baeck. It points to a different realm of experience from the scientific-ethical rationalism to which philosophy is limited by the Neo-Kantians. It echoes Friedrich Schleiermacher's interpretation of religion as a unique human experience. For Schleiermacher, religious consciousness is quite distinct from the sort of practical reason which Kant identified with morality. It is the feeling people have within them, naturally and properly, of absolute dependence, that is, on God. Such a consciousness is distinct from rationality for properly understood it is far more fundamental to human existence than reasoning. In this mid-nineteenth century theory, Schleiermacher pioneered the idea that religion was to be understood and validated as a matter of inner experience rather than of reason.

Baeck takes great pains to differentiate his approach from that of Schleiermacher—which is good reason to think he was not oblivious of his debt. Baeck may also have been influenced by Rudolf Otto's book, *The Idea of the Holy*. Appearing in 1917 to wide acclaim, Otto's study gave new vigor to the notion of religion arising from a unique level of consciousness. Otto sought to make Schleiermacher's somewhat diffuse identification of the religious consciousness much more precise. Religious consciousness, he argued, was a direct perception of the numinous, characterized by deep feelings of awe and fascination—our sixth empirical sense, so to speak. What surely influenced Baeck in his effort to move beyond Cohenian rationality was the new intellectual acceptance Otto had won for the idea of religion based on personal experience. Baeck could speak without hesitation of our consciousness of mystery as the deepest root of our religiosity. But Baeck rejected Otto's theory as inadequate to Judaism for it did not make ethics a primary ingredient of the holy. To Baeck as to Cohen, the two were inseparable.

Baeck's addition of this new principle of religious consciousness shatters the philosophic integrity of the Neo-Kantian argument. Cohen's carefully integrated system is fully dependent upon "pure" knowledge, "pure" will, "pure" feelings. These are defined as utterly rational, in need of no validation other than thought itself. Once that purity is broken, once an element beyond Kantian rationality can be decisive, the entire system falls. From the rationalistic philosopher's perspective, such thought ceases to be rational and hence becomes intellectually worthless. For Baeck to expound Judaism, even partially, in terms of special religious consciousness is tantamount to repudiating the chief virtue of Cohen's work. But by 1922 Cohen was dead.

Baeck surely realized that he had made a major methodological departure, but he was a rabbi in concern as in profession; and his primary interest was in the quality of the religious life produced by a philosophy of Judaism. Cohen's Neo-Kantian exposition had established the centrality of God in human existence but did so in terms of God as an idea or a concept. Cohen's God is the logical ground of our world view who integrates the divergent aspects of our rational activity into a coherent system. Such a God, Baeck felt, is too abstract to elicit piety and hardly provides a reason for expanding ethics into a broader pattern of religious observance. Of course, for an idealist philosopher there is no reality greater than that of a systematically required rational idea; certainly there is no more important idea in Cohen's system than the idea of God. Nonetheless, to the devout, there remains an unbearable distance between what philosophy says God is and what the religious life discloses. Whether in response to the yearning for personal contact with the deepest level of reality—a widespread phenomenon after World War I—or whether in simple reassertion of traditional Jewish piety, Baeck, by utilizing the notion of religious consciousness, now introduced the felt, subjective aspect of religion into his explanation of Judaism.

The Consequences of Having Two Major Premises

Baeck's exposition of the essence of Judaism is worked out in terms of two major motifs, human ethics and religious consciousness. As a direct result, he develops most of his ideas in a dialectical fashion, balancing one notion against another that moves in a somewhat different direction. For instance, one of his central ideas is that human beings have an elemental sense of being created (somewhat like Schleiermacher's sense of absolute dependence), and yet also know they are most true to themselves when they are creators, which is when they act ethically (an activism which is radically different from Schleiermacher's sense of religion). Such interplay of exposition in terms of ethics and religious consciousness is characteristic of Baeck's thought, though not all of the polarities he develops stem so directly from this basic dichotomy in human religiosity.

Baeck's unique, non-philosophic approach to human piety appears in his treatment of the ground of ethics. He situates this not in our rationality but in the mystery which a religious consciousness senses behind the creation. Both Kant and Cohen knew the philosophic desirability of extending ethics beyond its specific content. In Kant, ethics lead on to the practical knowledge that there is a God who guarantees moral fulfillment. In Cohen, the idea of God guarantees that the infinite moral task will have infinite reality in which to work itself out.

Those philosophic assertions pale beside the personal certainty of devout believers. They know that the commandments concern them individually, that they derive from what is most real in the universe, that failure to do them properly induces guilt, and that a day will come when righteousness will visibly triumph on earth. Religious certainty is incalculably richer than the rational assertions of philosophy. Religious experience testifies to what lies beyond the ethical, to the God who is more than the idea implied by ethics but is the One who has the right to issue imperatives and make them categorical. Reason cannot reach such a God.

For Baeck, ethics without this mysterious grounding in God is mere moralism. For Judaism, there can be no ethics which does not stem from such a living God who establishes relationships with humankind. With the rejection of a living God, Baeck contends, the rejection of ethics cannot be long delayed. Such has been the gloomy truth of modern history.

However, to glorify human feelings and allow them to determine the content of the religious life is dangerous, producing an a-ethical religion of self-concern or utter inwardness. Or, directed outward, such emotions might easily produce fanaticism or superstition. Having often suffered from human irrationality, Judaism knows better than to base itself on unbriudled feeling. Its religious consciousness, Baeck insists, receives authentic expression only in ethical acts. When it threatens to emerge in any other guise, it must be rejected as temptation. However, when feeling is channeled into the ethical realm, it brings power and strength to the ethical, receiving in turn the secure guidance it needs if our humanity is not to be perverted.

This dialectical tension between religious consciousness and ethics is Baeck's unique intellectual creation. In its assertion, Baeck broke with the Neo-Kantian, philosophic understanding of Judaism. In actuality, Baeck was more concerned to dissociate himself from Schleiermacher's sense of religion as absolute dependence. Baeck found this concept intolerable because it renders human beings ethically inert and so destroys our dignity. Practically, too, by Baeck's time German Romanticism had made clear its great potential for viciousness, not least by its close link with a growing anti-semitism. Schleiermacher would have despised such an extension of his thought, but thinking about these matters decades later, Baeck could not fail to be concerned about the danger of abandoning oneself to one's emotions. Baeck's debt to Cohen and the Kantian stream in German Jewish thought is most evident at this point. Due to their teaching, he insisted on containing religious experience within the structure of ethical command, even while defining it ultimately in romantic, not rational, terms.

God, Personally Sensed but Ethically Demanding

Baeck's exposition of Judaism remains typically liberal. It says much more about human beings, their ethical sense, and their consciousness of the Divine than it says about who God is and what, if anything, God does—but that humankind on which he focuses is spoken of in terms of its full range of consciousness. As opposed to Cohen, Baeck argues that the *idea* of God has little more religious value than any other pure idea. Our certainty that God is real comes not from our rational demonstration that God is the First Cause or the one who orders nature. We find it rather in what has happened to our lives, in the inner consistency, the moral power, and the sense of meaning and direction we now have gained. We know that our lives must be lived in response to a question put to us from beyond the mystery we sense at the heart of existence.

Can we say, then, that Judaism affirms a personal God? Of that, Baeck insists, nothing can be said today and nothing was said in classic Judaism. God is not to be understood as a God of qualities or about whom dogmas may be stated. Judaism has no dogmas, no explicit statements about God's reality which all Jews must accept. However, Judaism knows that since people are conscious of God as one close and responsive to us, one who penetrates our innermost depths, "He is therefore understood personally and regarded as personal." This is typical of Baeck's use of religious consciousness to reclaim aspects of traditional Jewish piety which were inaccessible to the Neo-Kantians.

Baeck naturally balances this emphasis on personalism with ethical rigor. Intimate talk about God engenders an anthropomorphism that believers can take seriously. This destroys God's transcendence, thereby vitiating the authority by which the ethical comes to us as a categorical demand. The medieval philosophers waged a protracted battle against this misunderstanding. They succeeded but only by turning God into an abstraction which denied the innermost reality of religious experience. Judaism overcame that danger by asserting a fundamental paradox about God: the exalted, transcendent God is nonetheless the present, personal God. Nothing stands between each individual and God—God is that close—but the very same God remains the God of the infinite heights and depths of creation. The ethical and the devotional are simultaneously affirmed in Judaism.

The sensitivity with which Baeck uses these two interpretive devices is well illustrated in his treatment of God's wrath or jealousy. Baeck feels we cannot reject these biblical terms simply because they are anthropopathisms, for then we would also have to give up such meaningful symbolic expressions for God as "Father." Encountering such disturbing language, we need to investigate what aspects of the religious consciousness are being articulated. God's anger is a way of expressing our sense that ethics must be uncompromising. Genuine morality always involves a protest against, and resistance to, indecency. It will not have any intercourse with evil. Every trace of unrighteousness implies a denial of God and a perversion of human dignity. Immorality brings one into a realm without meaning, value or ultimate reality. Against the Bible's admonition, we leave life and choose death. There is no compromise with evil or tolerance of it. God's jealousy powerfully symbolizes this aspect of the belief that God is one.

Baeck's Theory of Evil

Baeck is similarly categorical in his theory of evil. The source of evil is the misuse of human freedom. That people are fully free to do the good is an essential Jewish teaching—as well as the necessary premise of any serious ethics. So people are responsible when they do evil, even as they are praiseworthy when they do the good. Nothing may be allowed to impinge on this primary human need to be ethical or their capacity to do so. Baeck is relentlessly polemical against the Christian doctrine of original sin. He insists it utterly misreads human nature and that its promulgation provides people with an easy excuse for not summoning their moral power and doing the good.

Similarly, when people have done evil, this does not destroy their fundamental ethical freedom. They can change their way and make themselves again acceptable to God. The Rabbis termed this *teshuvah*, repentance. In Baeck's modern, ethical reworking of the doctrine, we are always responsible for what we do, even for turning from our sin and reestablishing our relationship with God. For good or for evil, the power is utterly ours.

Baeck set forth his theory of evil in the 1920's. His passionate commitment to ethical existence and his corollary emphasis on human responsibility form the essential basis for understanding his response to the Holocaust.

Baeck was the only major modern Jewish theologian to enter and survive Hitler's death camps. When Hitler came to power, Baeck was the leading liberal rabbi of Berlin and such a significant figure in the German Jewish community that he was named president of its representative organization. The dignity that he brought to a justly proud community about to undergo a tragedy unlike anything perpetrated by a civilized nation—and how can one compare this to what uncivilized people did in their barbarity?—has been movingly described by survivors of that period. Despite many opportunities to leave the country permanently, including several official trips abroad, he chose to stay with his people. In January 1943, he was sent to a concentration camp. His demeanor there; his concern for others; his efforts to keep them human by teaching them, from memory, the great humanistic classics; his refusal to be less than ethical, or to let the Nazis make him less than human, made him one of the heroic figures of an impossible situation. By error, chance, the sacrifice of others, by his spirit and the grace of Providence, the seventy-year-old rabbi survived Theresienstadt.

He went to London in July 1945 and in the years that followed, until his death in 1956, he continued writing and lecturing. Despite his experience, he did not feel that the Holocaust had changed anything he believed, and he did not see it requiring him to rewrite what he had said so powerfully in an earlier, happy time. Evil was the result of free human choice and God dignified us by not interfering with our freedom to determine what we would do. The Nazis had been more ruthless, more effective, more barbaric than other great evil-doers. Yet, they had not fundamentally changed the problem of

evil. Certainly they taught nothing new about God, though perhaps
they had shown something new about the human capacity or will to
evil. Even that drew no comment from Baeck. Perhaps having taken
the power to do good so seriously, he had known all along how
destructive the choice of evil could be.

The Continuity of Baeck's Thought After the Holocaust

Baeck published one book after the Holocaust, *Dieses Volk: Jüdische
Existenz* (in the English translation, *This People Israel: The Meaning
of Jewish Existence*). Much of its first part had been written before his
internment and while he was in Theresienstadt. Part two was the
product of the early post-World War II years. Its concerns seem already enunciated in "Theology and History," an essay he published
in 1932 in the face of the increasing rejection of rationalism in
Protestant theology and the alarming growth of Nazism.

"Theology and History" states the need for a theology of Judaism
to be new in its particularity, but not in its essence. Baeck warns
against importing into Judaism the new methods of particularistic
terminology of recent Christian theology, the Biblicism or Karl Barth
or the existentailism of Rudolf Bultmann or Paul Tillich. He sees
these as distorting any description of Judaism. Instead, he urges a
continued use of the science of Judaism with its critical, rational
approach to the Jewish past. In the present situation, however, it
needs to be utilized for the purpose of clarifying the continuing
validity of Judaism. The historic continuity of the essence of Judaism
is the one firm basis for Jewish theology.

What had changed for Baeck was not the method of doing theology, which still follows Dilthey, but only the focus of concern. He
now proposed to elucidate the particularity, that is, the distinctive
characteristics of the Jewish experience, but he still meant to explain
them in terms of the universal truth of human ethics and religious
consciousness.

This People Israel is the fulfillment of that program. His new interests are given by the full title. Where once he wrote about Judaism, here he is concerned with the Jewish people. Before, he searched for the essence. Now it is existence which matters. Yet for all the concern with Jewish history and even the Land of Israel, Baeck does not break with his former way of thinking. He explains and justifies Jewish particularity in terms of its relation to the essence of Judaism, which remains a generally available human truth, ethical monotheism. Baeck had not given up his universal-oriented ethical approach for an existentialist, particularist approach to Judaism. *This People Israel* is only an extension of what he had written in *The Essence of Judaism* a quarter of a century before. He gives the Holocaust less than one page of attention and the slightly larger treatment of the State of Israel is substantially taken up by two prophetically insightful questions: How will Israelis get along with Arabs? and will nationalism or religion be fundamental to the state? Baeck believed the theory of the Jewish people he had given in *The Essence of Judaism* remained correct. All he needed to do in the later book was give it more ample statement and apply it to the people's actual history.

Baeck's attitude to the Jewish people and Jewish law should be understood in the context of his analysis of Judaism's essence as a universal human truth. Only in the final pages of *The Essence of Judaism* did he treat the particularistic doctrine of Judaism in some detail. Clearly, he was not unconcerned with Jewish sources and what they had to say about the people of Israel or its practices. He continually cites the Jewish classics—the Bible, the prayer book, the Rabbis—making many an often quoted phrase refract a new light. He does so to carry out an ethical transvaluation of their meaning and disclose their hidden, universal message. Baeck studies the Jewish tradition to prove that the general human apprehension of ethics, extended to its religious depth, has been the creative force in Judaism.

Truth, for Baeck, remains universal. Whatever is true about

Judaism must be true for all human beings. Baeck does not believe the Jews had a revelation no other people had or could have had. He does not think anything their religious consciousness intuited and expressed in their people's way of life was unavailable to all other peoples. This being the case, Baeck is forced to confront rationalism's continuing challenge to all forms of particularism: If truth is generally available, why is your view of it, your people's particular sense of it, and your group's way of living it worthy of special devotion? The question is particularly poignant to Jews, for being a Jew not only carries with it many responsibilities, it involves the heavy burdens of minority existence extended to the point of potential special suffering.

Baeck's Understanding of the Jewish People

Baeck's particular mix of universalism and particularism emerges clearly in his treatment of the traditional Jewish doctrine of God having chosen this people "from among all peoples." In Baeck's system, religious consciousness allows us to conceive God through our sense of the mysterious depth to human createdness. This is not a sufficient philosophic basis for saying God acts in history. Rather, since God's relationship with people has a universal ethical structure, any notion of chosenness as preference is precluded. The God of Baeck's ethical monotheism must be equally available to all, a concept known to traditional Judiasm. Baeck goes further. His God cannot be particularly related to any one people—a negation of the classic Jewish doctrine, that the universal God has a special people. What then, constitutes Jewish "chosenness" for Baeck?

The universally available idea of ethical monotheism came to the Hebrews as it might to any people. In their case alone it became decisive for their self-perception as a people. They applied the universal demands of ethical monotheism to their folk life and staked their ethnic existence on their religious insight. Remaining faithful to their vision despite periods of infidelity, they became conscious of themselves as set apart from other peoples. They felt themselves uniquely pledged to God and historically identified with the idea of ethical monotheism. They thus became a people with a mission. They survived as a people not only for their own sake, but so that humankind might come to know and serve the one God. In this knowledge they found the strength to endure their suffering over the millenia.

Baeck does not assert Jewish particularity in terms of Judaism's essential content, which is universal, but only in the historic actuality of its appropriation and continuing expression. The Jews are "chosen" because they chose to devote themselves to God. They were confronted, as all people are, with God's command to be human, but they alone made that behest the foundation of their ethnic life. As this became their deepest consciousness of themselves, they called themselves God's chosen people. Again, Baeck's two principles balance out. What ethical theory had made improbable, the coordinate theory of religious consciousness has now explained.

Baeck's Polemic Against Christianity

Jewish particularity has existential rather than mere historical validity only if it can be argued that no other community carries the idea of ethical monotheism through history. In *The Essence of Judaism*, Baeck identified two types of religion—world-affirming and world-rejecting. He considers Judaism the classic example of the former type and he calls it a religion of ethical optimism. He does not deny that there are ethical teachings in the world-rejecting religions, of which Buddhism is the prototype, but their essential stance toward life is withdrawal. Buddhist ethics gains its objectives by eliminating human desire and thereby reducing contentiousness. However, its adherents no longer care deeply about anything. Their detachment keeps them from being passionate about righteousness or outraged by immorality.

Christianity seems to share Judaism's faith about God and ethics. But Baeck insists that Christian self-consciousness differs radically from its Jewish counterpart. He developed this thesis extensively in the essay "Romantic Religion," published first in 1922 and later somewhat expanded.

Baeck also employs the typological method to identify two varieties of religious experience. "Classic" religion is positive, activist, outgoing, social, ethical, deed-oriented, rational, masculine. "Romantic" religion is passive in the face of reality, individualistic, self-centered, inward, concerned with faith and its content, confirming itself in feelings, emphasizing grace. It has a feminine cast.

Pure types exist only in thought but history knows outstanding representatives of these possibilities. Judaism is closest to the classic type while Christianity is the finest example of romantic religion. Baeck ranges through the breadth of Christian history, Catholic as well as Protestant, to exhibit its non-rational, ethics-subordinating features. Since these are fundamental to Christianity as a religion, in principle it cannot hope to become a more activist, ethical faith by accepting liberal ideas. Judaism, by contrast, was always essentially the religion of world-transforming ethical monotheism, so its modernization is only the fulfillment of its classic stance. Baeck insists that he is making no value judgments in this essay but only describing the two faiths. But to anyone who cares about religion of reason, the message is clear.

Subjectivity is the problem of all typologies, and Baeck's argument is no exception. Why there are just two types, why these are romantic and classic, why Judaism and Christianity are the chief representatives, why all the countervailing evidence in both religions is ignored—none of these issues is examined; none of Baeck's premises is explained. Each is a mere assertion. Baeck speaks of Judaism in liberalistic terms as an ethical, rational faith. He contrasts this modern, German reinterpretation of Judaism with traditionalistic Protestantism and Catholicism. Baeck was so fully committed to this method that he believed his statement of the essence of Judaism to be objectively visible, not a highly subjective reading. But what he and

Harnack, in the self-assurance of their humanistic, scientific approach to the interpretation of history, took as self-evident now appears as self-justification masquerading as science. Baeck's argument for Jewish uniqueness says more about Baeck's love for his tradition than it does about reality. As a consequence, his resolution of the problem of Jewish particularity is seriously compromised.

The Jewish Role in History

Baeck drew a uniquely activist conclusion regarding the Jewish mission to humankind. Exemplification, the classic Jewish strategy, is not enough for him. He believes modern Jews should undertake a campaign of proselytization. Though Jews in medieval times did not seek converts and seemed rather to discourage them, he argues that this was largely the result of external pressures. While in talmudic times the Rabbis occasionally protest against proselytes, the overwhelming majority of their statements are positive. Baeck reads that history as saying that when the Jews were free, they proselytized. Therefore, he feels that today, in all dignity and faithfulness to their belief, they should do so again.

Baeck occasionally takes this line of reasoning one critical step further. He declares that the idea of ethical monotheism cannot now be detached from Israel. Significant spiritual notions become part of human reality by being borne by specific peoples or cultures. Other groups may come to know the meaning of ethical monotheism but the Jews alone, having identified themselves with it, are responsible for its fate in history. Since human beings are prone to relapse into paganism, the people of Israel's task is not short-term. Stubborn endurance is a Jewish ethical imperative; for a Jew, to exist is a commandment.

Typically, Baeck balances this realistic depiction of the world with Jewish optimism. Israel's service will not be in vain. Humanity can reach a time when it fulfills the command addressed to it. This messianic faith enabled Israel to survive over the centuries. The Jewish people now stands in history not only as a witness to the truth of messianism but to the efficacy of hope. A despairing humankind needs Israel to remind it that human ethical striving need not be defeated. Baeck devotes *This People Israel* to showing how the different stages of Jewish history contributed to this continuing Jewish service.

Jewish Law, a Means to the Universal End

This line of reasoning logically leads to Baeck's theory of Jewish law. Jewish law enables the people of Israel to carry on through history in devotion to its faith. The distinction between commandment and law is critical here.

Baeck normally uses the word "commandment" only for that which comes from God, namely ethical behests. People may come to know the ethical better or express it more fully but it is not subject to human will or imagination. Baeck uses the term "law" to refer to a broader realm of obligation, one whose precepts are legislated by people, essentially for their own purposes. Law therefore is subject to human evaluation and revision. Jewish law makes its most immediate claim upon Jews insofar as it states or leads to ethics, that is, to "commandment." In any tension between commandment and Jewish law, ethics has priority since it is the essence of Judaism.

Baeck is liberal. He favors change in the "law" to allow "commandment" to become more evident. Yet in all other cases, Baeck advocates our keeping Jewish law for it carries out another function. It helps the Jewish people survive history, keeping the people together and faithful through time and despite place. Though widely dispersed, in dissimilar climates, under differing economic systems, or disparate political orders, the law keeps them one Jewish people, dedicated to their universal mission. It also separates them from the paganism of humankind and enjoins a community life of warmth and beauty which is the most effective antidote to anti-semitism. If the law only served a social function it would have no compelling power. However, its high ethical content not only keeps Israel alive as a people but loyal to its task.

How Satisfying is Baeck's Reworking of Rationalism?

Baeck's thought may very well represent the last of the great Jewish universalist intellectual systems. At the moment it seems unlikely to have any significant successor. Thoughtful Jews today regularly call for a Judaism which emphasizes particularism, specifically, a rich appreciation of Jewish peoplehood, and a strong sense of ritual observance. If Jewish authenticity now requires such particularity, universally grounded Jewish theologies have been unable to provide it. Baeck's thought demonstrates this failing.

Though he went beyond Neo-Kantianism to create a system with a personally felt relationship to God, he remained in the world of philosophical idealism he had inherited. By grounding the essence of Judaism in universals, he left open a series of almost unanswerable questions regarding Jewish particularity. If ethical monotheism can be known by any person of religious consciousness, why does one need Judaism? If this universal truth is reasonably clear today, why chance distorting it by particularizing it? And, most dangerous and probing of all, if the essence of Judaism is available in direct, intellectual form, are we not ethically required to spare future generations of Jews the possible suffering entailed in perpetuating our people?

These questions arise directly out of Baeck's idealism: in his thought, the people, Israel, exists for the sake of its idea, ethical monotheism. If so, Baeck has made it possible to argue, particularly after the Holocaust, that one should choose a less dangerous instrument to accomplish the same end. Baeck might respond that the Holocaust proves how far from ethical existence even supposedly civilized people are. If anything, it demonstrates the supreme importance of the Jewish people continuing its humanizing mission.

Baeck's actual intellectual response to this argument, however, seems alien to his system. A Hegelian could argue, with some consistency, that an idea requires a people to carry it through history, but such an assertion cannot be made on the basis of ethics or religious consciousness which all people possess. Baeck's assertion that the Jewish people has become inextricably tied to the idea of ethical monotheism seems hardly credible when we recall the Kantian origins of this concept. At the very least it seems odd that a gentile German philosopher and his successors were able to clarify what is asserted to be "the essence of Judaism." If ethical monotheism can be recognized by all rationally competent and religiously attuned people, on what basis can one argue that the idea cannot survive without the Jewish people?

Jews Today and in Baeck's Vision

Baeck's notion that the Jews exist for their religious truth leads to added complications. Like Cohen, his universalism prevents him from seeing significant value in Jewish ethnicity, though unlike the philosopher he can see considerable instrumental worth in it. Thus, where Cohen was resolutely anti-Zionist, Baeck is only a non-Zionist. Baeck found virtue in whatever unites the Jewish people so long as it also contributes to their world-wide mission. So he appreciated and participated in the effort to resettle Palestine and to bring Jews there in escape from Hitler. There was a kind of Zionism for which he had little or no sympathy. He saw no point in ethnic activities for their own sake and opposed secular, nationalistic interpretations of Judaism. After his rescue from Theresienstadt he did not settle in Jerusalem but lived in London. The choice was not merely a matter of personal convenience. Like so much else of Baeck's life, it was symbolic and consistent with his philosophy.

The critique of Baeck's particularism can also be extended to his theory of Jewish practice. Assuming that the Jewish people is the bearer of ethical monotheism in history, why must Jews go beyond doing the good and believing in God? Is not all the rest of Jewish observance formality? If we are ethical and loyal to our people, why must we seriously attend to a lunar calendar, Semitic celebrations, and Hebraic liturgy? Although they might enrich our lives and solidify the Jewish people, they are also a special burden. By contrast, our society has many groups working for ethical ends. Membership in them is particularly appealing when they also consciously attempt to overcome the divisions between groups.

On a practical level the challenge is put this way: "Isn't it enough to be a good Jew if one is ethical and believes in one God?" In a day when so many ethical demands compete for proper attention, most people are quite satisfied if they can manage to live the simplest life, to do the essence. They are only too willing to abandon activities which are not essential though they might be useful, particularly when these are burdensome and require a special effort. And this competition for time and energy tells much of the story of modern liberal Judaism.

Baeck's system might have spoken to the needs of a generation so solidly Jewish that its universalization was no threat to its Jewishness. Our community is in another situation. We are substantially integrated into the general culture. An interpretation of Judaism which speaks mainly of our relation to humanity and gives little emphasis to our distinctiveness avoids the major problem of contemporary Jewish existence.

The broadest intellectual criticism is that Baeck never explains how religious consciousness and ethical understanding are bound together. Why does inner experience need to be limited in action to what the ethical can allow? Why must the ethical command rest on a mysterious ground? One cannot claim their balance is self-evident or even rational for, in substantial measure, they contradict one another. Philosophically these limits go against the teachings of the intellectual schools which created these concepts. In response, Baeck might argue that he is not a philosopher. He is only describing in modern terms the unity Judaism envisioned and taught through the ages. This brings critics to their most penetrating question: Just how does Baeck know this? What is the methodology by which he ascertains the essence of Judaism? What are the criteria by which he knows what is unessential and secondary? Why has apparently contradictory material been ignored? Surely his proposal, for all its persuasiveness, differs from the self-understanding of the Jewish tradition. No Jew before the nineteenth century talked about Judaism or its essence, no classic Jewish book mentions "ethical monotheism." Jews now doing so have a substantial burden of proof if they are to convince skeptics that their doctrine is authentically Jewish rather than a modern idea read back into the Jewish tradition.

Yet there is lasting greatness to Baeck's thought. In the face of the great philosophical accomplishments of Cohen, Baeck reasserted the right of religion to speak to the heart. Rationalism greatly appealed to modern Jews. It served to validate their participation in modern culture and their rejection of conversion to Christianity. For many Jews, reason alone was an adequate way of bringing modernity and Judaism into harmony. But not for Leo Baeck. While granting the virtues of the Neo-Kantian interpretation of Judaism, he dared to extend its scope and, in so doing, to make the religious life more substantial. He introduced the notion of personal experience into modern Jewish thought and insisted that personal spirituality was part of the essence of Judaism.

While his theories of the Jewish people and Jewish law have been seriously challenged, it is hard to imagine any contemporary Jewish thinker arguing that religious consciousness is peripheral to authentic Jewish being.

4

Nationalism: The Zionist Interpretation of Judaism

THREE events play critical roles in shaping modern Jewish thought. The Emancipation sets its context, the Holocaust remains its major unresolved theological issue, and the State of Israel by its success implicitly poses the questions of what constitutes authentic Jewish existence. One may say without qualification that nothing in contemporary Jewish life—and perhaps nothing in the last two millenia—has given rise to more Jewish pride and elicited more support than the State of Israel.

The Israeli accomplishments have been so varied, that they command world Jewry's admiration. Israelis have created a modern economy, reclaimed land, absorbed refugees, provided for social welfare, operated a government, fought wars, projected a humane image of the Jews, created an Hebraic culture, remained a democracy; and in the face of terror, contumely, threats and isolation, indomitably pursue a decent life for themselves and their children. This, in stark contrast to the callousness and barbarity which has characterized twentieth-century politics generally. Moreover, the State of Israel has largely been the product of refugees rescued from Hitler's death camps, or later from Arab countries. That people so maltreated by their enemies, ignored by most of humanity and neglected in their time of trial even by their own people, would now reassert their humanity, reaffirm their ethnic identity, and reenter history as a political entity, is awesome.

Since Israel did not exist until well into the twentieth century, an analysis of its place in modern Jewish though must begin with the thinking of the Zionist movement, out of which the state arose. Compared to the other systems which we are considering, Zionist thought was heavily ideological; it was not a systematic, academic search for the truth. No single Zionist thinker produced a coherent, theoretical justification of Zionism as an intellectual response to the meeting of Judaism and modernity. Nevertheless, Zionism had a lasting historical impact and positive influence upon Jewish life.

What If the Jews Are a Nation?

Zionism put forward a revolutionary premise: the Jews are a nationality. Or, to put this in European usage: the Jews are a nation. To Americans the term "nation" carries political overtones which imply that Jews are not wholeheartedly loyal to the countries in which they reside. Such an inputation of double loyalty, or worse, of a primary loyalty elsewhere, would be abhorrent to almost all American Jews. Some years back, the term "nationality" allayed such fears, for many immigrant groups remained attached to their national homelands while being loyal Americans. Today, when we are more accustomed to speaking of the diversity of America's ethnic groups, the radicalism of the original Zionist thesis would be lost if it were to be stated: the Jews are an ethnic group. The Zionists wanted to say far more. They were determined to rethink Jewish life and duty in strictly political terms.

In many countries, most notably in the lands of Eastern Europe with its dense Jewish population, the citizenry was often comprised of many national groups. Each folk might have certain rights, perhaps even receiving government support for the maintenance of certain of their national institutions and cultural activities. But with the spread of the ideology of nationalism in the nineteenth century, groups united by land and language often strove to achieve political independence as well. Italy is the classic case of such nationalism; and Zionism is the Jewish version of this nineteenth-century idea. It may also be called the characteristic East European response to modernity. Just as Western Jews, living in religiously pluralistic nations, modernized by equating Judaism with religion, so Eastern Jews equated Judaism with nationality and thus freed themselves to create an emancipated Jewish way of life.

Land, Statehood and Nationality

The Jews were united by languages, culture, history, and the problem of anti-semitism. But Jewish nationality had one obvious difference from that of other European groups: the Jews did not live on their ancestral land.

In its earliest stages, Zionist Jewish nationality was occasionally thought to be separable from the Land of Israel. In his revolutionary pamphlet, *The Jewish State*, Theodor Herzl, who initiated the modern Zionist movement, said that the problem of the Jews was national and required a political solution. When such a solution was offered by the British in 1903 in the form of a proposal that Uganda become the national homeland for the Jews, Herzl was prepared to accept. For him, "the Jewish state" need not be on the Jewish land; there was need for an immediate homeland to answer the pressing problem of anti-semitism. Indeed, for some decades thereafter a Jewish Territorialist Movement existed, nationalistic but willing to accept any country for Jewish settlement. Simon Dubnow, author of a ten volume history of the Jewish people, similarly envisaged a distinction between Jewish nationality and territory. In his theory, one great accomplishment of the Jewish people was its evolution beyond geographic fixation. The Jews were the first cosmopolitan nationality, a model for the future of humankind. Most Zionists rejected such universalizing conceptions, considering it unthinkable that the Jewish state could be established anywhere but on the Land of Israel, *eretz yisrael*.

For a long time, Zionists did not always equate Jewish nationhood with political independence. The program adopted in Basle at the First Zionist Congress in 1897 said only, "The aim of Zionism is to create for the Jewish people a home in Palestine secured by public law." It was conceivable that, as in Europe, national existence might be possible within the sovereignty of some other political power. When the 1917 Balfour Declaration publicly committed the British government to work for "the establishment in Palestine of a national home for the Jewish people," many Zionists thought that the movement had completed its work. Not until the 1942 Biltmore Program was adopted by a specially called conference did any but a minority of Zionists say that Jewish nationalism required a sovereign Jewish state.

David Ben-Gurion, who was responsible for the Biltmore statement, applied this understanding in deciding on the name of the new state established in 1948. Many had thought it would be called Judea, a continuation of the name of the last Jewish commonwealth. Ben-Gurion preferred the name Israel, *yisrael* (the declaration of independence also calls it the "State of Israel," *medinat yisrael*), since he wanted the name of the political entity to be identical with the name of the people. In Ben-Gurion's Jewish nationalism, political sovereignty was a fulfillment of national existence.

Can Jews Rely Upon the Emancipation?

Three intellectually significant notions were contained in the assertion that the Jews were a nation. The first was the proposition that the Emancipation was a tragedy, not a godsend, for the Jewish people. This negative assessment resulted from a shifted perspective. The Emancipation might be a boon to the individual Jew, but to the Jewish people, in terms of its culture and its community life, it was a disaster. Being Jewish was reduced to religious activity; the folk as such played no formal role in the social structure. The results in the West were already obvious: by the second liberated generation, emancipated Jews no longer shared a Jewish tongue as their primary language and Jewish styles were being shed for those of the surrounding people. Even in Eastern Europe where the *Haskalah* (enlightenment) movement had hoped to make Jewish culture attractive by active involvement with the world, this loss of folk vitality was evident. The *Haskalah* ideal was "Be a man abroad and a Jew at home," a prescription which unwittingly indicated how marginal and internal Jewish life would have to become in any society whose ethos was created by non-Jews.

Paralleling this Jewish assimilation was the emergence of a new type of anti-semitism. What had been essentially religious was now secularized. Jews were hated as unassimilable outsiders, perhaps even as national enemies. When race theories emerged toward the end of the nineteenth century, anti-semitism took on pseudo-scientific, biological hypotheses, thereby fatefully making Jews different in their very life stuff. This prejudice could not be met by the liberal Jewish strategies of education or assimilation for the more the Jews made their way into the society the more they provoked the host nation's anger at their intrusion. Some Zionists, like Vladimir Jabotinsky, carried this theory through to its logical conclusion, arguing not only that European Jewish life could not long continue but that a major calamity awaited Jews who did not immigrate to the Land of Israel. Most Zionists considered Jabotinsky an alarmist and his position extreme. They persisted in this naivete well after the Jews were already in the Nazi ghettos.

Ending Anti-semitism Through Zionism

Almost all Zionists agreed that only the establishment of a Jewish national homeland would solve the problems of Jewish life and anti-semitism. With Jews in their homeland, a proper Jewish national life and culture might be revived. In an influential pamphlet written in 1882, Leo Pinsker suggested to Russian Jews that the cause of anti-semitism was the lack of a clear social status. The establishment of a Jewish state would provide a national Jewish identity thereby ending anti-semitism.

Herzl's analysis placed the blame for "the Jewish problem" on Jewish population density and consequent economic competition with the indigenous citizenry of Eastern Europe. Zionism would remedy anti-semitism by moving large numbers of Jews to the Jewish state.

Clearly, both Herzl and Pinsker, like many of the early Zionists, believed that overcoming anti-semitism was a primary purpose for Zionism. In retrospect, this part of their program was doomed to ironic failure. Not only has anti-semitism remained alive since the establishment of Israel, but some have argued that political opposition to the state has given new form and focus to the old prejudice.

For Jews living in the post-Hitler era, it is difficult to comprehend why there should have been Jewish opposition to Zionism, why positive Jews opposed the effort to establish a Jewish state. One clue lies in the way in which Zionism opposed the adaptation strategy being utilized by the majority of Europe's Jews. The overwhelming number of Jews wishing to modernize either moved to countries where there was a greater degree of democracy or tried to adjust to their societies. The migrants, at great personal cost, based their hopes on the practicality of social integration. By rejecting the Zionist thesis that Emancipation was a fraud, they committed themselves to one of their major life decisions. In the Zionist arguments that true safety was possible only in a Jewish state, they perceived a threat to their claim that they could be wholehearted citizens of their adopted nations. Nor was this only true for Jews who had emigrated to Western Europe.

Those who came to America found a congenial ideology in the melting pot theory. Integration was the ideal for minorities and emphasizing one's ethnic existence put one's Americanism in doubt. The Reform Jews were the leaders of anti-Zionist opposition, for they had pioneered the ideal of Jewish integration into the general society. Classic Reform Judaism considered the Jews a purely religious group whose central teaching was ethical monotheism and who continued as a separate entity because they had a mission to teach this universal doctrine to all humankind. This theology was already under heavy attack when Hitler's intentions began to become clear. Disclosures of the horrors of the Holocaust and the establishment of the State of Israel effectively put an end to it, though the vestiges of this point of view remain preserved in the American Council for Judaism.

Politics as the New Means of Salvation

The fears of many Jews in regard to Zionism were further exacerbated by the method the Zionists adopted to accomplish their goal. This method, political activism—or, in philosophic terms, human self-assertion—constitutes the second major intellectual theme in Jewish nationalism. Herzl was not the first to advocate a Jewish state. His genius lay in projecting it as an open, collective effort to be carried out by the World Zionist Organization he created. The Zionist Congresses, with their worldwide representations, were utterly unprecedented in Jewish life. Such public political exposure immediately offended western Jews who had been declaring for a century that they were a religious group. They were sufficiently outraged to prevent Herzl from holding the first Congress at Munich, where it had been originally scheduled; and he had to shift its site to Basle.

Political action was the heart of Herzl's program, but more than that, it was the first manifestation that the Jews were a nation. It was also a direct challenge to inherited Jewish belief. It was traditionally held that God was responsible for the return of Jews to their land and the reestablishment of Jewish hegemony there. God would send the King Messiah to accomplish this only when God was ready to do so. Until then, Jews must wait patiently and not try to "force the coming of the End Time." (The notion of doing so by political action did not exist before the transformation of world politics in the nineteenth century.) This comparatively passive attitude to redemption was somewhat relieved by an activist strand in Jewish faith. There was a steady stream of would-be Messiahs in post-biblical Jewish history and the Lurianic *kabbalah* of the sixteenth century had radically reversed the rabbinic teaching, putting the power of achieving Israel's redemption in the hands of the mystic adepts. In a complex way, this made possible the worldwide Jewish response to the last great false Messiah, Shabbetai Tzevi (1626–1676). His ultimate conversion to Islam, particularly after having messianically introduced certain changes into Jewish religious practice, provoked a major reaction on the part of the rabbinate. Messianic activism was thoroughly rejected—the Hasidim transforming it substantially into a subjective goal—and taking the initiative to change Jewish practice was resolutely opposed. This mood of resignedly accepting the Jews' fate was reinforced by the economic and social deprivation in which most Jews lived.

Orthodox Tensions with Zionism

Zionism began as a self-conscious rejection of Orthodox Judaism and its passivity. For much of the nineteenth century, writers reviving the Hebrew language as a literary medium had savagely criticized the life style of traditional Jews. They attacked its superstitution, parochialism, worldly ignorance, and dogmatism. They accused the rabbinate of fostering and supporting these retrogressive elements of Judaism and contrasted them disparagingly to the love of nature, the appreciation of the body, the pleasure in human emotion, and the outreach to all humankind which characterized the modern spirit. Much of that negativism carried over particularly into East European Zionism where, as was often the case, it was influenced by the Marxist analysis of society with its view of religion as a reactionary force.

The Zionists defined the Jews as a nation in order to destroy the exclusive authority of the rabbinate to say what a good Jew was. Jews who wanted to be religious would surely not be prevented from it, but those who wished to adopt much of western civilization might do so in good Jewish conscience so long as they remained loyal to the nation. Specifically, the Zionists ridiculed the notion that Jews should accept their suffering as God's punishment or trial and wait for the King Messiah to redeem them when they were perfectly capable of taking action to improve their immediate welfare. Leo Pinsker entitled his pamphlet of 1882 *Auto-Emancipation*. Jews need not wait for some other people to free them as a nation; they could take responsibility upon themselves. The title may also be referred to God, for the Jews need no longer wait in utter dependence on God to grant them freedom.

The accommodation of Orthodoxy to Zionism was well under way before World War I and a party reconciling traditional Jewish belief with Zionism, *Mizrahi*, soon became a significant minority faction within the World Zionist Organization. Not all Orthodox Jews were convinced the two positions could be reconciled, of course. In 1912, when the World Zionist Organization decided to undertake educational and cultural activities, a group of Orthodox leaders withdrew from the Organization and established the *Agudat Israel* in opposition to secularist Zionism. Their party in the State of Israel has occasionally participated in government coalitions, but they reject the notion that the State of Israel can be Jewish if it remains steadfastly secular. Some smaller groups, notably the *Neturei Karta* and the Satmarer Hasidim, consider the establishment of a pre-messianic Jewish government on the Holy Land an act of heresy.

Turning Religion Into National Culture

This brings the third intellectual theme of Zionist nationalism into sharp relief. Because of their ideology, the Zionists wanted to secularize Jewish life. Classic Zionism was strongly anti-religious and anti-clerical. In addition to the positions already mentioned, most

Zionists equated modernity with the death of God and the end of religion. A self-confident humankind, taking history into its own hands and trusting in science to provide it with a reliable world view, had no need for religious faith, laws, or institutions.

The Zionists set about secularizing Judaism. The "holy tongue," Hebrew, became the language of everyday speech. "Redeeming the land" became the purchase of real estate. The Psalmist's cry, "Who can retell the mighty acts of God!" became the Zionist song (now associated with *Hanukkah*) "Who can retell the mighty acts of Israel!" The mystic credo, "Israel, the Holy One, Blessed be He, and the Torah are one" likewise became a song—omitting God. The examples could easily be multiplied, for the strategy largely succeeded. Much to the surprise of many American visitors who think of Judaism primarily in religious terms, the State of Israel remains substantially secular and most of its Jewish citizens have a nationalistic interpretation of Jewishness.

The three theoretical issues—the rejection of the Emancipation, the reliance on political activism, and the secularization of Jewish life—form the background for those questions which have been more openly debated by Jewish thinkers.

Do Most Jews Live in Exile?

The first group of such issues has to do with the rigidity with which Jewish nationalism should be defined. Chief of these is the argument over whether Jews living outside the Land of Israel are in Exile, *galut*, or only in Diaspora, the *tefutzot*. The difference seems at first linguistic, but major consequences for Jewish life follow on the choice of term. *Diaspora* is a Greek word meaning "scattered" and already in Roman times the knowledge that Jews were widely dispersed made the term useful. Some peoples do have their nationals scattered in many countries. Saying they are in dispersion is merely descriptive and attaches no judgment. But *exile* is an evaluative term. The bible authors use it with very strong negative connotations. If the Land itself is holy and given to the people of Israel by God as part of the Covenant, to be put off the land is a terrible punishment, religiously as well as nationally.

The Rabbis maintain and extend this attitude. They call other lands religiously impure, rule that residence on the Land and ownership of it have special legal priority, describe Jewish life elsewhere as hazardous, and depict Israel's Exile not merely as a local, national-religious matter but as a cosmic tragedy, for now God too is in Exile. With the increase in suffering by Jews in the Middle Ages, the term's negative significance intensified; Exile implied that the degradation of the Jews had a metaphysical root which only the coming of the Messiah could correct.

Mainstream Zionists rejected all the religious connotations of the term Exile and politicized it. The Jewish people was in Exile as long as it did not have its own state; individual Jews are in Exile until they come to live on the Land of Israel, particularly now that a Jewish state has been established there. Exile therefore is also a geographic term. Stepping out of the borders of the State of Israel, a Jew is in Exile; a step the other way and a Jew has left the Exile—an important part of the revised concept of redemption. The Zionists retained all the negative connotations of the term Exile, secularizing them now into a judgment on the deterioration of Jewish life and the persistence of anti-semitism outside the land of Israel.

How Many Centers Does World Jewry Have?

Several corollary questions emerge from this distinction. What is the destiny of Jewish life away from the Land of Israel? And how important a Jewish duty is immigration, *aliyah*, to the Land of Israel? If Jews abroad are only in Diaspora, some environments may make possible their continued existence as Jews. If they are in Exile, their Jewishness will not long continue. Similarly, Jews in the Diaspora may choose Jewish fulfillment through *aliyah* or be satisfied by the Jewish life off the Land. If they are in Exile and immigration to the

Land is practical, a loyal Jew must make it one of life's highest priorities. An interesting variant of these issues has been proposed by existentialist theoreticians. Utilizing the concept of general human alienation, they have argued for Exile as a condition of the self as well as of the Jewish people. Redemption therefore cannot be complete until the human self is restored to wholeness. Political action will not suffice because God is necessarily involved in completing human finitude. More surprisingly, the existentialist view depicts even Jews residing in the Land of Israel as in *galut*, until God's redeeming work is accomplished.

A parallel issue is the relation of the State of Israel to world Jewry. The pledge which qualifies one as a Zionist able to vote for delegates to a World Zionist Congress affirms the "centrality" of the State of Israel in Jewish life. As befits organizational language, the term "centrality" is broadly inclusive. Descriptively, it indicates the unique intensity Jews bring to Israeli affairs, thus embracing almost all Jews. In Zionist ideology it implies that nothing in Jewish life should take priority over the State of Israel's concerns. Thus, the World Zionist Organization Department of Education wants all Jewish school curricula to center around the State of Israel. If the Jews are a nation, what could be more important? Moreover, the doctrine of centrality has strong political overtones, suggesting that the State of Israel should lead all of world Jewry, democratically but with unique authority. At the extreme, it means that Jews off the Land have no right to criticize the State of Israel. Some Zionists find that illogical. They argue that if the State of Israel fulfills world Jewry's nationality, Jews everywhere have a stake in the manner in which it translates the Jewish heritage into social reality.

The Special Demands Jews Make of Jews

What should be the character of Jewish nationhood? Are the Jews a nation "like all other nations"? Or is there some special character to

Jewish life which must be maintained lest Israelis no longer be authentically Jewish? In many respects the Zionists aimed to make modern Jews a normal nation. They attributed many Jewish problems to abnormalities in Jewish existence, for example, the absence of a laboring class or farmers. Zionism attempted to restore Jewish normalcy economically, culturally and spiritually. For years the hero of the Zionist movement was the *halutz*, the pioneer who settled on the land. Contrast the artistic image of the Jew as a bearded, pale, frail, old man bent over a book, with the common expectation that the Israeli will be youthful, tanned, and vigorous, perhaps a soldier. A transformation has taken place, to the joy of most Jews.

Normalcy also implies that the Jews do not have to be better than anyone else. Politically, why should the Israelis be judged by uncommonly high moral standards while their antagonists are excused for practicing realpolitik? Yet would world Jewry be satisfied if the State of Israel conducted itself with the normal cynicism of governments? Would Jews everywhere passionately identify with it, if the State of Israel operated at about the level of the other Mideastern states?

Ahad Ha-Am: Zionism as Elitism

One early Zionist theoretician asked and responded to these questions. His answers endeared him to Diaspora Zionists. Ahad Ha-Am—the pen name of Asher Ginzberg (1856–1927)—was reared in a traditional family in Russia, educated himself in modern culture and became a leader in the Hebrew literary renaissance of the turn of the century. As an editor and writer he is credited with having developed the modern Hebrew prose style. Though many of his essays were prompted by events in the Jewish world in the three decades before World War I, they are distinguished by a philosophic cast of mind not common among other Zionist writers.

Ahad Ha-Am thought science had refuted religion. Unlike other

Zionists he substituted a high appreciation of the human spirit and a humanistic sense of nationhood for the old belief in God and revelation. His *cultural Zionism* contained several major priorities.

Ahad Ha-Am rejects as unscientific any supernatural motive for the continuation of the Jewish nation. Rather he points out that every people naturally wants to survive. A national will-to-live continues unabated in most Jews despite the misery of discrimination and the excitement of emancipation. By projecting a program leading to a revived Jewish folk life, Zionism could summon these latent national energies. Jews could abandon their unbelievable and unrealistic appeals to God's command or a Jewish mission to humankind as reasons for Jewish continuity.

At its best, every nation produces a culture of many dimensions. Jews are dissatisfied with the present state of Jewish life because of the poverty of Jewish culture. In the ghetto-*shtetl* period it had atrophied, retaining only a narrow religious focus. The fully developed arts of the general society, by contrast, have rendered irresistable the Emancipation's promise of full cultural self-expression. As long as Jewish culture remains unreconstructed, sensitive Jews will defect to the non-Jewish world. Zionism should draw on the extraordinarily variegated resources of the Jewish heritage to create a rich literary and artistic life. The positive response to the Hebrew literary revival proves that given a humanistic Zionism, Jews will once again make the good of the Jewish people the highest aim of their lives.

The People of Spirit Need a Spiritual Center

Ahad Ha-Am carried this concept one critical step forward. He offered a secular theory of the special character of the Jewish spirit. His intellectual resource was *folkpsychology*, the academic predecessor of sociology. It sought to understand peoples as if they were persons. As individuals have certain talents, so do ethnic groups and this produces their particular civilization. The Jews, Ahad Ha-Am proclaimed, had a genius for high culture centered on ethics. He not only identified this with the prophets' teaching, as the German Jewish liberals had done, but with Moses' leadership and talmudic law as well. The regeneration of the Jewish people, then, was a qualitative matter and could only be accomplished through cultural work of high creativity and ethical sensitivity. Ahad Ha-Am was a self-conscious elitist. For him Jewish culture was synonymous with the best in the human spirit. In that humanistic sense he considered Zionism a spiritual endeavor.

He conceived of the revived Jewish state as the people's "spiritual center." Only by returning to its homeland could the Jewish people reconstitute its culture in its own terms and express its natural genius. The spiritual products of the resettlement would reflect an authentic Jewish ethos that could be communicated to Jews all over the world. Local circumstances might permit them only a truncated Jewish existence, but, strengthened by the culture they received from the Jewish spiritual center, they could continue living as Jews. For Ahad Ha-Am, the word "spirit" has a fully secular, not a religious meaning.

Determining the Priorities of a Jewish State

Ahad Ha-Am tried to get the Zionist movement to implement his vision. Giving priority to culture, not political assurances or a changed Jewish economic profile, he resolutely opposed mass migration to Palestine. He was less interested in having Jewish farmers than in creating the cultural conditions which would keep them from becoming peasants. He proposed restricting immigration to those whose spiritual preparation was complete. These notions brought him and his followers into sharp conflict with the Zionist leadership which gave priority first to political tasks and second to migration and settlement. None of the practical Zionist accomplishments satisfied him for he envisioned the movement rebuilding the spirit of the Jewish nation by reviving its culture. For him, nationalism and humanism were indivisible.

In unforgettable fashion, Ahad Ha-Am insisted on the proper quality of a Jewish state. The bare rudiments of national existence—being on one's land, speaking one's language, perhaps having political sovereignty—were not enough. A nation had to be true to its history and folk genius. He connected the Jews with superior human achievement and insisted the national revival should settle for nothing less.

The Fate of Those Who Call for Quality

Ahad Ha-Am's ideas have been much beloved by Zionists who do not propose to make *aliyah*, for he propounds a theory of Diaspora rather than Exile. He does not advocate life outside the homeland, but he expects it to continue and believes a national spiritual center can keep it vital. Though immigration is a major Zionist responsibility, Ahad Ha-Am places greater weight on involvement with Hebrew culture. He is the spiritual father of American Jewry's efforts to benefit from Israeli art, literature and music.

He has markedly less influence in the State of Israel, though the Israelis' intense concern for culture may in part be traced to him. Due to the State of Israel's constant struggle to survive, political realities have taken precedence over the Zionist aim of reviving Jewish life everywhere. Something of Ahad Ha-Am's fate also befell the three other notable theoreticians who sought to introduce an element of quality into Jewish nationalist theory. All were religious thinkers. Aharon David Gordon (1856–1922) had a spiritual appreciation of the life-power invigorating nature and created a quasi-mystical doctrine of the importance of a nation working its soil in non-exploitive, socialistic relationships. Rabbi Abraham Isaac Kook (1865–1935), the chief Ashkenazi rabbi of Palestine for the last twenty-one years of his life, had an all-encompassing mystical vision of the universe and the central role of the Jewish people in it, for which return to the Holy Land as a nation was a prerequisite. Rav Kook's combination of Orthodoxy and Zionism was unusual because of its mystical grounding and the sympathy he showed the mainline Zionists despite their determined secularity. The third such thinker was Martin Buber, and his Zionist philosophy will emerge from the general discussion of his thought given later in this book (see chapter 7).

Zionism as a Reversal of Judaism in Exile

Some Zionists criticized Ahad Ha-Am and his followers as continuing *galut* ideals of proper Jewishness. Instead, they advocated a radical turn from the values of European Judaism. These thinkers were too extreme to have their philosophies widely adopted, yet their vigorous advocacy of nationalism influenced Zionist ideology more than did the cultural elitism of Ahad Ha-Am. Yoseph Hayyim Brenner (1881–1921) is often considered the foremost exponent of the theory of *shelilat hagalut*, the negation of Jewish life in the Exile. He had almost nothing good to say about the Jewish experience since the days of an independent Jewish existence on the Land. He considered *galut*-culture valueless for it reflects the servile status of its creators. Its religion largely denies the elemental, natural forces of human life. Contemporary Jews in Exile hardly constituted a living people, having allowed their national will to degenerate to a resignation he considered more animal than human. The Emancipation, which supposedly civilized Jews, only showed their capacity for mimicry and their willingness to deny their own identity in the futile dream of social acceptance. Such hope as Brenner had in Zionism required it to radically transform the Jewish spirit from what Exile had made of it over the centuries.

Micah Joseph Berdichevski (1865–1921) similarly decried the *galut* and excoriated what he saw as its perversion of the true Jewish spirit. He drew intellectual inspiration from Friedrich Nietzsche's call for a radical human change, for a "transvaluation of all values." In his many literary works Berdichevski sought to expose the hidden vitality of the pristine Jewish spirit. This he found in the Jew's relation to the life forces animating nature and the human body. He read the Bible as an effort to repress this natural Judaism in favor of a false Judaism of spirituality. In his anthology of talmudic legends, he featured those which showed the passional, mythic underside of Jewish life. Against the usual glorification of intellectuality and piety, Berdichevski stressed the virtue of physical development and military prowess. He considered Jewish universalism the major intellectual reason for the continuation of the Exile and therefore wanted to end "Judaism" so that the Jewish nation might be redeemed by return to its soil.

In Defense of Jewish National Normality

The most extreme position with regard to Jewish nationalism was probably that of Jacob Klatzkin (1882–1948). Where the two previous thinkers were essentially literary figures, Klatzkin was essentially a philosopher. His theory of nationalism is elegantly simple. A nation is defined by having a common land and language; all other factors of national life may be desirable but they are not essential. Klatzkin was no opponent of Jewish culture and by his many literary efforts sought to promote it. But unlike Ahad Ha-Am, he considered Jewish culture an embellishment of national existence not one of its distinguishing characteristics. Only what gave any nation individuality, its land and language, separated Jews from other people, in their case the Land of Israel and Hebrew.

Klatzkin was an uncompromising advocate of *shelilat hagalut*. For nearly two millenia the Jews had been in Exile and suffered from its deleterious affects. Until the Emancipation, persecution kept them alive. They had managed to survive as a nation by the self-destructive strategy of restricting Jewish life to religious bounds. The Emancipation now dooms that tactic. As persecution declines into mere social antipathy and religion grows ever more unbelievable, the Jews in Exile will die out. Immigration is the central Jewish duty of our time; Zionism and *aliyah* are as good as identical.

Once settled on their land and speaking their own tongue, the Jews may create whatever they wish, or nothing much, and still be authentically Jewish. They will have fulfilled the definition of nationhood and their Jewishness ought not to be judged in any other terms. Klatzkin, though himself a highly sophisticated intellectual, provided Zionism with its most thoughtful statement of the Jewish State's right to mediocrity or worse.

All these issues and others—most notably that of a proper relation to the Arabs in Palestine—were on the agenda of concerned Jews by the early 1920's. Since that time, Zionist philosophy stood still, almost certainly because most Jews cared little about theorizing while the lives of Jews or the survival of the State of Israel was at stake.

When Do I Listen to My People?

Despite the emergencies which world Jewry has faced, the past decade or so has witnessed the slow surfacing of a previously subterranean issue, one which often is at stake in discussions between Israelis and American Jews. When does ethnic or national loyalty properly impose duty upon an individual? Zionism asserts that the nation may rightly make great claims upon its members, for example, immigration to the State of Israel. What if the demands of the nation conflict with one's conscientious judgment of what one ought to do?

For example, the abstract issue of corporate authority has disturbed Americans with particular power ever since the Vietnam War. The U.S. government demanded that citizens risk their lives in what many found to be a senseless or even evil conflict. Many Americans concluded that one ought to give up one's nationality if it substantially contradicted one's mature sense of personal responsibility. The American psyche remains scarred by that experience. And the presumption of the past is now reversed: if collectives do not serve individuals' needs, why should individuals be expected to respond to them?

Or, in terms of our discussion, why should being a Jew mandate making *aliyah* or building one's Diaspora life around Israeli culture? Either would be good for the Jewish people but each also conflicts radically with the life goals of most American Jews. As a result, Orthodox Jews comprise the overwhelming majority of American immigrants to the State of Israel. Their religious belief motivates *aliyah*. If Zionism remains secular, how can one justify giving priority to one's group rather than to one's autonomy?

A common Israeli response has been to sound the classic Zionist theme, the prevalence of anti-semitism in the Exile. Espousing *shelilat hagalut*, many Israelis argue that anti-semitism will inevitably destroy Jewish life overseas. The United States may be unusual but it is no exception to the law of modern Jewish life. Anti-semitism remains persistent and virulent in America—and these Israelis are sensitive to every incident of it. One has a simple moral duty to go where one can live in safety and without apology. Since one must be a Jew, one ought to do so most positively, by participating in the vibrant life created by Jews living in self-determination on their ancestral soil.

American Jews have not been convinced by such arguments. Theoretically, they evade the issue of individual versus corporate authority. Practically, they argue that "America is different." This inevitably precipitates a debate comparing European nations to America and German anti-semitism to that in America. The quality of life argument is also hotly disputed. For all its Jewish virtues, the State of Israel faces a collective anti-semitism of world nations and very often has more people leaving it than come to settle there from the United States.

Making the Case for Liquidating the Exile

Since Ahad Ha-Am's day, most Zionist writers have piously described only the movement's accomplishments. But, as the State entered its fourth decade, Israeli-American disputes were raised to a new level by the sophisticated statements of two writers who had long since made *aliyah*. Their candor about the realities of existence in the State of Israel was remarkable.

In *Letters to an American Jewish Friend*, Hillel Halkin offers a major restatement of *shelilat hagalut*. A former American, Halkin understands and forcefully rebuts arguments for a meaningful Jewish life in the United States. He docs not deny that many projects once considered visionary—like university chairs of Jewish studies—have become reality. In the long run, he claims, such accomplishments mean little. Despite talk of pluralism, America demands that its various ethnic groups largely assimilate to the national ethos. He ruthlessly reminds American Jewish optimists of the rising rate of intermarriage and the community's endemic ignorance and apathy. Its current resurgence of Jewish ethnicity is a response to the State of Israel's emergencies, not an indigenous Jewish folk passion. Most important, religious belief will not long survive a secularized world. Already most American synagogue affiliation masks a deepening agnosticism and hypocrisy.

Refreshingly, Halkin makes no counter-claim that life in the State of Israel is humanly satisfying or Jewishly exalting. He concedes that one's Zionist ideals make the tawdriness and discomfort of everyday Israeli life rather unbearable. Israeli culture is mostly a second-rate imitation of international styles and the Hebrew language itself is undergoing adulteration in its polyglot social situation. With hostile neighbors and poor demographic prospects, the very survival of the State is thrown in doubt. Why then should Jews come to the State of Israel? Because it is the last, best hope for the Jewish people. Committed Jews can find no better way of expressing their Jewishness. Halkin is self-critical enough to admit that such commitment to one's people must be called a matter of faith, a secular one to be sure. He does not explain why any nation deserves a devotion entailing such self-sacrifice. The further development of his classic Zionist position requires that he confront this question.

Zionism at Heart Must be Religious

In *The Zionist Revolution*, Harold Fisch has taken a similar stand from a radically different perspective. A British immigrant, Fisch, concentrates his argument on the Israeli's special suffering. Terrorism makes suffering a part of daily existence and wars inflict it *en masse*—this for a people still wounded by the Holocaust. How does one explain the devotion and heroism with which Israelis have faced up to their pain? Why does this nation exert a passionate will to live despite the sacrifices demanded of it? The secular theories of Jewish nationalism professed by most Israelis are utterly incompetent to motivate such dedication. The Israelis' insistence on doing their Jewish duty regardless of its human cost can have only one basis, though they are unconscious of it or hide from it. They are responding to a Transcendent Reality which has laid Its claims upon them. At its core, Fisch argues, Zionism has always been an act of faith. Once this had to be masked in secular form. Now, when the long range, maximum devotion of Jews is needed for its fulfillment, secularity can no longer serve to motivate Zionism. The faith that moves Zionists must be exposed in its true depth. Belief in God and God's Covenant relationship with the Jewish people makes maintaining the State of Israel the chief collective duty of all Jews.

Interestingly, Fisch's deeply felt and cogently argued position gathers some strength from the Israeli courts. In two widely publicized cases—the Brother Daniel and Binyamin Shalit cases—the Israeli Supreme Court denied that a complete separation could be made between the Jewish religion and ethnic Jewish identity. In the first case, the Court ruled against both Zionist theory and traditional Jewish law. It said that the Israeli government should respect the common Jewish opinion that a Jew who has converted to Christianity is no longer part of the community. Hence an apostate has no right to immigrate to the State of Israel under the law of Jewish return. In the second case, a furor resulted from a decision that the Shalit child might be registered on the Israeli population rolls as Jewish in nationality but of no religion. The government then promulgated a regulation that, unless a Jew converts to another faith, the religious registration will be "Jewish." Taken together, these cases made it apparent that Jewish nationalism contained more religious content than its secularistic ideology had heretofore conceded.

Fisch's own argument is fully Orthodox. His faith, that God gave this Land to the Jews as the Torah teaches, is absolute. He denies Arabs the rights not only to Samaria and Judea (the West Bank), but to Eastern Palestine (Jordan). Faith here resolves the issue of motivation and sacrifice. We suffer and act for God's sake. What remains in contention is the sort of faith modern Jews can accept and particularly the role of human conscience in it.

Happily, these controversial issues arise in the context of the State of Israel's extraordinary human and Jewish accomplishments. In a few generations, the Zionist movement revolutionized the Jewish community. It made the tone and quality of Jewish life immeasurably better as the twenty-first century nears than anyone dreamed when the twentieth century began. Largely for good, then, the questions raised by Zionism remain high on the contemporary Jewish intellectual agenda.

5

Naturalism:
Mordecai Kaplan

IF PHILOSOPHY is the child of leisure, 1934 would seem a strange year for the appearance of the first major American philosophy of Judaism. The United States was deep in crisis, and so was Jewish life. The economic depression had shattered morale, provoked hostility, and suffused the country with an anger born of frustration. Every stress was felt with special force in the American Jewish community. Anti-semitism was an open, publicly approved, well-supported movement.

Much of American Jewry fled its Jewish identity. Participating in Jewish life kept one an alien while investing one's energies in democracy enabled one to gain from a system which rewarded talent impartially.

Into this disheartening scene came a message of Jewish hope. With the publication of *Judaism as a Civilization*, Mordecai Kaplan emerged as the intellectual focus of the generation. He had not been unknown before the book appeared. For many years he had taught at the Jewish Theological Seminary of America, influencing scores of men entering the burgeoning Conservative rabbinate or being trained as educators in its Teachers' Institute. He also exerted great influence on Jewish social workers because of his efforts to transform the settlement house into what became the Jewish center. Now, maturing as a thinker, he challenged American Jewry with a full-scale analysis of its situation.

Mordecai Kaplan's continuing response to crisis in Jewish life has been to redefine Judaism and thus redirect Jewish activity. Kaplan proposed to articulate a social philosophy for the Jewish community. He was a rationalist, yet he differed from the German rationalists by focussing not on the autonomous, thinking individual but on the Jewish people. Zionist theory influenced him greatly. He agreed that one cannot usefully speak of individual Jewish identity without talking about the corporate nature of the Jews.

The Two Premises of Kaplan's Philosophy

In Kaplan's eyes, contemporary Judaism's difficulties arise from the upheaval that has affected all Western peoples and religions in modern times. Two terms epitomize it: nationalism and naturalism. Both are used quite broadly.

Nationalism means more than the nineteenth-century ideal by which ethnic groups sought political self-assertion, that is, to become a state. For Kaplan it encompasses the entire process by which monarchy gave way to democracy. The concept of society as divinely ordered—and hence unchangeable—gave way to that of a secular state founded on a social contract. Everyone, therefore, was entitled to equal rights in it. Nationalism brought the Jews Emancipation, the end of ghetto existence both physically and spiritually. After centuries of segregation, full participation in the life of their country entailed a radical change in their accustomed way of life and their manner of thinking about it.

Kaplan uses the term naturalism to identify the way people in secular states think about the world. At the simplest, naturalism is the rejection of supernaturalism. Moderns limit their thought to this world and structure it in terms of the natural order. They consider the scientific approach to reality, including human beings and society, the most reliable method of ascertaining truth. As a consequence, naturalistic religious thinking focuses on people and their welfare rather than on God or God's purposes. Modernity involves a radical shift from theocentrism to anthropocentrism and Kaplan often employs the term "humanism" in this people-focused but not God-denying sense.

Theological humanism revolutionizes the classic religious emphases on supernatural revelation, miracles, and otherworldly salvation. Not just God's word, but God too, must now be found in, not above, the natural order; miracles are dismissed as unscientific; and this world, the only one human beings can know, must be the place in which they seek salvation.

Change Assures Survival

Most moderns live by these views, though some are unconscious of it. Kaplan therefore has no patience with religious leaders who timidly still use the old religious terms. Their very evasion of definition or philosophy indicates that they no longer hold a traditional faith. A truly contemporary understanding of Judaism must be naturalistic so as to be coherent with our modern world view. Liberal Jewish thought has proved that change has always been part of Jewish life. Kaplan also agrees that the unconscious evolution of the past is inadequate to the dramatic change brought about by the Emancipation. Judaism needs to be rethought in terms of the philosophy implicit in modern science. In turn, the reconstruction of Jewish group life must be based on the scientific study of social development. Sociology thus becomes the critical science for Kaplan's interpretation of Judaism. He explicitly cites Durkheim—from whom much of his social orientation is taken—in affirming that religion must now receive its function and character from scientific observation.

Religion cannot be dispensed with. It significantly supplements nationalism and naturalism. The nation has purposes other than the well-being of its citizens. Particularly when the state has failed to serve persons but has demanded instead that they serve its needs, religion can rise in prophetic judgment against it. Religion's mystical element can also usefully complement naturalistic thinking. Applied rigidly, naturalism reduces the universe to an amoral mechanism, thereby negating human freedom and undercutting human aspiration. Religion, without reverting to supernaturalism, can evoke an awareness of the mystery of existence and the reality of spiritual values, thereby assuring people that the universe supports human striving. Personal and social progress are unthinkable without some form of religious life.

This brief statement of Kaplan's basic intent demonstrates that Kaplan's rationalism has it limits. He is not as skeptical of reason's claims as was Leo Baeck. Kaplan appears to have undiluted trust in the adequacy of human rationality and thus in humankind's potential. Yet in rejecting the strict naturalism that denies God's existence and human freedom, he appeals to religious intuition. Why one should accept such unscientific premises is unclear, unless one does so for their usefulness. But how can one scientifically know what is good for people before these premises are accepted? The circularity of the reasoning hints that Kaplan retains something of a reliance on faith.

The Social Scientific View of Religious Groups

What do the social sciences teach us about religion and peoples? An open examiner cannot help being impressed by the universality of religion in human society. In primitive or high cultures, or in societies which are animistic, polytheistic or imagistic, religion is found wherever there are records of human existence. Modern thinkers need not proclaim there are gods who impose themselves upon people or attribute religion to the clever manipulations of priests or capitalists. Its source is human need.

We have a natural urge to self-fulfillment, to utilize our capacities fully. Life itself cannot be the highest value for there are ideals without which we would rather die. The good life is a continual quest for self-realization and self-expression; religion is the human institution that helps us to achieve it. And as our need for such consummation is universal, so is our need for religion. For us the accomplishment of the basic human striving for fulfillment is "salvation." In a naturalistic, this-worldly era, that old religious term cannot mean getting to heaven. It must be freed from all such mythical notions and reinterpreted to refer to self-actualization in this world.

Though human beings are individuals and religion is social, the two are inseparably joined, for salvation must be communal as well as personal. How can individuals be serene when they live in a wretched world? Conversely, no society can claim to have reached its goal as long as its individual members are frustrated and unhappy.

Much of the present-day confusion over religion arises here. We moderns will sometimes admit that aspects of our life are as socially determined as they are personal. Yet we often insist that religion is a strictly private matter. Emile Durkheim, the first great modern sociologist, had argued that individuals do not create religions. Rather, their personal needs and desires are given shape and expression by their culture. A people is prior to its religion. One first shares its way of life and consequently shares in its religion. Kaplan was overwhelmed by Durkheim's insight. He called the social reorientation of the origins of religion the "Copernican turning point" in his thinking. He followed its implications rigorously. Where traditional Judaism spoke of God giving the Torah, thereby constituting the people of Israel, Kaplan argued that the Jewish folk created its culture, Torah, including its religion, climaxed by its idea of God.

What fundamentally differentiates religions is not their theological content so much as their social elaboration. Since science views the universe as an integrated whole, there can be but one God and one ethics. Religious truth is as universal as the operation of human reason. Some peoples have not yet attained the level of monotheistic, ethical religion. That is a historical accident or social lag, not an indication that reality is not equally available to everyone. Each folk clothes the universal content of religion with the garb of its unique symbolism. As a result of its ethnic experience it has come to revere certain people, events, places, books and acts. These are its *sancta*, its channels of reverence. Through them a people expresses individualistically the religious feelings common to all humankind. Religions have different sancta because the articulation of human reverence necessarily takes particular form. Ethical monotheism, by contrast, is as common to humanity as is the human nature on which religion is ultimately based.

A social emphasis pervades Kaplan's philosophy. He has a passionate commitment to folk existence. Since a civilization can survive many generations, its death can only be compared to the death of an individual. Similarly, Kaplan can conceive of all religions one day having the same theology and ethics. He denies that this would mean the end of separate peoples for they are an enduring feature of human existence.

Defining Judaism as a Civilization

Following the theories of the renowned sociologist Sumner, Kaplan boldly identifies Judaism as the Jewish people's civilization. Religion is not its only or even dominant content. A civilization is the organic unity of the people and its land, its language, its literature, its mores, its folkways, its laws, its sanctions, its arts, its religion—in sum, the social forms through which a folk expresses itself. Previous liberal Jewish thinkers erred by identifying Judaism in church-like terms. Kaplan's ethnic perspective leads to a far broader conception of the rebuilding of Jewish life. Following the usage of the social pragmatists of the 1930's, Kaplan called his theory Jewish Reconstructionism. Its creative implications emerge from a consideration of its uncommonly far-ranging component aspects.

A people generally comes into being by virtue of living in a certain territory. Its land then becomes a critical factor in the development of its civilization. The Jews are no exception to this pattern. The Torah speaks continually of the importance of the Land of Israel to the

Jewish people and of the life it must create because of the Land. When the Jews were dispersed, they prayed for a return to their Land and celebrated festivals based on its agricultural cycle. An other-worldly religion might be able to dispense with its tie to a specific country. Judaism, as the civilization of a people, cannot.

Kaplan can now make a strong case for the identity of Judaism and Zionism. A civilization as contrasted to a religion requires a place where it can be fully lived and only its homeland will do. Were Kaplan's social philosophy a simple nationalism, land and language would take precedence over culture and only *aliyah*, immigration, would be the preeminent Jewish duty. Kaplan's theory of peoples and their culture does not require him to "negate the Exile" but allows him to hope for a positive Jewish existence in the Diaspora. Like Ahad Ha-Am, Kaplan argues that once the folk center has been established, Jews elsewhere will benefit from its civilization, thereby perpetuating their Jewishness.

With a land goes a language. Hebrew never died as the Jewish tongue *par excellence*. Of all the ancient languages which modern national movements have sought to resuscitate, it alone is truly alive. Worldwide Jewish civilization is increasingly united by it. On this score, too, Kaplan's teaching is in full accord with Zionism.

Once Judaism is seen as the civilization of the Jewish people, the arts, too, have a significant place in it. Religious interpreters of Judaism have been puzzled by Jewish folk songs and dances. Secular theoreticians have been embarrassed by the largely ritual concern of Jewish art and poetry. Both sorts of thinkers fail to grasp the breadth of Jewish self-expression. To the contrary, Kaplan argued, everyone should have been shocked at the lack of Jewish artistic expression in the 1930's or its limit to ritual activities.

Social habits form the bulk of a civilization. Jewish life possesses abundant folkways, ranging from ethical customs to honored recipes. In pre-modern days the major folk acts were authorized as religious duties. They were, *mitzvot*, "commandments (given by God)." For modern Jews with their this-worldly orientation, the term *mitzvot* can only be a metaphor, testifying that these acts arouse or articulate a Jewish religious mood. We are far more likely to perform *mitzvot* when they are freed from any connection with a commanding God and seen instead as our ethnic ways to self-fulfillment and folk-survival. This humanistic view of "commandments" has the added advantages of allowing them to be changed as needed or created as seems fitting. In a democratic society, Jewish law must be the community's participatory legislation of its standards. The folk creates "law" as another facet of its civilization; against tradition, the law is not the criterion or creator of the people. Kaplan is that liberal in his reinterpretation of Judaism.

Any group is obligated to manifest high ethical standards. When it does not reflect these universal values, individuals lose their humanity and the group, its rationale. The glory of Judaism has been its exemplary ethical concern, personal and communal as well. Nothing less will do today. Here too Kaplan follows Ahad Ha-Am. He is so committed to ethics that he limits the right of a people to develop its civilization as it sees fit only by this ethical consideration.

The People Takes Precedence Over All Else

If modern Jews are to live as a full-scale civilization they require an appropriate pattern of community organization. Kaplan suggests creating an American version of the European Jewish community structure, the *kehillah*. Abroad, it was an autonomous, governmentally authorized body. Here it might be a voluntary association of all Jews and Jewish institutions committed to the people's survival. All Jews should have their basic loyalty to the community. It, in turn, should be responsible for meeting the diverse needs of Jews in the community. Thus, congregations should no longer be independent entities, as if religion were not another part of Jewish civilization. In Kaplan's "organic community," they would be maintained for the groups desiring them. Rabbis, too, would be retained by the community to serve its various religious needs.

A fully integrated organizational structure makes the Jewish people itself, not any single facet of its culture, the focus of Jewish loyalty. Operating democratically, the organic community would develop our modern Jewish equivalent of law. With the people legislating for themselves, the living relationship between the folk and the law would be reestablished. This would bridge the present day gap between the rigidity of the traditional requirements and the permissiveness of modern Jewish living.

The secret of Jewish survival has now become clear. The Jews continue from generation to generation not as bearers of an idea of God or because they have a mission (à la Cohen and Baeck). Kaplan does not conceive of the "essence" of Judaism as an idea. He is not that sort of rationalist. Judaism's essence is its social base, its ethnicity. The Jews survive because they are a people. Jewish culture changes. The Jewish folk endures. Peoplehood has provided Jewish identity over the centuries. If properly understood and reinvigorated, it will do so today. Kaplan is certain that the Jewish people can survive the present age of transition. Its civilization may adopt many of the ideas of the surrounding society, but as long as it remains a healthy, self-affirming people it will express them in an authentic Jewish civilizational form. Kaplan therefore dedicated himself to "reconstruct" Jewish peoplehood.

Religion has thus far been omitted from this discussion of Kaplan's theory only to emphasize how radically he had departed from traditional and liberal philosophies of Judaism. Kaplan does not deny the central role of religious belief and practice in Jewish life over the centuries. He is determined, however, to put them into proper sociological perspective.

As Durkheim demonstrated, all civilizations have a religion at their core. It integrates the people's way of life. It gives cosmic authority to the values it cherishes. It empowers the institutions and laws which effectuate these goals in people's everyday lives. The religion also inspires and motivates individuals to strive for these ends. Religion, while only one element in a civilization's variegated activities, is the most important of them, "the first among equals." For Kaplan,

Judaism must be a *religious* civilization. He did not substantially alter that position during the next forty years in which he continued to write.

Kaplan's Response to the Changing Social Mood

Since Kaplan wrote his magnum opus, the intellectual climate of western civilization has lost much of its previous reliance on science and human reason, and something of a turn to religion has been under way. One might have expected this changed evaluation of modernity to cause a major readjustment in Kaplan's thought. Instead, he was among the sharpest critics of the synagogue-focused Judaism of the 1950's and 1960's. He envisaged this trend stemming from a need to belong to a Jewish community, not as an outcome of any deeply held belief. As religion it would not go very deep until there was a naturalistic reconstruction of Jewish theology. As an expression of solidarity with the Jewish people it was ineffective because it used the church instead of folk civilization as its model.

Kaplan also rejected the effort by some Jewish thinkers to substitute existentialism for naturalism as the philosophic context for modern Jewish thought. Kaplan criticized the surrender of rationalism, damning it as a weary society's typical "failure of nerve." For the moment, human beings have lost faith in themselves and their capacities. Thus naturalism, which is founded on that faith, has seemed less appealing than non-rational philosophies. Kaplan has no doubt this mood will pass and naturalism will once again be the handmaid of modernity.

The Zionist aspect of his 1934 social perspective could not help requiring serious reconsideration after the State of Israel's establishment. Its subsequent growth and development posed many problems for Kaplan's understanding of Zionism as a civilizing force. His continuing power as a thinker was evident in his willingness to confront these issues. Mostly, Kaplan was disappointed by the Israeli refusal to reorient Diaspora Jewish life to a full range of cultural self-expression. Kaplan believed Zionism must serve the welfare of the Jewish people and not essentially seek world Jewry's support of the State of Israel. To insist that the movement focus on *aliyah* or preparation for it, vitiates Zionism's greater possibilities and ruins the morale of Jews who will not immigrate. Kaplan has gone so far as to suggest making clear that the State of Israel is not properly described as a "nation." There is rather, an Israeli state, while world Jewry is an international people, rooted in the Land of Israel but with branches everywhere.

Kaplan's criticism went even further. If Zionism seeks to enrich the life of the Jewish people, then reconstructing Judaism is a problem for Jews within the State of Israel as well as for the Jews of the Diaspora. Despite the advantages of land, language and Jewish social context Israelis too need a properly balanced Jewish religious civilization.

Responses to Kaplan's Program

Time has not dealt kindly with Kaplan's organizing program for American Jewry. No organic communities have been established or are likely to be in a society where congregational affiliation and independence remain the general norm. However, with a static or declining Jewish population having great difficulty financing independent Jewish programs in the 1980's, some greater pooling of local resources seemed indicated. Should the economic pressure intensify, Kaplan's proposal for organic communities might yet come into its own.

Kaplan's social theory has likewise had shifting fortunes. In the middle decades of the century, America assimilated its immigrant communities and became pluralistic, primarily in religion—the famous "Catholic, Protestant and Jew" which often adorns even the inauguration of American presidents. With economic expansion benefitting almost everyone, the American dream displaced the older concern for one's ethnic roots. In the 1970's a radical shift of mood took place. The once pervasive confidence in democracy was shattered and a resurgence of ethnic interest took place. Among Jews this attitude was heightened by the perils of the State of Israel and by the occasional public signs of anti-semitism. With much of American Jewish life centered on the State of Israel, Kaplan's theory of the Jews as a people received fresh substantiation. Surprisingly, reconstructionism now had less intellectual appeal than in its early, radical days. Kaplan's message about the significance of ethnicity had been absorbed by the major religious movements while its sociological reinterpretation of Judaism was discounted by a generation largely critical of science.

Despite his own goals, future Jewish generations may well consider Kaplan more important as a theologian than as a social philosopher. His effort to rethink the ideas of the Jewish religion in naturalistic terms remains one of the distinctive, creative theological options available to inquiring Jews.

Fashioning a Naturalistic Jewish Theology

Naturalism begins with an act of humility. The human mind cannot provide answers to ultimate questions like, What is the essence of being human? What is death? Why is there evil? What are the limits of our freedom? Most important of all, reason cannot tell us what God *is*. We cannot understand ourselves, much less comprehend God as God truly is. Agnosticism is the only honest posture on the metaphysical issues concerning God—existence, nature, will. Working from our own experience in this world, we simply cannot know anything substantive about God.

Kaplan is not stymied by his intellectual realism. Rather, it prompts him to distinguish between a belief in, and a conception of, God. The belief precedes the conception. Faith is an intuitive human response to the universe. Ideas of God result from people seeking to understand the world in a way that will allow them to live the fullest possible life. They are the outward cultural expression of inner experience; hence, ideas of God need to be socially understood. Knowing how God functions in our lives is, in essence, all we need to know about God. Belief in the Divine confirms and motivates our drive to self-fulfillment. A naturalistic faith will begin with our highest human hopes and identify God with them.

Belief in God is a corollary of our search for self. The self can fulfill itself only by dependence on the external world, by trusting that nature supports its inner upward strivings. To affirm that creation is hospitable to human growth is not an assertion about ultimate reality. Kaplan is not offering a proof of the existence of God, though he says we all need religion. He is only positing that our nature drives us to live abundantly and we therefore naturally trust that reality enables us to do so.

Kaplan's View of God

In what sense, then, does Kaplan use the word "God"? He rejects any description of God as personal, for to him a personal Divinity is an anthropomorphic one. No naturalistic thinkers could accept such a God. Some philosophers have therefore identified God with strictly impersonal scientific concepts such as force or energy. Kaplan rejects this view on two grounds: first, as an unwarranted metaphysical assertion, albeit a naturalistic one; and second, because it renders God morally neutral. Kaplan's God must be related to human self-realization and that, Kaplan believes, inevitably has an ethical component. For him, God is everything in nature we rely on to fulfill ourselves. Kaplan condenses that into, "God is the Power that makes for salvation." The assertion is remarkable. No other Jewish thinker has ever given a definition of God. Kaplan has done so not because he believes that these eight words are adequate to describe God, but so that he can rationally communicate his basic religious insight to others.

God is not a mere wish or an illusion. The term refers to those real processes in nature which support our efforts to live abundantly. Our faith is subjective in being based on our hope that we might fulfill ourselves. It is objective because by God we mean those forces in nature which make it possible for us to achieve our ideals.

Kaplan cannot be criticized for speaking of his God as real. What should not be assumed as a consequence is that God is *a unity which is real*. Kaplan abets this possible misinterpretation by referring to God in terms that seem to describe an entity. He calls God variously the Power, the Process, the Force, with both article and capitalization indicating he is referring to a special "thing." Unity in Kaplan's conception of God cannot be a description of God's being but only of our way of looking at Divinity. Kaplan makes no statements about God's nature for that would be metaphysics. Asserting the unity of God reflects the consistency of our inner, subjective response to the universe. In its objective, "real" sense, the term God does not refer to an entity, but to many different forces in nature—hence, to disparate objective realities. We may summarize, then: insofar as Kaplan's God is real, God is not one, and insofar as God is one, God is not real. Many Jews have found this an insuperable difficulty in Kaplan's conception of God.

A second problem arises from his view of the function of the God-idea. If one can accept the reality of Kaplan's God, one has faith in a God who is fully impersonal. Anthropomorphism and naive religiosity are immediately ruled out. But can an impersonal God involve people personally? Or, conversely, can people take personally an impersonal God? Indeed, what happens to our standards of human development when God is declared to be impersonal? Kaplan's response is in terms of his definition: God is those natural realities which promote the highest human values. Hence the impersonality of God does not vitiate the importance of full human personhood. Kaplan's critics then charge that this God cannot serve as a model for people to emulate for it is only a means we have created for our self-fulfillment. Can one worship such a Divinity?

Humanly, a religion centered on an impersonal God seems a contradiction in terms. Religion either touches all one's heart, one's soul, and one's might, or it is nothing. Why should one be utterly involved with a God who is utterly unresponsive in return? Kaplan does not see why the impersonality of God should create such a problem. God is no more impersonal than any other lofty idea. People take their country very seriously. They address it personally and speak of it with deep affection. They will even give their lives for it. God, being far more involved in human existence, should be even easier to relate to personally.

Kaplan's Theory of Evil

Kaplan reinterprets all the major themes of Jewish belief. Of particular interest are his treatment of the problems of evil, prayer, the chosenness of Israel, and Jewish law.

Kaplan's theodicy is kept thoroughly rational by again substituting function for metaphysics. Had he approached the question metaphysically, we might expect him to say that God cannot be held responsible for the evil in the universe because God is not omnipotent. Kaplan's God is finite, limited to those powers in nature which make for human fulfillment. If God is restricted to what makes for good, how then can we blame God for the evil that befalls us? Kaplan does not take this approach, apparently because it would imply that he has a metaphysical knowledge of precisely what God is and is not. Instead, he prefers to deal with the functional question of how we should meet evil. He worries lest evil deprive people of the will to better themselves or their world. Regardless of our suffering, we need to find sufficient faith in the positive aspects of the self and nature to continue to fulfill ourselves. We transcend evil by not letting it deter us from further self-realization. Here Kaplan yokes his theory of human nature to the liberal's moral argument that evil is primarily a challenge to our ethical courage and creativity.

Kaplan saw no need to modify his views about God and evil as a result of the Holocaust. The history-ruling God that some people now said was dead, Kaplan had given up years before as unbelievable for any person of sophistication. The suggestion that the world was empty of God, specifically that it was morally and humanly neutral, contradicted everything Kaplan understood science to teach about human nature. A negative "faith" would function counterproductively. It would confirm people's fears that the universe was bound to frustrate their efforts at self-actualization. Their consequent passivity and resignation would be utterly unworthy of human beings as conscious moral agents. The Nazis had used their freedom of will to become murderers, and the leaders of the democracies, by doing nothing, had acquiesced in their evil-doing. No iniquity, regardless of its horror, proves that our ideals are false or cannot succeed. To the contrary, we indignantly protest the Nazi savagery and recognize the paramount importance of fighting evil everywhere precisely because we know the evil which people can do. Moral activism, not metaphysical speculation, is the fitting human response to the problem of evil.

Kaplan's View of Prayer and Chosenness

Kaplan's treatment of prayer is a logical outcome of his view of God. Prayer must be understood in terms of the worshiper. Kaplan states boldly:

> All thinking—and prayer is a form of thought—is essentially a dialogue between our purely individual egocentric self and our self as representing a process that goes on beyond us . . . when we wish to establish contact with the Process that makes for human salvation, we can do so only by an appeal to the higher self that represents the working of that Process in us. From that . . . we seek the answer to prayer.

One prays to oneself, so to speak, but to oneself as a locus of the consciousness of the realities which cooperate with us, those natural processes we call God. Why will we pray if we are only communing with ourselves? Because our nature as self-transcending creatures will always lead us to intense inner reflection about the goals and direction of our drive to improve.

Even so, prayer is not primarily a personal matter. Kaplan stresses its social context. Communal worship not only aids the individual but relieves the single self of the special pressures of private prayer. The group supplies one with perspective, channel, and incentive. No wonder the great religions have always advocated both solitary meditation and institutional services. Jews will naturally wish to express this universal human social need as part of their people. In the Diaspora, synagogue services provide one of the most important regular occasions for Jews to gain a feeling of ethnic solidarity. To give effect to his philosophy Kaplan and his disciples have composed new prayer books. They are largely traditional *siddurim* with a number of alterations and omissions, as well as some creative additions, all based on Kaplan's teaching.

Neither Kaplan's view of evil nor of prayer has called forth such controversy as his vigorous opposition to the concept of the chosen people. He rejects it as an immoral, divisive, arrogant notion. Jews ought to renounce it as generating hatred, or at least suspicion, between Jews and non-Jews. At its best, chosenness may once have meant special moral responsibility and thus presented a spiritual challenge to the Jew. With time, it has become an assertion, even if unconscious, of Jewish superiority. It functioned to give the Jews a defense against their enemies and a rationale for their continued existence. Neither use is desirable or necessary in the modern world. Minorities should be safeguarded by securely establishing democracy. They need no justification for their will to survive. They have a right to do so which derives directly from the natural order of things.

Moreover, the idea that God chooses a people is today as meaningless as the notion that God has some sort of conscious, personal will. The study of comparative religion, Kaplan believes, has demonstrated the falsity of claims to exclusive revelation by the inconsistency of the many doctrines asserted to be "the only truth." The higher ethics of the contemporary world, with their universal horizon, makes such tribalistic notions unthinkable.

Any religion genuinely interested in the unity of humanity should renounce particularistic doctrines of salvation. The Jewish people, which has suffered so grievously from those who held exclusivist ideas, and whose civilization has been permeated by ethics, ought to take the lead in this direction. Kaplan concedes that a sense of unique communal purpose does offer added inducement for Jewish living. Let the Jews choose a vocation for their people but not disguise it as as supernatural act of God. By an open, communal decision, let them dedicate themselves to serve humankind. Since nationhood has often meant chauvinism, exemplifying the moral potentialities of collective existence could be a worthy goal for Jewish life.

Law in Kaplan's Reconstruction

A similar liberalism pervades Kaplan's conception of Jewish law. He demands that the law serve the needs of the people, not the people serve the institution of the law. He would modernize it by making it entirely voluntaristic and eliminate any sense of compulsion behind it, either heavenly or human. An active community can be built in stages. In the beginning we must try to help Jews regain a strong loyalty to their people. Then they will naturally want to express their human concerns in Jewish fashion. As participants in Jewish civilization they will also want to share in Jewish religion. If its practices are made as meaningful as possible and if pluralism in ritual is accepted, many could be won to faithful observance. A democratic assembly of the organic Jewish communities should lead this process. Their legislation would determine what constitutes "law" for Jews today. Because these would now be living folk decisions, they would carry special weight with all loyal Jews.

Kaplan has maintained this position consistently though it has brought him into tension with the Conservative movement, with which he was long associated. Its position on Jewish law was more traditional, holding that contemporary decisions be fixed by a body of rabbinic experts and interpreted by local rabbis. The theological issue of the source of the law's authority was by-passed in the hope that enough Jews remained loyal to the classic Jewish legal process to accept as binding modern decisions made in its spirit. Kaplan has been scornful of this theory. Limiting change to what the traditional processes of the law might allow is often retrograde (as shown by the problem of granting women full-scale rights in Jewish religious life). Kaplan's protests against the Conservative movement's failure to develop new patterns of practice were ineffectual. He and his followers finally decided to develop their own institutions to further Reconstructionism. Their pattern of observance is considerably more liberal than that sanctioned by the Conservative movement. For the time being, that is as much of the Jewish community as has been brought into Kaplan's democratic process of setting contemporary Jewish law.

In sum then, Kaplan utilizes a comprehensive humanistic framework for his interpretation of Judaism. All our knowledge of history, of society, of the self and its development are relevant to his modernized Judaism. Every aspect of Jewish communal, cultural and spiritual life is touched and affected by his reinterpretation of the Jewish heritage. He has not hesitated to adopt positions previously unknown to Jewish thought, many of them quite unpopular. His philosophy is irradiated by his integrity and commitment. Yet it is Mordecai Kaplan, the person, who has been his most extraordinary creation. The seriousness and formality of his writings generally mask his warm and lovable nature. In the various decades of his long life, the man himself has always been present, giving, open. He is that rarity, a genuine person—and rarer still, an authentic modern Jew. His words are the words of naturalism but their overtones echo Sinai.

Questions Jews Ask About Kaplan

Having demonstrated in great detail what naturalism might make of Judaism, Kaplan has convinced his critics that it cannot adequately explain the nature of Jewish life.

Kaplan begins his thought with a general understanding of humankind and moves on to justify the continuation of Jewish life. In typical rationalistic fashion, he has greater confidence in the superior truth of a universal theory—sociology—than he has in a particular tradition—Judaism. The abstract, broad-scale approach commends itself not only as modern and scientific but because of its greater comprehensiveness.

His critics charge that in beginning with the abstract Kaplan has ignored another strand in modern thought. Other thinkers have argued that truth never is available in a general form. In reality, truth is inevitably particular. Thus, religion in general is something only academics talk about. The rest of us know "religion" through particular religions. If truth is to be found in specific instances and not just in abstract theories, then Judaism has as much right to determine what is valuable in modern thought as modernity has to instruct Judaism on its proper form. Why should Judaism be so obsequious to modern social science when it is ethically agnostic and denies the realm of the spirit? If anything, science's moral neutrality has become one of the great human dangers of our age. Humankind, teetering on the brink of nihilism, needs its religions, including Judaism, to give it an independent source of value. Science might then not abuse its awesome new power over nature and human life so badly in the future as it has done in the recent past.

Critics also deny Kaplan's view that people by their very nature are oriented to self-fulfillment. The American dream of happiness through self-improvement has proved deeply disappointing. Most lives necessarily remain unfulfilled since worthy human goals are infinite. Kaplan's optimism seems naive. Traditional religion balanced a ceaseless, unsatisfying servitude to self-fulfillment with a serene joy in the fact of being. Over the ages, religion has proved most valuable to people by helping them deal with an existence which was not ultimately self-validating. A mature view of life and religion needs both dark and bright tones.

Kaplan rejects the new realism as unnatural. He insists science has discovered certain lasting truths about basic human nature. Leaving aside the issue of whether psychology has demonstrated that there is an essential human "nature," Kaplan's use of science itself has been challenged. He treats it as if it were prescriptive, assuming that the patterns it shows people have followed are the ones we must or ought to utilize in the future. But what of human freedom? Once we know the way social forces have operated, do we not have the possibility of choosing to act against them? For example, in a world desperately in need of internationalism, perhaps separate peoples are an anachronism we should now speedily transcend. Kaplan appears to have turned description into command, deriving a moral "ought" from what merely happened to be the case.

Besides, Kaplan's social science derives from its earliest modern discoveries—those of Durkheim and Sumner. Decades later, many truths which he accepted as permanent are rejected altogether or subsist in one theory among many. His very claims for the reliability and consistency of the social sciences are rarely heard among the practitioners themselves.

Finally, the entire Kaplanian discussion of human nature is dominated by the term "self-fulfillment" or its equivalent. He apparently thinks its meaning is self-evident. In a simpler day, it may have been. In a time beset with identity crises, little is more problematic. Surely the self is not an entity in us. If it is a potential, how shall we know which of our drives and powers properly fulfill it? Nature only gives us conflict. Unless we have a standard external to our troubled selves and on a superior level, how can we ever know what fulfillment might be? Since Kaplan's God is interpreted in terms of human self-realization, God cannot set a goal for us. Kaplan's God disappears, the critics allege, just when our society needs God the most, when we no longer are certain what we ought to be.

Criticisms of Kaplan's Judaism

Kaplan's proposals for the reconstruction of Jewish life have also drawn rejoinders. One arises from his strict identification of peoples and religions. Kaplan maintains that if America is to become a proper civilization it needs to develop its own faith—what recent followers of Durkheim have termed its "civil religion." Until that has been fully accomplished, Kaplan contends, American Jews have good reason—and democratic warrant—to live in their two civilizations. Kaplan's antagonists have not been persuaded by his plea for dual cultural life. If Americans as a people ought to develop their own religion, should not American Jews give their major energies to that goal? They have a special inducement for such concern. By finally being part of a mature American folk they could end the perils of minority status. To respond that every people ought naturally seek to survive disregards the utterly unnatural, incomparable persecution of the Jews. Without a compensating reason for remaining Jewish, morality dictates that this dangerous social status, being a Jew, ought to be brought to an end.

Furthermore, if the Jews are primarily a folk, then their secular activities are as valuable as their religion. Is folk dancing the Jewish equivalent of study of the Bible or Talmud? The great American Jewish folk act is gossiping over coffee after synagogue services. By contrast, the worship rarely gives most Jews a strong community feeling. Should prayer, then, give way to more socializing? Kaplan properly feared that considering Judaism a "religion" might lead to a loss of ethnicity. To make religion only the first of many folk activities seems to delimit it unduly.

Two theological criticisms must also be noted. God once functioned in people's lives because they believed, consciously or unconsciously, that God was real. Can Kaplan's God have the same effect on people's lives when they know God's unity is only a mental construct and God's reality is a disparate series of natural processes? To argue from our alleged need for a God is already to lose the case. Of course, we moderns would like to believe in God and know that our efforts to live abundantly are supported by that God. Having been trained by Feuerbach and Freud that all our talk about God is only a projection of ourselves into a cosmic realm, we are sceptical about God. The more we hear about human needs the more we wonder whether God is real. Only when we are convinced that God is not just a mental prop we have created, will God be significant enough to us to affect our lives. Functionalism does not allow us to avoid the metaphysical issue.

The concept of the chosen people also seems poorly handled by Kaplan, certainly in its historical development. Rarely has religious particularity been as hedged by moral considerations. The prophets categorically denied that Israel's chosenness supervened God's justice. The rabbis repeatedly defined chosenness as receiving Torah and hence being obligated to do commandments. Jewish "superiority" to others was occasionally asserted as a response to the persecutor, not as a product of Jewish theology. In any case, giving up one's doctrine is no way to change general social realities. A doctrine ought to be evaluated in terms of its intrinsic merit, not in terms of what one hopes other religions will do about their similar beliefs. At this point the dangers of dealing with religious truth essentially in terms of its social context become vividly clear.

The very intensity of the criticism testifies that Mordecai Kaplan has made a lasting contribution to modern Jewish thought. His legitimization of a secularized Jewishness enabled many post-immigrant Jews to integrate into American culture while retaining Jewish self-respect. When religion was on the defensive from a metaphysically imperialistic science, he created a theology in which a de-anthropomorphized God could be understood in terms of human needs. In a day when liberal Judaism and Zionism seemed intellectually incompatible, he found a way to combine a strong Jewish ethnicity with a fully universal faith. In a troubled and confused time, Mordecai Kaplan had the daring and capacity to confront his people's problems realistically and to propose solutions. For decades he challenged the will and the intelligence of all who cared about Jewish life. His unique combination of Jewish heart and mind remains a spur and a challenge to all succeeding Jewish thinkers.

PART III
The Six
Systematized
Positions:
Non-rationalistic
Models

6

The Pioneer Existentialist: Franz Rosenzweig

SOME Christian theologians—Sören Kierkegaard or, centuries before, Augustine, or, more recently, Karl Barth, for example—have been connected with existentialism because of its characterisitc criticism of the human situation. The existentialist analysis exposes our bent for self-deception and self-exaltation, giving the doctrine of original sin fresh meaning. Suddenly, liberalism's doctrine of humankind's perfectibility seems a rationalization of our aggressive self-esteem. Classic Christian terms such as "sin," "justification," and "redemption," seen in an existential light, take on a contemporary, personal tone. More, they explain much of recent history. Social analysts, political scientists, and other intellectuals who normally eschew theology have turned to Christian existentialism to comprehend a humankind that could produce the horrors we have seen. By contrast, religious liberalism's essentially optimistic view of people has failed to account for the depth of malevolence in educated, cultured people.

The general Jewish view of humankind differs radically from that of Christianity and many scholars consider this the root disagreement between them. For Judaism, sin is heinous but not the central reality of humanity's relation to God. The classic Jewish sources reveal no more than an intellectual flirtation with the doctrine of original sin. They depict human beings as pure-born and fully capable of responding to God's demands. Even should one sin, one retains the capacity to reconcile oneself with God through the practice of *teshuvah*, repentance (better, "turning"). Judaism rejects the concept that people are sinners, either in essence or by the necessities of existence. In Jewish usage the word "salvation" does not, therefore, customarily denote helping sinful individuals justify themselves before God, their judge. With its more positive attitude to the human situation, how can Judaism appropriately utilize existentialism to explicate Jewish faith?

Many thinkers also insist that Jewish modernity and rationalism are inseparable, that reason has played an indispensible role in the development of modern Judaism. Historical analysis demonstrated that Jewish practice and belief had changed over the centuries, suggesting the validity of contemporary adjustments. Philosophy argued that an unchanging ethical devotion was central to the Jewish tradition, whereas the ritual forms in which it was expressed were secondary and ought to be adapted to a new social ethos. Reason also motivated the Jew's continued rejection of Christianity. Miracles— the virgin birth, the incarnation of God in human form, the resurrection, the ascension—are central to Christian teaching, as is dogma (e.g., that God is a trinity that is yet a unity). Any rational mind, operating without prejudice, should deny them. Ethical monotheism, particularly in its rationalistic reinterpretations, posed no such difficulty. If anything, reason spurred the Jews to adhere to their minority faith.

The Place of Rationalism in Jewish History

Even a cursory view of its history refutes the notion that Judaism has historically been as rationalistic a religion as has been suggested. If reason is identified as the kind of systematic, abstract thinking associated with Greece, then its use in Judaism is late, not early;

sporadic, not continuous; syncretistic, not indigenous. The Bible is not a philosophic document but a collection of histories, stories, law, poems and wise sayings.

Philo aside—he remained unknown to Jewish tradition until modern times—rationalist expositions of Judaism arose only in the ninth century C.E., a thousand years after the last biblical book was written and centuries after the editing of the Talmud. Moreover, this rationalist awakening took place not in response to a Jewish need, but at the polemical prompting of, and as a response to, the Moslem culture in which Jews then found themselves.

Similarly, today, the Emancipation brought Jews into a society that alleges a high regard for rationality. Jews again had recourse to philosophical patterns of self-description. From roughly the fifteenth to the eighteenth century, there was little or no Jewish philosophy, though much speculative Jewish mysticism. Thus, Jewish history offers ample evidence to refute the contention that Judaism cannot be divorced from rationalism.

The gains rationalism brings to Judaism—a changeable tradition and a rejection of Christianity—might equally well be accomplished by a non-rational existentialist theory of Judaism. Franz Rosenzweig was the first Jew to explore this intellectual possibility.

Beginnings of Jewish Existentialism

Rosenzweig was born in 1886 and died at forty-three in 1929. His Jewish background was inauspicious. He was the only child of a reasonably well-to-do German family, with typically little interest in Judaism but great devotion to German culture. After a shift from medicine to philosophy, he wrote a doctoral dissertation published under the title *Hegel and the State*. The work evoked considerable acclaim and influential professors were ready to sponsor his teaching at a university, though Jews were still unwelcome there, particularly in that native discipline, idealistic philosophy.

Rosenzweig rejected a career as a professional philosopher because of his turn to religion. He gained his intellectual maturity by giving up the rationalistic gods of his early philosophical faith. His major contribution to religious thought, *The Star of Redemption*, was written during World War I. Many thinkers then were seeking a substitute for idealistic rationalism as a result of its failure to prepare them for the human realities they had experienced. Rosenzweig's book must be read less as an existentialist statement than as a German idealistic philosophy seeking to overcome itself.

The young thinker opens his argument with an uncommon philosophic topic, death. Why, he ruminates, should it trouble the individual? If Hegel is correct that all people are included in the Universal Spirit which is working its way through history to ever greater self-realization, why should they be disturbed at dying? Their cosmic significance will not perish, for their individuality is carried along by Absolute Spirit on its purposeful way. Death cannot rob individuals of their part in its magnificent, all-encompassing, forward flow.

What poor consolation is such philosophy, as we contemplate the frightening reality of our inevitable, evernearing death!

Surely an individual's disappearance has no real significance for idealist philosophers, for they dissolve its reality into an idea and turn our concrete existence into an abstraction. In an instant the hidden function of Hegelian philosophy is revealed. It exists to help people convince themselves that death is meaningless and may conveniently be ignored. Such philosophy is generated by our fear of dying and our unwillingness to face it. We are terrified lest we be forced to acknowledge the startling paradox of our individuality. Nothing in the world is as real to us as our own being—and we are steadily losing it. No abstract concept, no matter how universal or all-embracing, can ever be as significant as that. No idea can ever match the reality of "me" here and now. Proper philosophy—"existentialism"—begins with the reality of this incomparable but perishing self, with the recognition that true existence is concrete, individual and particular, not abstract, general and universal. Rationalism can no longer be a useful way of contemplating existence. A new sort of thinking must now begin.

The Three Givens of Existence

Death makes us aware of the first given reality of being, the self. Similarly it discloses that the world, too, has existence in its own right. Some idealist philosophers were so taken with the creative power of reason that they had reduced "the world" to the intellectual construction of reality created by a human mind. Rosenzweig argues that "the world" is real even as the self is real. Individuals can have a separate existence because they are independent of the world about them. Thus, our death fills us with anxiety but the death of "the world," were we able to survive it, has another effect upon us. The self and the world are different and distinct. Neither is a creation of our reason or will. Both are simply there, realities given with our very existence. They precede our reason. Hence the hardheaded thinker must cope with them.

How can this be explained? How can one make sense of the existence of two such irreducible realities? German idealistic philosophy tried to do so with its concept of the Absolute whose universality embraced them both. The concept of the Absolute did give a comprehensive meaning to existence. In the process it robbed persons and the world of the individual reality that it reserved for itself alone. The significance it had claimed to confer, it thus subtly took back. Rosenzweig concludes that we must renounce traditional philosophy's goal and hope: a single concept universal enough to embrace persons and the world in their distinct realities. Instead, we shall understand them only when we acknowledge a reality beyond them and independent of them. Religion calls it God. As suddenly as that, without proof or definition or even pointing to any special realm of religious experience, but simply by contrasting the work of modern philosophy with the reality of human existence, Rosenzweig posits a real, existing, independent God.

Rosenzweig's does not begin with Descartes' notion of an empty, doubting mind. He posits three given, distinct realities: first, "me", the individual (which he calls "man"); second, the world, (in which one lives out one's existence); and third, God (the ground and guide of all existence). Rosenzweig once termed his method of reaching these three entities "absolute empiricism." That is; they were the unavoidable realities yielded by a direct confrontation of the conditions of personal existence. We, the world, and God are simply there. Our reason cannot hope to explain them in terms of some master abstract principle. Ideas are always less than life. Responsible thought must build upon that recognition. The task of philosophy is humbly to follow after what exists and utilize reason to explicate its structure insofar as that is possible. This approach is proto-existentialist, the sort of thinking that a few years later Martin Heidegger and others would systematize into what we call existentialism. Commenting on his own thought, Rosenzweig also described his intellectual approach as a "new thinking," a methodology which made the situation of one's actual life the basis for all one's ideas.

Some Characteristics of The New Thinking

We cannot use European philosophy to capitalize on Rosenzweig's insight into what is given with existence itself. If the individual self is its very core, the new thinking must be personal, not impersonal, as philosophy customarily is. It must proceed in terms of particulars, not in terms of the universal categories rationalistic thinkers utilized. It must be open and dynamic, thus able to cope with living, shifting relationships between individuals, the world and God.

Rosenzweig found human speech a close analogy to the kind of thinking he was advocating, going so far as to characterize it as "speech thinking." In true interchange the individual is personally involved, not passively present. In the course of speaking, people say things they did not previously know they believed or affirmed. Speaking from one's depth is therefore a variety of revelation. Taking place between partners, speech unites human beings into a momentary society. Dialogue is the living sinew of relationship, binding one partner to the other in genuine togetherness.

Rosenzweig wants to think about human existence in this participating, revelatory, relational way. Note that Rosenzweig does not propose abandoning all rational guidance at the point of human commitment but, beginning there, to construct an intellectual understanding of existence. After World War I other thinkers similarly explored the possibilities of speech as a guide to existential thinking. Martin Buber's somewhat different exposition of thinking in terms of dialogue has become the most widely known and accepted of these philosophies.

Rosenzweig carried his exposition a bold step further. In effect he tried to create an appropriate logic for existential thinking. He argued that three primary words were necessarily involved in every statement. The first is "yes," the affirmation that something is real, that it has significance. The second is "no," which applies even in affirmation, for it indicates that the object is not something else but just what it is. The final word is "and" since, after all, the thing is both its "yes" *and* its "no."

Rosenzweig's structure for the new thinking is suspiciously close to the rationalistic logic of Hegel. Here as elsewhere, Rosenzweig is not as free of German idealism as he desired to be. Rosenzweig might have responded that Hegel's logic applied so well to reality because it stemmed out of the structure of speech, not from purely mental considerations.

One significant example indicates how Rosenzweig's "logic" shapes his religious thought. To say a "yes" about God is to say that God is "there" and real, that God is what God is, thus making God "God." The affirmation also implies a certain "no"—that God is not any one thing, not merely this or limited to that. Transcending thingness, God is free to be and do whatever God wills to be and do. To this must be added an "and." God "is" *and* God is "free." God is the free being; the one whose being is freedom; who, through freedom, expresses God's particular being.

For Rosenzweig, God cannot be mere abstraction, a concept that summarizes or grounds all other ideas. God wills; God acts. In the language of Jewish tradition, God is a living God.

Time and history are critical to this sort of religious thought, for the relations between people, the world, and God are not lived out in static, unchanging being. Existence takes place as dynamic duration and, as the confrontation with death revealed, it finds its meaning only as one event succeeds another. Truth cannot then be merely the logical coherence of ideas or a static correspondence of thought to what-really-is. Truth now must be understood as a true relationship. Truth exists when a self is willing to live it and ascertain its existential reality. The important truths are those on which one stakes one's life. More important truths are those for which one is willing to die. And the greatest truths are those to which generation after generation will pledge their lives and for which they will risk their deaths.

By virtue of God's relation to people and the universe, God is involved in time and works in history. Thus, despite the modernity with which the new thinking operates, Rosenzweig's existentialistic God is a personal God, one very much like the God described in the Bible.

The Three Relationships of Existence

What exactly is the relationship between God and the world? The ancients called it creation and thereby stated a continuing truth. Nature is not independent of God but receives its existence from God. God "calls" it into being and is its source and origin. Creation may largely be spoken of as referring to the past, though it cannot take that meaning exclusively. God sustains creation and keeps bringing new things into being, though largely in a derivative way. As the Jewish morning prayer puts it, properly utilizing the present tense, God "renews each day the work of creation." Nonetheless the creation-relation is fundamentally an event of the past.

The relationship between God and people is revelation. God makes us aware of God's presence and, out of that knowledge, of what is demanded of us. Unlike traditional Judaism, Rosenzweig does not believe God communicates verbal statements. All God gives in revelation is Self, God's being-there-with-us. As we all know from being in love, the presence of our beloved awakens in us a sense of aspiration and unworthiness, of dedication and resolve. Revelation as being-there-together means command, judgment, and acceptance as one. Jewish tradition depicted it in objective, factual terms, "And God spoke, saying . . . ." In Rosenzweig's existentialist interpretation, revelation has been given new meaning in terms of personal relationship.

Even as one lives in the present, not in the past, revelation is a very present exchange. It cannot have happened only once or occur sporadically. It must be a contemporary reality—if people will open themselves to it as presence and not as idea. Of course, revelation has occurred in the past and history has been changed when groups have been decisively influenced by it. Such special moments have the quality of a continuing present, for revelation is most appropriately spoken of in the present tense. For Rosenzweig, God tells the Jews today, as at Sinai, what they must do. The contemporary experience of God, not that of the past, is ultimately critical to him, producing a dynamic and evolving Judaism. Rosenzweig's thought indicates that an existentialist theology can generate criteria enabling Jews to deal with the question of meaningful change.

The remaining tense, the future, applies primarily to the relationship between people and the world. Standing before God, we know we must transcend our present level of existence. Our work in the world ought to reflect our knowledge of God better. Each person needs to reach out and find others. Ultimately a community will appear whose members, through knowing one another in full individuality, will live with one another in peace and harmony. In turn such communities will overflow to reach all humankind and then out to nature until a final concord of people, the world, and God is achieved. The relations between the three existential realities are consummated in this messianic fulfillment. The Jewish sages termed this redemption and often pictured it as humanity's work as God's partner in history.

Some people consider messianism impossibly remote and utterly unrelated to our present existence. They underestimate the power of life. It struggles to maintain itself despite all change, to attain permanence amid the flux of existence. A living thing is that unique natural locus where individuality asserts itself, even if only briefly, against unremitting change and decay. Our daily, lifelong experience testifies to our continuous triumph over non-being. We remain; the self continues; life is transcendent. The redemption of the entire world is the ultimate victory of the life principle. Effective only in a partial and incomplete manner now, it will one day be perfected in a harmony of people the world, and God. Not without deliberate intent does Rosenzweig begin his philosophy with an evocation of death and end it with a call to life, a life dedicated to the work of redemption.

The Star Which Illuminates Existence

Rosenzweig's "metaphysics" may be depicted by a diagram. The three realities are set at some distance from one another to indicate their genuine independence of one another. Their active interrelationship must also be indicated. Balancing the static realities and the active relationships, our view of reality looks like this:

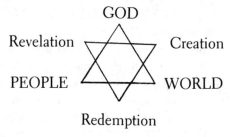

This is the star of redemption!

Rosenzweig's abstract conception of reality must now be applied to history. How did it receive concrete application in time? What do human records disclose of God's acts and people's response?

In pagan cults as in great religions, people everywhere have truly known the living God but only dimly. Rarely have they fully grasped the three realities and their interrelations. A true religion must build its way of life on creation, revelation, and redemption. Many religions have some truth, but thoughtful people will adhere only to those religions which know and live by the star of redemption.

Rosenzweig cannot accept the Asian religions for they do not know and reflect the dynamic of creation, revelation and redemption. Rosenzweig also denies the ultimate merit of Islam. Though heir to the Jewish understanding of history, it no longer demonstrates that active, creative relationship with God set forth in the star. He considers Islam's formalized and culture-bound condition a parody of a true religious relationship. Obviously, though Rosenzweig had firsthand experience and academic expertise in Judaism and Christianity, his knowledge of Islam was slight and his contact with it nearly non-existent.

Two True Religions of History

Though a loyal Jew, Rosenzweig comes to an assertion probably without parallel in modern religious thought to this day. He declared that there are *two* true religions, Judaism and Christianity. Each emphasizes one aspect of truth. Judaism remains aloof from other religions to protect its integrity, to retain its vision against the distortion that would result from adopting perspectives from the outside world. Christianity is expansive, seeking at all costs to win the world for God, even to the extent of compromise or adulteration. Judaism is the fire of the star, Christianity its rays. Neither has the whole truth, for they stand in history, not at its integrated conclusion. Now human beings can achieve only part of the final perfection. To realize the harmony of knowledge and action, of self and community, which is redemption, we must utilize our present religion, awaiting its culmination in messianic days. Only then will we know and live God's truth in all its fullness. Until then we must live in such partial truth as we can find in our finite state.

Many people are shocked to hear that two religions, highly divergent in teaching and practice, are true. That defies logic and outrages consistent thought. But not by Rosenzweig's definition: that we find truth not in ideas but only in the concrete living out of history. Which of these religions is finally true can be known only when the generations of men over the millennia of history have lived by them and given their lives for their truths. Then either or both, transformed perhaps, will participate in that fulfillment called the Kingdom of God.

Does Rosenzweig's existentialism deprive its adherents of a justification for maintaining Judaism rather than accepting Christianity?

Rosenzweig does acknowledge the legitimacy of Christianity. Considering its history and the lives it has molded, he feels he cannot honestly do otherwise. Must not every believing Jew face up to the significance of Christianity's (and Islam's) place in God's purposes? So, too, the devout Christian must puzzle over Israel's continued existence in faith and service despite its rejection of the Christ. Rosenzweig has given a candid response to a perplexing reality. He would want to know how other modern Jews could give any less positive a judgment.

Rosenzweig simultaneously affirms Judaism's special truth. He would emphatically deny that Christianity is truer than Judaism. It can offer Jews nothing they do not already possess. All they need spiritually is already in Judaism. Indeed, what every Jew has at birth, the Christian must yet acquire, for a Jew is born into a living relation with God, the Covenant. No one is born a Christian, for without baptism one dies a heathen. To become a Christian, one must come to the Father through the Christ. For heathens Christianity is an effective means to God. But what can baptism bestow on a Jew who already shares an authentic relationship with God?

Rosenzweig claimed further that the Jews are already at the goal for which Christians are still striving. Christianity is only on the way to the Kingdom. The church must be reconstituted with each new birth, each generation. It justifies its present unfulfillment by the future return of the Christ. Then Christians will finally be fully united with God. The Jews are in a quite different situation. They are already with God. Having God's revelation, Torah, enables them now to live, so to speak, in the Kingdom of God. This constitutes

Israel an eternal people. Time and place, the political and social events which make up ordinary history are of relative indifference to the Jews. Living in eternity, why should they seek temporality? For a Jew, to desert Judaism is not only unnecessary but a retrogression.

The Uniqueness of Rosenzweig's Theory of Judaism

Rosenzweig's existentialism contradicted the theories of Judaism dominant in his day. The liberals insisted that Judaism was a pattern of belief centered about the concept of ethical monotheism. The traditionalists countered that a Jew was identified by observance or neglect of Jewish law. The Zionists rejected both religious positions, affirming rather that Jews were a secular, national group. Loyalty to the folk, its land and its language were the primary signs of Jewish authenticity. Rosenzweig consciously dissented from all three views while incorporating some of their major concerns. For him, the Jew's religious existence was not simply personal. Each Jew shares the Jewish people's Covenant with God, made at Sinai and renewed through centuries of loyalty and practice. The idea of the Jewish people without God is utterly unknown to the Jewish past and unthinkable in any genuine Judaism. A living relationship with God must be its center and no idea, not even one as noble or exalted as "ethical monotheism," can substitute for it. The Covenant relationship is naturally expressed in deeds and thus Jewish law is its necessary expression. One cannot, however, compromise people's human dignity by requiring them to do an act which, despite knowledge and general commitment, they find themselves unable to do. For Rosenzweig, relationship, not performance, is the test of Jewish legitimacy. He therefore was more concerned with piety and observance than the liberals, with autonomy more than the Orthodox, and with religion more than the Zionists.

Rosenzweig's philosophy grew out of his experience. Immediately before World War I, the young university student had been directly challenged by the religious affirmations of some friends and relatives.

Their thoughtful probing destroyed his middle-class, self-righteous secularism and made him see the need of religious commitment. Though born Jewish, they felt one could find living religiosity only in Christianity. Rosenzweig agreed to join them, yet somehow felt it more authentic to do so as the early Christians had done, to come to the Christ as a believing Jew. He spent one last Yom Kippur day in an ordinary, traditional synagogue in Berlin. When the full day of services was over and that day of Jewishness had been lived, the resolve to convert made no sense. He no longer felt that he needed Christianity or that he could ever become a Christian. Rosenzweig never discussed that day's events or described what transpired. His many other writings make plain that religion ought not be based on special experiences, whether the genteel ones of Baeck and Otto, or the extravagant ones of the mystics. He rejects such grounds for a proper faith. For him, being, not feeling, should be our guide. I suggest that, having once opened himself to the reality of living as a Jew under the Covenant, he realized that he had always possessed that which he though he must convert to find. Existence, not experience was critical.

The present task of Jewish leadership, as he saw it, was to lead Jews back to the Jewish roots of their existence. In culture-oriented German Jewry he felt this could be accomplished best through adult education, by exposing people to the ancient sources, wherever possible in the original Hebrew. After his war service he desisted from theologizing and devoted his life to Jewish education, most of it as head of the adult Jewish academy in Frankfurt, which he founded. His philosophy demonstrated that deeds, not ideas, are the primary way a Jew responds to God and he was determined to exemplify it.

Rosenzweig's Debate With Buber

In the early 1920's Rosenzweig had an extraordinary debate with Martin Buber, in which they exchanged a series of letters on the issue of Jewish law. (Rosenzweig frequently used letters to express his ideas, since it allowed him to practice speech-thinking with his correspondent.)

In a long open letter, Rosenzweig challenged Buber to adopt the same standard for Jewish law that Buber had urged Jews to apply to Jewish study. With telling effect Buber had argued against the liberal notion that only the ethical teaching of Judaism was worthy of serious lay study. Jewish history dictated otherwise. The Jews were a people, as the Zionists said, not a philosophic school as the liberals implied. A people records in its literature what it has learned and valued in life. To grasp its folk wisdom, one must study its texts in all their variety, openly and without preconception. To set limits by genre or theme as to what will or will not be of value produces more of an encounter with oneself than with the spirit of the Jewish people. A serious inquirer will first study the material and accept whatever lessons may emerge from the encounter.

Rosenzweig urged that modern Jews come to Jewish law in the same way. They should observe it not according to any prejudgment of what remains valid in it, but insofar as they are "able" to do so. A living, personal relationship with God as part of the Jewish people mandates a life of Jewish duty, of the discipline delineated by the sages. Life under the Covenant is existence under "the yoke of the commandments." The liberals had required only the practice of ethics, judging all other acts by their usefulness in sensitizing one to morality. Rosenzweig now advocated a full-scale commitment to carrying out the traditional law, allowing the doing to produce its own validation.

Buber firmly rejected this line of argument. He wanted no precondition, not even the content of the law, to stand between him and what God might or might not command. In a living relationship one responds to the other in terms of what is demanded of one now, not what once seemed appropriate. A given precept of the law is probably what God once asked Jews to do and may be asking them to do now. It may also not be what God wants now. Buber made a distinction between study and action. Facing a text, one may reasonably suspend judgment about its worth and accept the discipline of giving oneself to the study. Action is different. It involves the commitment of the whole self. Often our deed reveals who we truly are—even to ourselves. When acts are at stake, Buber insists, people can only be required to do what, in their encounter with the Eternal Thou, they find themselves called to do.

In this correspondence Rosenzweig did not develop further his thesis that traditional Jewish law is binding, at least in principle, on non-Orthodox Jews. He could not easily do so because he and Buber shared a common theoretical understanding of revelation and law. Both thinkers affirmed autonomy, that only the immediate moment of relationship with God was authoritative. Only the encounter with God, with its address to the individual self, could command. Once the living moment was reduced to a rule, what had been an authentic behest became an impersonal and hence dead regulation. Or, to put it another way, a law addressed to everyone and thereby to no person in particular, had no religious validity. Rosenzweig conceded that command must be existential. (We shall take up this matter again in Chapter 7.)

Resolving the Issue of Autonomy and Law

In other writings, Rosenzweig suggested a way around this dilemma. He did not abandon either his identification of authentic Jewish existence with accepting the authority of the law or his existentialist notion of the personal, present quality of revelation. Instead he argued that in the doing, what previously might have seemed only a lifeless statute, became God's personal command to the doer. Against Buber's insistence that the imperative must precede a genuinely required religious act, Rosenzweig asserted that stated Jewish observance, carried out in Jewish being, created its own sense of commandment.

Had he said no more, Rosenzweig would have been an apologist for traditional Judaism. But his position is particularly intriguing since he remained a liberal by dialectically enunciating the notion that Jews need not undertake any duties they found themselves "unable" to do. His comment on the topic was brief and cryptic. He surely did not mean Jews should desist from observances that did not appeal to them. No trivial considerations could carry weight in his serious approach to authentic existence. His personalistic philosophy would normally make the criterion for a proper act the ability to devote one's whole self to it. Against Orthodoxy, Rosenzweig could not demand that Jewish law had sway over a Jew who, at the very deepest level, was "unable" to perform a given practice. In Rosenzweig's understanding, the law momentarily exempted from it—and that as a matter of authentic modern Jewish duty. For such a Jew, the unobserved law was in a special category: a commandment, but one "not yet" fulfilled.

Rosenzweig is the only major modern Jewish thinker to have created an unqualifiedly non-Orthodox interpretation of Judaism which takes traditional Jewish law so seriously. He has therefore been highly esteemed by those Jews who see law as the central feature of Jewish history but who no longer can accept the doctrine of its divine origin and continuity. Rosenzweig's intuition in this regard seems in conflict with the rest of his thought and with much Jewish experience. Even as his theory of revelation does not validate Jewish law, neither does observance usually do so. Many well-intentioned Jews testify that doing rarely produces the sense of personal command that Rosenzweig told them would occur. Rosenzweig raised, but could not answer, a question which continues to perplex liberal Jewish thinkers: How can one grant the individual self the dignity of making independent decisions yet require law for the Jewish people?

Rosenzweig's doctrine of the Jewish people has also drawn much criticism. By making the Jews essentially a people of revelation, he withdrew them from normal history. Living in eternity, they had no need for a land of their own or the protection that acquiring their own sovereign state might grant them. Rosenzweig was a confirmed non-Zionist. He saw no significant virtue in ethnicity and he worried lest the revival of the Hebrew language secularize Judaism and thereby empty it of its unique spiritual content. If anything, Rosenzweig seems here to be less authentic to Jewish tradition than to have made an ideal of Diaspora existence, if not of a Christian theological view of the Jews. Half a century later—in a time which has seen the establishment of the State of Israel—Rosenzweig's attitude toward peoplehood seems particularly naive.

Rosenzweig has had few intellectual disciples. For one thing, his thought, reference and argumentation is thoroughly Germanic. He has not transplanted well. Many of his key assumptions appear more as proclamation than as the result of reasoning or by way of experience—for example, his treatment of God's reality. His later, Jewish, thought also suffers from being developed only in fragments. We often cannot tell what he meant and do not know how we can apply his works to our quite different situations.

Rosenzweig's own life was powerful argument for the value of an existentialistic commitment to living as a Jew. In 1921 the first signs of a progressive paralysis were detected, and as the years wore on he became completely incapacitated, barely able to move a finger, finally able to signal with only his eyes. Despite this, he lived until 1929, and did so as an incredibly active, concerned, creative human being. With his wife's aid, he wrote innumerable, discursive letters, reviewed records and books, and worked with Martin Buber on a new German translation of the Bible. A circle of friends, admirers and disciples gathered around him, offering him the Jewish community that was basic to his being. The various accounts of the group who regularly came to Rosenzweig's home and enabled him to carry on his Jewish practice are among the most moving documents of modern Jewish life.

Rosenzweig's thought stands on its own as a special example of Jewish existentialism. That his life bears its own special testimony to the validity of his ideas is an existential consistency one hopes to find in thinkers but dares not expect. For Rosenzweig, death ended existence only as men know it. It could not overcome life itself.

7

Religious Existentialism: Martin Buber

EXISTENTIALISM proceeds from the premise that the whole person, not merely one's mind or conscience or emotions, must be the standard of our thought and action. By analyzing the structures of human existence and describing our existential needs, it provides a new justification and elaboration of religious faith. Though this emphasis on the self gives existentialism great power, it also produces its great weakness. Turning to the person may teach the necessity of belief; it tells us nothing about the proper substance of our affirmation.

With attention concentrated on the virtue of faith, every religion seems acceptable, even the most bizarre. If existentialism only produces faith in faith, it can support great evil. Naziism had a powerful effect on many Germans. Its ideology seemed a saving truth to vast numbers, even though it produced a corrupt society and a ravaged continent. Is there no guidance to what is worthy of our existential commitment or why our personal stand in faith should be here rather than there?

If human existence were rationally comprehensible, our concerns about the content of faith could receive sure and explicit answers.

141

Classic philosophy utilized the mind to supply us with judgments about life as dependable and certain as the logic upon which they were based. If existentialism is correct, the human condition cannot ultimately be explained in purely cognitive constructs, no matter how grand. Despite the pain, we must surrender the hope that reason might yet give us the safety and assurance of having an intellectual understanding of existence. If we are honest with ourselves, we will acknowledge that our lives always retain a substantial element of risk and venture.

Recognizing the difficulty inherent in their position, various existentialists have sought to explain what constitutes a worthy faith. Negatively, they have proceeded by offering an intensive analysis of the depersonalization of the individual in contemporary society. By exposing the ways we have been robbed of our sense of personal dignity and unique identity, they have pointed to needed social change. Positively, working from their new insight into the self, they have suggested what it means to be a genuine person, to have true relationships and to create a social order which fosters authentic individuality and community. No one has contributed more to this project than Martin Buber.

He was born in Vienna in 1878, and until his death in Jerusalem in 1965, his life was marked by his steadily increasing influence. Before World War I, he was already a significant figure in European and Jewish intellectual affairs. His writings on religion and culture, religious socialism, and particularly mysticism, appealed to the broad public engaged in spiritual search. In the Jewish community, he was an early adherent of Zionism and a leader of its cultural activities. His emergence as an existentialist came with the appearance of his brief classic I and Thou in 1922. In the following decades, he applied his new theory to every aspect of human and Jewish existence. No Jewish religious thinker since Biblical times more substantially influenced his culture than did Buber; though it must be noted that his influence outside the Jewish community was much greater than that within it.

Origins of Buber's Thought

Buber's thought shows no symptoms of the personal or social trauma often called a "failure of nerve." He came to existentialism in the decade following the appearance of his mystical work, *Daniel*, in 1913.

Buber once related an incident that was symptomatic of his development, from one concerned with immersion in The All to facing real people in their immediate situation. In late autumn, 1914, a young man came to see him. Buber had just spent a morning basking in mystical exaltation. Still warmed by his intimate communion with God, Buber received the youth cordially and answered his questions in friendliness. Afterward Buber was troubled. He realized that he had not truly heard or genuinely responded to his caller. The young man obviously had questions he burned to ask but could not articulate. The older man, more concerned with the afterglow of his morning rapture than with the person in front of him, had inhibited rather than promoted their exchange. Sometime later, Buber heard from his friends that his caller had died in the war. Experiences such as this forced Buber to the admission that mysticism, far from disclosing reality to us, obscures it. The people who confront us moment by moment and make their demands on us are far more significant than any subjective occurrence might be. Authentic human existence, Buber realized, is found in "meeting," in the reality that arises between people, not a reality suggested by theories or sensations.

Some scholars have maintained that Buber's ideas developed from his early and lasting affection for the Hasidic movement. None has shown how Hasidism might engender Buber's philosophy rather than offer convenient illustrations for it. The possible Jewish roots of Buber's unique insight into the human condition remain unclear. Yet his affirmation of the interpersonal as more significant than purely individual being repeats the priorities of traditional Judaism. A religiosity that can obscure one's responsibility to one's neighbors is uncongenial to the Jewish spirit. In stressing engagement, rather than solitariness, Buber affirmed the Jewish heritage in a new, existential way./

Buber directs our attention to the inner life of personal relationships. This has led many critics, particularly rationalists, to call his teaching mystical. This can easily lead to profound misunderstanding. If a mystic is one who wishes to transcend individuality by union with Deity, Buber is no mystic. He envisages meaning arising from what transpires *between* two persons. One must take this statement literally. If either person does not steadfastly maintain individuality, there is no meeting, only merging, probably involving the submerging of one in the other. Rather than surrender oneself in dialogue, Buber believes that only maintaining one's particularity while sharing it with another truly calls relationship into being./

Persons Not Ideas Are Critical

With intellectual communication no substitute for person-to-person encounter, Buber sometimes writes in an odd style. Seeking to direct people to I-Thou meeting, he cannot convey his meaning in impersonal, objective, philosophic prose. He presents his comments on the human situation in short, poetic observations, more musing than arguing with his reader. He had no desire to be considered a theologian or philosopher as he did not want academic convention to keep him from engaging reality or his readers. Again, a personal experience is illuminating.

Buber once gave some lectures attended by working men. Recognizing they were uncomfortable in the milieu of the university students, he later met them at a separate place. In response to his presentation, one man commented that he did not require a hypothesis such as God because he felt at home in the universe. Buber responded with a withering refutation of all the man's preconceptions, particularly his naive insistence that sense perception exposes reality. After Buber's philosophically devastating speech, the man said, "You are right." And then Buber knew he had been wrong. He had merely convinced the man that he needed a new set of ideas, perhaps even that he required a concept of God. But Buber's goal had not been conceptual; rather, it was to bring the man to a personal relationship with God.

In moments such as these Buber came to know the vast difference between knowing an idea and knowing a person. Buber's fame derives from his unique twofold understanding of relationship, which may with some liberty be called his theory of knowledge.

Our Dualistic Approach to the World

Buber suggests that there are two ways of knowing or relating to the world. The more obvious one, on which we base our everyday lives, Buber terms the "I-It" relation. People usually relate to things by observing them, examining them, testing them. They are measured, taken apart, put back together again and thus comprehended. This can involve ingenious manipulation of the object or the use of sensitive instruments to yield a precise understanding. During this process we make a conscious effort to put a distance between ourselves and the object we seek to understand in order not to disrupt our perception by emotional or personal involvement. As a sophisticated technique, this becomes modern science. On an ordinary level, it is our common modern manner of relating to our surroundings.

Buber does not belittle the value of this kind of knowing. Without objective understanding, people become the victims of superstition and magic, never attaining the freedom that a scientific understanding of the natural order makes possible. Technology may have caused many problems but those who daily benefit from its wonders—enough food to eat, pure water to drink, medicines to cure disease—should not condemn it as worthless.

Buber can pinpoint our difficulty with objectivity. It arises when advocates of the I-It relation imperialistically claim it is the only legitimate form of knowing. The dogma is highly tempting. Dispassionate observation offers to give us control over the world. Place the tremendous social and economic power of a technologically oriented age behind this proposal and the drive toward the dominance of the I-It becomes almost irresistible.

Buber adamantly refuses to accept the sovereignty of the I-It relationship. Consider again the two incidents previously described. Are detachment, analysis, manipulation capable of opening us up to the human being who stands before us who might, if we are accessible, speak to us from the very depths? In special circumstances we may agree to be treated as objects, for the I-It relation may disclose which chemicals or operations are indicated to remedy certain of our disabilities. Normally, we are offended when someone who should treat us as a person will only relate to us as if we were a thing. Then we know that the I-It relation cannot enable us to know a person as a person.

Think of a common personal experience. Something troubles you deeply and you want to discuss it with someone. You hesitate talking to anyone about it but finally know you must and you go to visit a certain trusted person. After the ritual preliminaries and the pause in which you summon up your courage, you begin to speak. What you wanted to say comes slowly at first, but then easier, perhaps in a rush. You begin to say things that, to your surprise, you did not know you wanted to say. Now that they have come out, you realize that they are even more important than what you had consciously intended to say. You are speaking from someplace very deep within you when you suddenly notice that your friend is staring at the run in your hose or the pimple on your chin. You break off speaking; you probably cannot continue. If he asks why you stopped and you respond that he was not listening, he may be shocked. He may even be able to repeat your last words. It makes no difference. You came to have him listen not merely to your words, but to *you*. That is why no long letter, no telephone conversation, or casual meeting could substitute for a face to face meeting. You wanted him to pay full attention to you—and he didn't. How frustrating such an encounter can be!

Genuine Meeting, the Less Common Experience

You know what did not happen because you have occasionally had the opposite experience. You try to talk to someone but you simply cannot express what you want to say. The words will not come. You say many things, even wrong things, but never what you really had hoped to say. In the midst of your frustration you may stop and have the joy of realizing that your inarticulateness makes no difference. Your friend understands what you want to say, even though you never put it into words. You know that. You know that your friend understands you. More, he knows that you know that he knows. And *you* know *that*. The two of you have truly come to know each other. In authentic encounter—meeting, dialogue, relationship—two individuals come to understand and appreciate one another, not just the words or signs they exchange. Buber called this the I-Thou relationship.

Encounter arises in a far different way than does I-It knowing. It demands participation, not distance, giving oneself, not objectivity. If the other person is to know you, and not merely part of you, you cannot hold back part of yourself from the communication. You can be truly known as a person only when someone knows you as a whole and that can happen only when one is addressed by another person, and responds on that level.

Buber cannot, therefore, accurately describe the I-Thou relationship to us. If all of you is in it, there is nothing kept back to observe and record what is going on. Many people say they cannot even dimly recall an I-Thou encounter. From earliest childhood, we have been trained to remain on guard with other people. In everything we do, we keep part of us on sentry duty, hoping we are being properly noticed, fearful lest we blunder, wary of the great judges within and without us. This inner-outer, schizoid existence may have its virtue as making possible the objectivity which can bring stability and structure to our existence in the I-It realm. (Thus, I must watch as I write these words to make certain that they are set down in correct grammar and syntax, that they are logically ordered and properly convey my understanding of Buber's teaching.) In personal relationship such detachment is fatal. Operating behind our facade we wonder who is really behind the limited self the other has disclosed to us. Mask encounters mask, not I-Thou (you singular, you in all your individuality.

Some Signs of Genuine Dialogue

Much of what people value most in I-It knowing disappears in the I-Thou realm. Precision is impossible and public communication is difficult. Language cannot easily convey so uniquely personal an experience. Perhaps that is why all cultures have honored good poets and considered music indispensable. Ultimately, the I-Thou relationship is ineffable. My description here and Buber's own writing cannot substitute for your personally experiencing it or recalling having done so. They are meant as helpful gestures, offered in the hope of pointing you toward similar events in your own life.

Buber himself would object to characterizing his basic insight as a distinction between knowing objects and knowing persons. He maintains that the form of our relationship is not determined by the apparent nature of the partner. Just as one may have an I-It relation to a person, so one may have an I-Thou relation with an object. Many people occasionally respond to nature with I-Thou sensitivity and others have a similar openness to ideas, to art or other cultural activities.

I-Thou relationships yield far more significant meaning than do those which remain I-It. Becoming a person fully and seeing reality in responsiveness impresses one with a richness of quality in oneself and thus potentially in all things. To take the climactic case, love brings us incomparable affirmation. We know ourselves and another to be of inestimable worth. Our world is full of such value, given or achievable.

Love also commands. We must live up to the self we have come to know ourselves to be, through our relationship. Our beloved may legitimately make demands on us and we quickly come to know what is expected of us. For fear of shattering our relationship, we will feel obligated to do certain acts and refrain from others. No verbal exchange may occur to define our duties. Sometimes articulation blemishes rather than enhances our communication. In any case, the dearer the person, the more responsible we will feel. Now we know when we revert again to the usual I-It situation that it is not ultimate. Rather, what we discover on the uninvolved, analytic level receives its proper human context from what is revealed to us in true dialogue.

As desirable as it may be, the I-Thou encounter cannot be forced. A person is essentially free or effectively an object. To demand other people to be fully present or to manipulate them to do so, denies their freedom and destroys the possibility of an authentic encounter. All we can do is try to remain open to dialogue. Knowing that it occurs and remembering our previous experiences can help us stay available for a fresh meeting. Fortunately, the I-Thou moment often comes on its own to grace our lives with its gift of meaning.

Buber envisions life as highly dynamic. We cannot persist in the I-Thou experience but continually revert to the I-It. For all the loss entailed in that movement, it blends continuity and structure with glimpses of value and direction. At any moment we may again be relating to the world of in I-Thou fashion. Encounter comes and goes in quite prosaic fashion. It involves no mystic state, no emotional peak. It is an ordinary ingredient of our lives when, say, we spend a few moments with someone we truly care about.

We Come to Know God as We Come to Know People

Buber declares that we need to relate to God in an I-Thou way if we wish to know God at all. Most philosophers have sought God in I-It terms, as if God were an object. Turning God into a thing is idolatry—the most fundamental denial of God's reality, according to the Bible, though the modern images are mental, not stone or wood.

If God is not known as objects are known, our customary intellectual questions about God sound misplaced. We would not ask them about any given individual. Does one prove the existence of a person? Can one give the concept of one's sweetheart or the definition of one's friend? Persons can never adequately be conceptualized. They are found, addressed, lived with, and only then truly known.

Far more important, intellectual understanding is not a prerequisite of relationship. People cannot know everything about their prospective friends before they put their trust in them. Despite our necessary ignorance, we rightly reach out to one another and accept the risk of life's most significant commitments. Our minds may help us live responsibly but if we limit living to what is rationally conclusive, we shall not be fully human.

Buber's argument is simple: apply the wrong way of knowing to people or to God and they remain hidden. Reach out to God as one does to another person, and a surprising yet obvious fact emerges: God may be found everywhere. We discover God in the same place we might make a friend, wherever we are, as ordinary as that might be. We do this in the same way we reach out to another person, not forcing the encounter but by being there and letting whatever happens happen. Religion ought to be a commonplace, the basic stuff of everyday existence. The point could not be more important.

Buber Is Against Special or Religious Experiences

Buber rejects the term "experience" for the I-Thou relationship. He is wary of its romantic, sensual connotations. He wants to make certain that we do not identify encounter with God as an exceptional event—one characterized, perhaps, by tingles or tongues, overwhelming bliss or overcoming power. Perhaps dialogue with God will leave a residue of serenity; it will certainly command one involved in it. If we measure significance by sensation, we shall utterly misunderstand the I-Thou relationship with God. The analogy with love or friendship is exact. Coming from a chat with a person we hold dear, we are certain our companion is, as we often now say, "a real person." Not because gongs chimed, or a ray of sun broke through the clouds, or through any other romantic sign or event. Persons met—that is all, and everything. So it is with God. Most religious traditions teach that if we would but turn to God, in whatever ordinary place we find ourselves, God would be there with us.

People often prefer to have a special realm for God—most likely in the secret hope of confining God to it. To recognize God's presence in our ordinary lives would mean exposing ourselves to the responsibility and spontaneity of genuine relationship. Religion, our institutional way of relating to God, easily becomes an elaborate scheme to limit God to given times, acts, and places, excluding God from interfering in the rest of our lives. Religion, like theology, may easily become the foe of the religious. On the whole, Buber advocates abandoning religion in the hope that we will once again be open to personal involvement with God.

What should one expect from an encounter with God if not rapture and ecstasy? Many people wait for words. Taking the Bible literally, they assume they will hear a voice. To them dialogue must mean a verbal exchange. The remembrance of human relationship should disabuse us of such mythic expectations. Encounter may begin with words, but if it is limited to language, it may never proceed very far. In our moments of greatest intimacy, what is most binding and mutual is expressed silently. Thus, when we undergo great sorrow or suffering, words tend only to belittle reality. Good friends know when not to talk—yet, they also intuit how important it is for them to be there. Were they not present, there would be a painful emptiness that even mute presence fills with comfort and consolation. Presence, not verbiage, is given when I and Thou commune. "I" know that "Thou" art with me—and I with Thee. From being there with one another—and that alone—all else derives. Seeking God, we should not await a voice but only God's presence, God's being there with us—no more but also no less.

For some few people, finding God ends all doubt and answers all questions. Most of us are not so blessed. Our faith remains mixed with questioning, our moments of certainty alternate with new scepticism. Buber's own understanding of faith as relationship makes understandable this strange dialectic.

Love always provides the best analogy. Many a marriage survives the shocking discovery that one's spouse is capable of hateful and abusive acts. How can people face that and still say they are in love? Their confidence in one another is not ended by such a trauma because they set love into the totality of their relationship. Their love grew in those many repeated moving occasions when they found themselves truly I-to-Thou. Now, momentarily standing in I-to-It negation, they trust that it will pass and the confirming I-Thou will return as it has before. When faith in the dialectic departs, love is gone.

Encounter with God follows the rule that we cannot abide in the realm of the I-Thou. God's presence gives way to God's absence, a loss made all the more severe since, unlike the beloved, God is never present as a body. In Buber's pregnant phrase, God is the Eternal Thou, the only Thou we know which never becomes an It. God being absent, we have no immediate warrant for faith. When our doubt arises in the context of trust that we will yet find God again, disbelief is painful but acceptable. Every serious personal relationship knows such oscillation between its highs and lows. Faith, Buber opines, is not a permanent state, something gained once and forever like a college degree. It is like a great love, found and lived in a continual alternation of knowing and wondering, losing and regaining, and believing and doubting and believing once again.

Buber's Understanding of Evil

Before the Holocaust, Buber explained evil as the result of our refusal to relate to one another personally. When we can treat people as abstractions and thus deal with them impersonally, exploitation and manipulation cease being sins. As soon as we face outsiders and enemies as individuals and open ourselves to them as persons, we cannot easily continue treating them with indifference or hostility. Human interaction can counter hatred since relationship is the foundation of morality. Conversely, willfully withholding oneself from others is the first step on the road of evil.

Buber suggested that immorality arises in people in two stages. In the first, we are merely aimless. We cannot make up our minds what to do. We are victims of the infinite possibilities which human freedom opens up to us, and can do nothing. Our evil consists of our passivity. In the second stage, we do casual, occasional evil acts, eventually even being untroubled by willful and habitual wrongdoing. At that point, we have allied ourselves with the demonic in us and have dehumanized ourselves—at least for the present.

Persons being ultimately free, we can always stop and change our ways. We "turn" back to other people—and to God. The Rabbis termed this *teshuvah*, repentance, or in Buber's existentialist reinterpretation, the "turning." If we will make the effort, relationship can be restored. God, Buber taught, fulfilled the Divine responsibilities in the relationship with people by always remaining available for its restoration ("atonement"). The difficulties in finding, maintaining and reconstituting the covenant were always on the human side. Instead of turning to God, the everlasting open One, we resolutely turned away.

After the Holocaust, Buber could not remain so optimistic. He no longer was able to declare that it was people's fault if they lost faith or did not find God present in their lives. The unbearable evil of the Holocaust forced Buber to the tragic recognition that God sometimes, somehow withdraws from humankind. What could be more evil? Buber used two images to describe this. The blacker one was biblical: God sometimes hides God's "face" (presence) from people. The other was a bit more positive. To use an analogy from nature, in radically evil times, God is eclipsed. God is not dead, then, for though we stand in darkness, we await God's return. Buber did not seek to explain this. Instead, like a faithful, wounded lover, he neither lied about his pain nor abandoned a relationship that was real though incomprehensible.

Buber does not propose to explain why in normal times, God is so readily available. He does not argue that God, in some metaphysical sense, *is* a person. All objective assertion about God deviously turns God into an "it." As an existentialist, Buber can only speak of the reality we know as part of our living experience. Thus, what he can profess is that we know God the way we know persons. He further maintains that when persons encounter one another truly, God is also present.

Describing so subtle a presence is even more problematic than trying to find words for a direct I-Thou encounter. Buber says that in true meeting we may sense an other, who stands behind the dialogue partners and makes it possible for them to meet one another. People who are blocked from approaching God directly should try the path of love and service to their fellows. Often the best way to bring people to God is not by describing the I-Thou relationship but by making oneself personally available. Should the encounter occur, not only will the basic paradigm of meeting be experienced but an intimation of God's presence will be gained.

The New Spirit of Liberal Piety

Existentialism's personalization of religion gives it a tone which, though modern, has many traditional echoes. For example, it mandates personal piety without the encumberment of an anthropomorphic God. To avoid describing God as a person, some theologians have insisted on an impersonal understanding of God. The intellectual gain was generally exceeded by the human loss, most people finding it difficult to relate personally to a God who is neutral to them. Buber predicates a God but does not mean that literally. All literal statements are I-It—hence, in Buber's philosophy, they are necessarily false, including all anthropomorphisms. When understood as I-Thou poetics, anthropomorphic statements may direct us with great power to the God who is known as persons are known.

Another example of the personalist reinvigoration of tradition is found in its attitude to the Bible. Liberalism was based on the Bible being a human work. It was the greatest book humankind had created in the course of its spiritual development. Why that was so, why the modern classics—Darwin, Freud, Dostoevsky, Ibsen—were not really more relevant to the religious quest of people today than Holy Scripture never could be explained. Buber's view of revelation enables the religious person to take the Bible seriously, though not literally. The words are human, but they result from authentic encounters with God. They are unique in human literature in their transparency to what transpired between the prophets and God. Reading them today in I-Thou openness, we can often recapitulate the experience which engendered them. Over the centuries, the Bible has brought people into relationship with God in a way that no other literature has ever done or is ever again likely to do.

Something similar happens to the practice of prayer in Buber's reworking of it. People have often turned prayer into a means of appeasing God or flattering God into a favor. In reaction, modern philosophers have limited it to an exercise in mental hygiene or the integration of one's inner resources. Buber's Eternal Thou can as little be manipulated as can anyone with whom we wish to have a genuine relationship. More, God cannot now be denied independence, the critical characteristic of one who participates in dialogue. Answering our prayers cannot now mean that God does what we ask. When one always must do what another requires, it is slavery, not covenant. God, too, must be granted the freedom to answer our petitions, even to give a negative answer by saying "No." We pray not for results but to renew the most important relationship of our lives. In prayer we seek to open ourselves up to God's presence. Learning again that God is with us in what we are going through provides all the answer a mature person can ask.

Having the classic religious terms and practices revitalized creates a contemporary religious practice which is more pious than the older liberalism and more believable to moderns than unrefurbished traditionalism.

Relating Religiosity to Reality

Too many people never go beyond this point in Buber's thought. They are fixated on what may be called Buber's theory of religion-in-general. Since it can produce a warm involvement with God and people, since it knows no limitations of circumstance or situation, it possesses broad appeal. Many Americans particularly esteem Buber because he seems to justify religiosity against religion, the private practice of the I-Thou, over against institutional pieties. Buber is not that unhistorical. Because he is an existentialist, Buber concerns himself with religion in the concrete, lived human situation. He probes humankind's actual experience with God in time, climaxing in the record given in the Bible. By I-Thou standards, it is the Bible that best tells how God was first fully known. Reading its pages with I-It eyes, as is done in so-called scientific biblical study, yields data only of some antiquarian interest. It necessarily caricatures the Bible's own concern, the continued involvement of the living God with individuals and a people. Read with I-Thou openness, the historic reality and contemporary truth of the Hebrews' experience with God is revealed.

The Covenant of Sinai, the climax of the exodus narrative, was a unique event in human history. At the mountain, the raggle-taggle band of erstwhile Hebrew slaves, moved by the incredible experience of exodus and the leadership of a man of extraordinary vision, entered a Covenant with the one God of creation. This was no mere ritual of offering sacrifice and accepting legislation so as to give structure to the mob. True, through rites and laws a new nation emerged to seek its destiny. It did so out of the unique consciousness that this people, Israel, had faced and known God. In the strange and overpowering events it had experienced, the Hebrews had become open to the presence of the Eternal Thou operating in their history. At Sinai, corporately, in one great moment of recognition and acknowledgment, they, individually and collectively, bound themselves to God. They pledged themselves, as a nation, to be God's own people, to serve God in human history, to carry the knowledge of God in their midst and exemplify it before humankind. They dedicated themselves to this service until all people would similarly recognize God and live in that knowledge.

What was not specified at Sinai became clear to the people of Israel through its history in the wilderness and on the Land. Much of its education in the meaning of the Covenant came from suffering and chastisement. The Sinai, golden calf, punishment, return cycle runs through the Bible. The genius of the Jewish people was not that it was inhumanly saintly but that it never fully broke its relationship with God. It acknowledged God's truth even when that truth was used to condemn them. Its glory lies in turning its chastisers into its heroes. Other historic religious movements have kept their inspiration alive for two, perhaps three generations after their founder. Israel's span of fresh revelation runs through at least eight centuries after Moses. Despite backsliding and stubbornness, even Exile, the people, as a people, managed to return to God and renew the Covenant. In those historic trials the people of Israel mastered the art of maintaining loyalty to God and their destiny despite the tribulations history might bring. Succeeding generations built their lives as a folk on the Sinai experience and through their reliving of it knew that it was true.

The Covenant Remains the Basis of Jewish Existence

The Covenant relationship is the foundation of Jewish existence. It has taken different form as Jews have moved from one society and culture to another. Sometimes it has not been expressed in its full power, only again to burst forth with renewed vigor, most recently, according to Buber, in the Hasidic movement.

Buber declares that Israel's Covenant with God is as alive and needed today as it has always been. Humankind remains radically unredeemed. People do not know the Eternal Thou. They do not seek to treat all others as "Thou's" and bring community, the Messianic Age, into being. With the major forces of society moving in totalitarian and technopolitical directions, Israel's stubborn loyalty to humanity through God is desperately important. Christianity may be a true faith, but it is mediated and indirect, essentially individual and not strongly social. Israel's faith is direct and communal; it has not been superseded or rendered obsolete.

Today, the Jewish people faces a major spiritual danger. In the secular western world one's nation and one's religion are kept in separate spheres of existence. Buber derides this as blasphemy. Exiling God from social existence to the halls of institutions set aside for that purpose desecrates human life. Everyone suffers when such radical secularization occurs, as is obvious from the continuing efforts to remove human considerations from the realm of politics and think essentially of what is most efficient or technically desirable. The Jews should be particularly disturbed by this trend for their unique character and historic destiny derive from the biblical fusion of religion and nationality so as to set an example for humankind.

In medieval times, the Jewish community was able to integrate folk life with religious understanding. In the emancipated modern world, that unity is no longer visible. In the State of Israel many insist that Jewishness is adequately expressed as civic loyalty, God being a private if not irrelevant matter. Elsewhere, in the democracies, Jewish identity is largely defined in terms of an institutional religion, one which often lacks an inner sense of God's presence and an outer commitment to social responsibility. Buber, the Zionist and believer, demands that the two realms interpenetrate. When he immigrated to the Land of Israel, he aroused considerable hostility by his insistence that Israeli politics must be humanistic. He advocated a binational, that is, joint Arab-Jewish state, as the only legitimate way of dealing with the just claims of both peoples to the land. Buber was also critical of contemporary Jewish religious life. He saw its primary stress on the observance of Jewish law as divorcing religiosity from the broader realms of modern existence. Worse, the practices had as good as become ends in themselves and thus an impediment rather than a help to gaining the presence of God. In this situation, Buber refused to accept any objective, external set of standards to structure his service of God, and did not follow Jewish law.

Problems with Buber's Philosophy

The major critics of Buber's existentialism see its personalistic gains more than offset by its intellectual and Jewish failings. The central issue is structure. His opponents judge Buber's ideas too insubstantial to be considered a serious system of thought and are disturbed that his theology is individualistic to the point of anarchy, thus Jewishly inauthentic.

Intellectually, the clash is the familiar one between the schools of rationalism and existentialism. Personalistic, its reasoning is so subjective, its logic so individual, its categories so fluid, how can one know what the thinker truly has in mind or be able to debate it? If the I-Thou relationship is ineffable, how can Buber or anyone else talk sensibly about it? No one denies an individual's right to create an evocative, private pattern of speaking about life and its meaning. Buber wants his thought to be taken more seriously than that, yet refuses to accept the usual standards of evidence and clarity employed in intellectual intercourse. This line of attack may be pressed home on two specific fronts, ethics and coherence.

Making the I-Thou relationship the basis of ethics conveys no useful content to anyone seeking moral guidance. Its subjectivity does nothing to prevent possible horrible abuses. The fanatic and the inquisitor regularly claim a private sense of God's authorization. Reason alone provides an objective defense against the fiendishness propagated by self-delusion. Rejecting rational ethical rules for commands, which arise only in a given situation, removes our best check on the demonic potential in all of us.

Buber cannot deny that his antagonists have understood him correctly, and this admission is particularly troublesome since the problem of evil is not academic in our generation. Buber's own efforts to rule out intolerance under his system are impressive yet inconclusive. His most telling response might be that the greatest evils of our day have come from *applying* reason, not giving into subjectivity. Auschwitz and Hiroshima are equally results of deliberation and calculation. Many of our current social problems arise from our zeal at rationalizing human affairs. Human reason and its rules are not immune to our talent for perversion.

On the other hand, following the dictates of the I-Thou involves an element of freedom and, hence, risk. The risk of evil may be mitigated by Buber's principle of applying to the I-It world the values learned in one's I-Thou moments. We should always strive to accept others as fully human and treat them with mutuality and responsibility. This would surely create a greater moral climate among us. Of course, such a procedure converts the I-Thou encounter into an I-It law, a move inconsistent with the fundamental premises of Buber's theory. Consequently insofar as Buber can respond to the critics of his ethics, his system loses coherence. But Buber does not claim to be a system builder—which he considers an I-It intellectual goal— but one who lets thought follow the realities of human existence.

Do We Live in One World or Two?

Buber's dualism has also troubled many thinkers. Our world, as he describes it, seems to be two discrete entities, differently encountered and differently structured. One is in either the I-It or the I-Thou realm. They never intersect or merge. How can one gain a comprehensive understanding of so contradictory a universe? If the "logic" of the two is radically dissimilar, what becomes of the fundamental unity of existence which most people desire and which philosophy has always prized?

As applied to God, the puzzle deepens. In the realm of the I-Thou, we may know God as the ground of all that is, the source and foundation of all existence. But we cannot know God that way in the world of I-It. God does not enter the world of the I-It, for, by definition, the Eternal Thou is that which can never become It. As long as we look with I-It eyes, we never see God at all. Then how does God relate to the world of I-It? What is God's place in that dimension of being in which we must spend most of our lives?

Buber might respond that he is not a metaphysician and has not alleged that the I-It world is real. He is only describing one of our "attitudes" toward the world, a sort of Kantian analysis of how we think, not of reality itself. This turns Buber into an idealist philosopher, a stance that contradicts his insistence on turning to our concrete existence to search for truth.

He might also argue that while the I-It world is real, so to speak, the I-Thou world is "more" real, that is, it provides the greater context within which the I-It world must be comprehended. But that is just what we do not understand. How can the Eternal Thou be related to a world in which God has no place and in which God cannot be seen? As science increasingly supplies mechanical or electrochemical explanations of phenomena, the world of I-It seems ever more fully closed against God's entry. If that world has reality, how does the Eternal God rule it, guide it, provide for it, or simply enter it to make the I-Thou possible? The least charge one can make against Buber is that he does not take the scientific view of reality very seriously and disposes of the issue by assigning it to a second level of significance.

Buber has no further rebuttal. This anxiety about dualism has little meaning for him. He is satisfied to take our strange dualistic situation simply as he finds it. He cares more about living in sanctity than on attaining a unified intellectual world view. His critics doubt that such a divided understanding of reality for all its high humanity, will satisfy the modern mind.

Can There Be a Serious Judaism Without Law?

The major Jewish criticism of Buber is directed at his rejection of the validity of Jewish law.

His controversial stand emerged most clearly in his famous correspondence with Franz Rosenzweig on this issue. Their debate hinged on the place of corporate experience in personal responsibility. Both men agreed that their relationship to God was part of the Jewish people's Covenant. They had no difficulty with the individual Jew's need to study and personally appropriate Jewish literature without preconception as to what might "speak" to one. In that realm, discipline legitimately preceded meaning.

Rosenzweig then analogously urged such a standard with regard to Jewish law. He admitted that revelation was only personal, that we are required to do only what we know God wants of us. He further acknowledged that law was the aftereffect of encounter, not its content. God did not reveal the rules themselves. People created them, having been involved with God. With all that, he argued that a Jew was bound in principle to live under the law, that the classic codes had authority over the individual even though some of their regulations did not "speak" to one's personal sense of duty. Rosenzweig called for doing the law first and awaiting its personal validation in the process of its performance.

At this point, Buber demurred. He insisted that action involved the fullest commitment of the whole self. No external criterion should therefore be permitted to interpose itself between the I and what the Eternal Thou might now be understood to command it. Perhaps a given law might serve to open the individual Jew to the presence of God. Once, such an encounter gave rise to the practice and gave it legitimacy. Where one still retained that connection, the law was valid. Otherwise—the usual case—it was impersonal and hence, invalid. All such structures place barriers between the individual and the Eternal Thou. Buber thus denied that, in principle, Jews were obligated to perform the stipulations of the Jewish law. Indeed, considering its present proponents behavioristically rather than spiritually directed, he was an opponent of observance as a means of revitalizing Judaism.

A Personal Response to the Problem of Law

I have argued that Buber is inconsistent in this area. He predicates Israel's Covenant as corporate reality that continues from generation to generation. In some sense, the people of Israel's religious destiny is distinct from the decisions of individual Jews. There must be, then, a level where the individual as such is not the final arbiter of appropriate behavior under the Covenant. If not, Jewishness should be subject to judgment just as every other social accident and therefore could be discarded, to the point of ending the Covenant. Yet Buber often indicts modern Jewry for its refusal to identify individual Jewish being with personal acceptance of Israel's Covenant. He implies that one's individual being has a corporate dimension. One is true to oneself as a Jew, therefore, only as one is true to one's folk. There cannot be any ultimate distinction between the two aspects of Jewish existence.

Much of the ambiguity and tension of modern Jewish life arises from struggle to pacify the warring parts of the Jewish soul. If so, Buber is overly strict in limiting legitimate Jewish responsibility to what the socially isolated I "hears" as it stands over against the Eternal Thou. Existential Jewish duty results rather from what the I/Jew is called upon by God to do in the I-Eternal Thou relationship. That may not generate external law but it authorizes common patterns of practice, for the Jewish "I" does not function in utter isolation, but as part of the Covenant community.

I am suggesting that the Jewish I in an I-Thou relationship is substantially determined by being situated in the people of Israel's historic-messianic relationship with God. Support for this inference exists in the unexpected, variant description Buber gives of the personal exchange between good teachers and their students. Buber denies that effective education can be confined to I-It competencies. It must help students become persons. Teachers need to find ways to engage their students as Thou's. Buber surprisingly maintains that teachers should not make themselves fully present to the pupils. Rather than become friend or companion, a Thou, teachers must always maintain a certain distance from their students or they will be unable to function. In the classroom the I-Thou relation is real but one-sided.

This account violates Buber's regular dictum that only with both persons fully present can "I" meet "Thou." How then can teachers evoke the students as Thou's while denying full mutuality? I believe the answer is to be found in the concept of role. Teachers enter the classroom precisely in order to teach, pupils in order to learn. Teachers can be true selves in teaching only as they follow their vocation, not as they abandon it to be persons-in-general. To borrow a Kabbalistic conception, teachers constrict their full personality for the sake of accomplishing this important task, teaching. In the task, good teachers can find themselves as selves and not as its. As teacher-selves they offer but do not complete the mutuality that makes a genuine I-Thou relationship possible. Perhaps this violates Buber's canon that only the presence of the whole self can make the I-Thou relationship possible. If so, then I have only reduced but not eliminated the inconsistency he introduced into his thought when he sensitively described the reality of the fulfilled student/teacher relationship.

As I see it, then, a Jew is one who stands athwart the Eternal Thou, not as universal self, but as Jew-self, individual and member of a people simultaneously. The Jew's duty will always be as much a matter of folk as of self, of what the Covenant of Sinai requires of me at this particular moment as of what I personally feel as commanded. Such Covenantal existentiality does not restore the complete validity of traditional Jewish law or reestablish a basis for objective, impersonal standards of Jewish conduct. It does channel personal autonomy in terms of God's demands as the Covenant people ought to respond to them. Buber did not go this far, but those whom Buber has made self-consciously believing Jews may now well learn it from him.

8

Neo-Traditionalism: Abraham Heschel

IF THE BIBLE is our standard, Martin Buber has the most classic theological stance of any of the liberal Jewish thinkers. His God is real and personal, far more like the living God of traditional Judaism than any idea, mystery, or process could be. His concept of the people of Israel encompasses its multifaceted nationality without belittling its relationship to God. In revitalizing the ancient sense of Covenant through his understanding of personal relationships, he showed a way beyond universalistic religiosity, or secularizing particularity.

What Buber did not do was far from insignificant. His philosophy has the least power of any liberal doctrine to validate Jewish law or communal standards. Cohen knows social ethics to be required; Baeck adds the obligations imposed by mystery and shared with a unique people; Kaplan makes the folk authoritative for all who are its healthy members. Buber, in his strict immediate individualism before God, is the most antinomian of them all. He acquires a rich Jewish faith at the price of any rule or norm of Jewish obligation.

Traditional Judaism gave precedence to action over belief when a conflict between them was unavoidable. Here again the flaw of the classic liberal theological strategy reasserts itself. Jewish reality is unilaterally subordinated to modern truth, in this case, Buber's understanding of the I-Thou relationship. Inevitably, one or another fundamental aspect of classic Jewish faith has been slighted, thus prompting efforts to create a more adequate contemporary Jewish theology. Baeck went beyond Cohen to restore a felt relationship with God. Kaplan added ethnicity and Buber reaffirmed the Covenant as a relationship between two real and independent entities. Yet in taking modern Jews that far in belief, Buber makes the issue of Jewish practice so central that his version of Jewish duty—for all its inner possibilities of development—must now be surpassed.

The realities of Diaspora Jewish existence lend special urgency to the creation of a ground for community norms of practice. If Jewishness is merely a personal, existential stance, though related to the Jewish people, what will give structure to Jewish life in the Diaspora? In what sense do these Jewish individuals function as the people of the Covenant? Buber, though recognizing this problem, wrote very little about the possibility or method of creating a vital Diaspora Jewish life. His Zionism called for living among other Jews, on the Land of Israel, a situation which he hoped would keep radical individualism from destroying the people he cherished. Diaspora Jews, facing the fragility of their communal life, know that the corporate Jewish act establishes and signals their continuing peoplehood and relationship with God. Without a repertoire of communal practice, Jewish existence off the land ceases to have meaning. Those American Jews who seek to reclaim Jewish identity in depth find no theological issue more pressing than that of the proper form of Jewish observance and the authority behind its delineation. As long as liberal Jewish thought redefines Judaism by an externally determined, perhaps secular criterion, how can their concern ever receive a significant response, much less an answer? They require a post-liberal approach to Jewish theology, thus setting its central problem in the last decades of the twentieth century.

Heschel's Unique Stance and Style

Abraham Joshua Heschel consciously devoted himself to creating a philosophy which learned from the liberals but reversed many of their basic premises. He used the intellectual tools of modernity to move beyond his predecessors' procedures to a contemporary justification of traditional Jewish faith.

Heschel was a professor of Jewish ethics and mysticism at the Jewish Theological Seminary of America (Conservative) from 1945 until his death in 1972. His apparently odd combination of competencies reflects a biography and career devoted to commonly divergent religious interests. Scion of a distinguished Hasidic dynasty and steeped in Jewish learning of the East European style, Heschel gained a doctorate from the University of Berlin with a phenomenological study of prophecy. His piety unshaken by the move to the West or the university, his earliest publications dealt with technical problems in medieval Jewish philosophy. Another stream of his researches focused on Hasidic leaders and doctrine. While his thinking reflected Hasidism's emphasis on subjective piety, his major books sought to provide an intellectual structure for Jewish faith. In person, he powerfully communicated the possibility of mystical awareness, yet he was also the Jewish thinker most actively involved in such public issues as civil rights, the Vietnam war, and the oppression of the Soviet Jews.

He was a superb stylist in Yiddish, Hebrew, German, English, and, it is said, Polish as well. He published in all those languages and his linguistic brilliance was an integral component of his method of communicating the proper depth of modern Jewish faith.

Readers can so easily be overcome by the unique quality of Heschel's word play that they miss the cognitive development going on behind it. To complicate matters further, Heschel develops his ideas in an uncommon manner. Modern arguments normally proceed in linear fashion. One sentence follows another cumulatively, each thought building on the previous one until the conclusion is reached and, by this process, considered well established. Heschel rejects this procedure as inconsistent with his understanding of religious insight. His paragraphs may deal with one theme, but their sentences are radial, not additive. They center about a given motif, pointing to it or away from it so as to disclose various of its facets. By a sort of sculptor's shaping, the notion itself appears. In the same way, the paragraphs that combine to form a section—and the sections that comprise a chapter—are not joined in ladderlike progression to reach a new level of thought. They multiply the insights and expand the vision, evoking rather than demonstrating, disclosing but not delineating. Yet, unlike Buber in *I and Thou*, Heschel carefully builds a logically ordered intellectual system in his major books. His work, *Man is not Alone*, bears the subtitle, *A Philosophy of Religion*; and its more substantial companion volume, *God in Search of Man*, is subtitled *A Philosphy of Judaism*. The books are philosophy in a very special sense, for Heschel repudiates the self-sufficient rationalism with which that term is usually associated. More helpfully, he used the term "depth theology" to describe his intellectual method. In common with the religious existentialists, he believed thinking ought to proceed from one's given human situation, analyzed to its deepest roots, which were, for him, religious.

Though Heschel utilizes the customary existentialist attacks on scientism and rationalism to clear the way for his teaching, he refuses to accept the human self as an independent given and think in terms of it as Buber and Rosenzweig do. Instead, selfhood prompts Heschel to wonder and gratitude, and hence to God, who becomes the fundamental axiom of this thinking. Heschel's unique sense of the radical "depth" of the self transforms person-centered existentialism into "theology." He reverses the standard liberal argument and denies the legitimacy of arguing from human experience to the reality of God. This inversion of an accepted point of view is common in Heschel's writing. He wants us to change our perspective totally in order to comprehend Judaism. Heschel's unique style seeks fundamental change, not a mere alteration of substance. Once he has established his religious premises, Heschel explicates them as rationally as he can. His philosophy consists of thinking about their content and consequences in a way which is coherent with them and acceptable to any open mind.

Heschel's Three Paths to God

Heschel predicates three ways to religious truth: through nature, revelation, and the holy deed. In the pious life they operate as one. Due to our modern spiritual disabilities, we find it desirable to analyze them separately, identifying what each lends to and borrows from the other two.

Were the term not so easily misunderstood, Heschel's first, most generally available path might be termed mysticism. He exhibits an extraordinary sensitivity to the hidden reality inherent in the seemingly ordinary. He denies that one must attain a special level of experience to know this. The religious perspective is quite normal. If anything, such a response to the universe is the natural one, as children and primitives show us. Modernity has trained us to repress our instinctive awe at the world and our part in it. Our most important spiritual task today is to liberate ourselves from the scientism which has taught us an unnatural skepticism. Then we will once again ask with a higher incredulity: Why is there anything at all? Why is it so wondrous, so unexpected? Why do we human beings have this astonishing power to ask and marvel? Regaining "radical amazement" will enable us to be true to ourselves and open to the reality of God.

Heschel's felicity for images is most impressive as he seeks to arouse a reader dulled by the secular demythologization of nature. Argument will not work. It does not evoke awe, only another level of technical understanding. Heschel writes to illuminate, and like the great painters and photographers, he makes us see anew what we have blindly glanced at a thousand times before. In an age so jaded it has forgotten that nothing should be taken for granted, Heschel's approach to reality must be called therapeutic.

Regaining the Wonder That Anything Is

Heschel directs our attention not only beyond rationalism to experience as Baeck did, or onward to encounter, as Buber did, but away from ourselves altogether. Personhood is too wondrous to be accepted as self-evident. Our reasoning, our sensitivity, our ability to engage in dialogue are not self-evident principles from which we can confidently search for meaning. They themselves refute all liberalistic complacency. Whatever we might choose to start us on our religious quest itself is given to us and directs us to its source. Nothing is self-explanatory; everything points beyond itself to a Giver. God necessarily precedes every effort we might make to search out Divinity. God must, in a post-liberal way, be understood as an "ontological presupposition." That is, God is the basis of any being, the utterly basic premise for anything that is. Only when we affirm God's greatness and reality do we ourselves, and our minds, our sensations, even our doubts and our skepticism, become worthy of serious self-investment. God is the premise of our existence, not the possible outcome of our inquiry.

A God so fundamental to our lives is far beyond human powers of description or definition. God overwhelms every effort to explain God for the very act of explanation itself drives us to its Divine ground. Heschel denies that we are capable of useful judgments as to what God is like. The God who gives us our capacity to judge ought rather to fill us with a sense of the Divine greatness and glory. Our most exalted praise is necessarily an understatement. On this first level, Heschel brings us to God's sublimity. With this preparation, he can move forward in a way the liberals could not, to proclaim the reality of a contentful revelation.

The Move from the Universal to the Particular

Modern theologians who must come to terms with the universal phenomenon of true religion must then validate their specific religious tradition. For Cohen, particularity was as good as a historic accident. For Baeck, spirit enters history through groups. For Buber, the people of Israel had a unique ethnic response to God's presence. For Kaplan, Jewishness is a matter of social form, which in itself is a necessity of nature. Heschel explains the ubiquity of faith on the level of radical surprise. It provides him with a broad base from which to appreciate the variety of human religiosity. How then does he validate his particular Jewish faith? He is too traditional to accept a liberalistic explanation of Jewish identity. While existence reveals God universally, "there is no speech, there are no words," but these are granted with revelation. The greatest miracle in the Bible is the Bible itself! In it, what was perceived mutely in creation rises to the level of direct communication. Through its pages a new type of religious understanding is born, one that can recognize the truth of radical amazement but also knows the direction of its fulfillment. Moderns can hardly be expected to recognize God's revelation if they have not been awakened to its possibility through knowing God's nearness. Until then they consider the Bible another technical problem, a set of conundrums about literary sources, the dates of their editing or the social setting which produced them.

When one's understanding begins with the God who grounds all being, an encounter with the Bible is itself a revelation. Reading its words, one quickly recognizes that our private intuition has here been given its fullest exposition. Now we are prepared for its central, astounding claim: instead of a human quest for religion, the Bible declares that God has been in "search of man." People in the Bible are as we know them. They seek to avoid God and, failing that, rebel against God's rule. God will not be put off. The God we know from our openness to self and creation comes to people to command and console, to judge and forgive, to direct and give hope.

So traditional an affirmation of biblical revelation instantly raises the old liberal questions concerning the humanity of the biblical text. Heschel will not deny the human element in Holy Scripture but this should not obscure its Divine origin or accuracy. When we read its books in openness to the One who speaks through the text, we will realize how much more it knows than we do. If radical amazement replaced scientific dogmatism about what could have happened in ancient days, many of our modern questions would vanish.

Prophecy, the Ultimate Act of Sympathy

Heschel's unique conception of prophecy ingeniously resolves the problem of an accurate Divine revelation cast in human form. Heschel deems the prophet to have attained a special height of religious sensitivity which he calls "sympathy." The subjective overtones of that term properly indicate that prophecy transcends all cognitive enterprises and lies beyond technical analysis or explanation. The prophet is turned toward God in utter existential depth and responsive to what is happening in the Divine. Prophetic sympathy has nothing to do with human emotionalism, self-abandon or ecstacy. The prophet remains sufficiently self-possessed to respond to God as an individual, sometimes to the point of resisting or arguing with God. A contrast with Buber's theory of I-Thou encounters will clarify the distinctive intellectual contours of Heschel's formulation.

Three major differences must be noted. Heschel claims a certain reflective or cognitive aspect to the prophet's experience. Taken within the context of sympathy, we may say the prophet gains understanding. The prophet does not merely encounter God person-to-person but gains knowledge about God. Second, Heschel assigns God a far greater role in the moment of prophetic sympathy than Buber finds in the I-Thou relationship. God's reality dominates the prophet, though not to the point of the prophet's loss of self. How can God, the one real Master of the Universe, the presupposition of every aspect of human existence, not be the overpowering, overwhelming reality of such a situation? Third, Buber claims, the prophet only experiences God's presence during the encounter and later provides a personal, verbal expression of what transpires. Heschel disagrees. The prophet accurately records what God is going through or demands at a given moment. Though expressed in a personal style and in the symbols of the culture, God's reality, not the prophet's person, determines the message. The prophet reliably re-counts what God wants of us. Sympathy is receptivity to God, not projection of self.

Heschel's position has, therefore, fairly been described as a sophis-ticated fundamentalism. The biblical text is taken as true to God's own reality without requiring a defense of every aspect of our Hebrew text as the equivalent of a photocopy of God's dictation. Heschel's differences with the religious liberals are clear-cut. More certain of human reason or experience than they are of God, liberals mandate substantial human initiative in determining what religion ought to be. Heschel knows that God has disclosed to us what believers ought to know and do. God's revelation, not human creativity or con-science, ought to determine the content of religion.

God Has Feelings, Particularly About the Good

Two consequences of Heschel's theory of revelation give his philoso-phy distinctive shape. First, we may be astonished but we ought not deny the steady prophetic pronouncement: God has feelings. Again and again, the prophets describe God as distraught, unhappy, angry, indignant, and, less frequently, overflowing with tenderness, com-passion, mercy, or affection. With some embarrassment, liberals have termed these anthropopathisms and considered them, when not mere poetry, a symbolic way of pointing to transcendent reality. Heschel will have none of this. The prophets may speak poetically but their concern is truth not literature. Indeed, we can now see that to speak of revelation as sympathy meant that the prophets felt what God felt; they had *sym-pathos*. God is a God of pathos, of emotions, for that is the God the prophets described.

Heschel sees no need to apologize for what seems to non-believers and liberals a mythological notion. To the contrary, he vigorously rebuts the idea that God would be superior for not having feelings. Such a stand has no Jewish foundation. Greek philosophy derogated emotion as a source of wisdom, and the Stoics, in particular, spread the idea that a calm detachment from one's feelings is the best way to face life. As philosophers became more rigorously intellectual, they created the idea of God being impassable, insensitive and emotionally unreactive. Jews should not let Hellenic predilections outweigh the clear message of prophetic revelation, especially when they contradict major commitments of the modern mind. Thought without emotion is a caricature of personhood. Worse, the proliferation of people who merely function in roles or efficiently pursue calculated ends is one of the great evils of our era. Our major social task is to restore people to full personhood. Pathos, not distance, needs to play a major role in our lives.

The same is true of our icy God-ideas. We have become as unfeeling as the God in whose rationalistic image we have sought to recreate ourselves. In our urge to become whole as persons again, we are responding to the reality the prophets long ago accurately described. We ought to be feeling beings for God is a God of pathos.

Heschel's second emphasis is surprisingly liberal. Having established the accuracy of the prophetic message, he might have then devoted himself to discussing the teachings of Moses, "the chief of the prophets." Instead of concentrating on the Torah, Heschel gives most of his attention to the later prophets. He reiterates all the familiar themes of "prophetic Judaism" so powerfully enunciated by Hermann Cohen. God's feelings are aroused by human action, in most cases by their ethical or unethical conduct. We can judge the heinousness of our sins by the intensity of God's reaction. Unethical acts are not a petty annoyance to God and righteousness does not evoke casual Divine satisfaction. When we judge the prophetic accounts of God's reactions to our behavior as extreme, we only testify to our loss of a proper measure of their cosmic importance. Nothing is more important to God than ethical conduct between human beings on a social and personal level. To be sure, Heschel rejects the liberal thesis that ethics alone is revelation. God's self-disclosure produces one body of truth in which law is the central substance and ethics the most significant concern. Heschel is unique among those who have upheld the accuracy of the biblical message, in giving ethics this predominant place. And his teaching was made all the more impressive by his record of political activism.

Responding to the Holocaust He Escaped

The Holocaust death-of-God discussion of the late 1960's did not cause Heschel to revise his philosophy. In one respect, his attitude toward evil was essentially that of the liberals: evil results from the human abuse of the freedom God gave us. For God to take away that freedom because we have badly abused it would itself be evil of God. The world's indifference made the Nazi bestiality possible and Heschel made that destructive moral sloth the model for his calls to humanity and Jewry to take action against the evils around them.

In another critical respect, Heschel struck out on his own. The liberals, judging people to be basically good, assumed that education and culture would bring humankind to behave ethically. Heschel, here reflecting his Hasidic background perhaps more strongly than anywhere else, was no optimist with regard to human nature. He considered the evil urge in people to be far more sinister and effective than the liberals had ever imagined. He believed it affects everything we do, even our righteousness. He acknowledged a close affinity with Reinhold Niebuhr's Christian theory of human nature as existentially though not biologically fallen. But for all his realism about the human will to do evil, he never claimed people were sinful in essence. They always remained free to return to God and, with prayerful effort, to do the good. The Nazis could not blame their perverse human nature for what they did. They were fully responsible for it. They chose to perpetrate the Holocaust and "rationally" determined to keep it going at all costs. Their awesome guilt is a direct consequence of their moral freedom.

Heschel denied that people had a right to question God about our suffering. Apparently he did not think us righteous enough to offer such challenges. He certainly believed that God was so much greater than we are that we should maintain a respectful, appreciative silence in God's presence. Interestingly, too, he did not apply his theory of God's pathos to the problem of evil. In talmudic times some Rabbis assuaged the agony of the exile by saying that God accompanied Israel in *galut* and shared its sufferings. Heschel could not bring himself to explicitly revive that idea. Perhaps he felt our pain was too great for such consolation. Or his general reticence about speaking about what God does may have kept him back from such a theodicy. Or, he did not essay the stance of a modern Job or Levi Yitzchak because he knew too well that God was the very premise of our doubt and indignation. Having lost much of his family in the Holocaust, he suffered greatly over it. His sense of our proper humility before God kept him from writing very much about it.

We Meet God in Doing the Commandments

Revelation is only the second of the three paths Heschel sees leading to God. Heschel could not stop the development of this thought at this point for Judaism is not the only religion of biblical revelation. Christianity, perhaps even Islam, could join Judaism as a religion seeking to be faithful to the prophets. Heschel was open to the truth in these traditions and frequently participated in interreligious activities. Yet he also affirms the distinctiveness of the people of Israel's relation to God. The move from revelation to holy deeds, the third level of religiosity, finally exposes Heschel's doctrine of particularity.

Traditional Judaism is grounded not only on the revelation of the written Torah, but the oral Torah as well. The writings of the Rabbis and the rabbinic traditions down to this day have God's authority behind them. If the recognized rabbinic authorities today speak in God's name, then only such changes as they allow are authentic Judaism. If, as the liberals argue, all the Rabbis operate with is essentially human power, then past decisions may be altered and contemporary ones disputed if there is good reason. Heschel maintains the inseparability of the written and the oral Torah, but does not explicate his meaning. He merely notes, "The prophets' inspirations and the sages' interpretations are equally important"—an Orthodox stance. At the least, his theory of revelation would substantiate right wing Conservative Judaism. In any case, he teaches that for Jews, the fulfillment of the Bible is the Rabbis, not the Gospels or the Koran.

He mitigates this doctrine in two ways. First, he insists on a careful distinction between revelation and interpretation. The former is quite limited in extent when compared to its amplification by the Rabbis. Perhaps Heschel implies that the process of interpretation might permit us to move on to practices somewhat different from those previously sanctioned. He further argues—with considerable vigor and passion—that ethics should receive priority in the life of Torah. He claims this has traditional warrant and illustrates the inner tension in the Bible and rabbinic literature which led many great teachers to assert the preeminence of the ethical. Despite these liberalistic concerns, Heschel never specifically indicated when and under what conditions he would countenance a break with rabbinic law.

Fulfilling the commandments brings one to God. Neither experience nor existence nor encounter but devoted doing is the central concern of Judaism. Heschel produces a phenomenology of observance which opens up the inner life of the pious and moves beyond the liberals' concern with the doer to what transpires between the believer and God during the holy deed. Modern students of religion usually concentrate on religious feeling or faith. Heschel examines the sacred act as the meeting place between God and humankind. Heschel, fully self-conscious of this uncommon approach, summons Jews not to the risk of faith but to a "leap of action."

In a pious deed, we confirm and fulfill the fickle subjectivity of faith. We transcend our limited selves by responding not to our desires but to God's. The climax of human religiosity is learning to make God's needs our own, to want so much to do what God wants that we are continually doing it. In such responsive living our private relationship with God is renewed for Jews as individuals and a community. Observance is the ongoing renewal of Israel's ancient Covenant with God.

Heschel does not insist that emphasis on works is distinctively or exclusively Jewish. Though he speaks of *mitzvot*, divine commandments, and cites rabbinic sources liberally, he refers continually to "man," not to the Jew in this analysis. Perhaps he is making room for that understanding of Christianity which sees gospel as including, if transcending, law. Perhaps he only wishes to show the universal human effect of Jewish living. Whatever the reason, Heschel's third way of coming to God is most fully expressed in the traditional Jewish observance of law and commandment. Heschel's system reaches its goal in identifying the particular Jewish way of life as an incomparable response to the revealing God, a position anyone with general faith now ought to be able to see.

Where Is The Jewish People In This System?

The revelation to Israel dominates Heschel's understanding of Judaism. The Jewish people, as such, hardly has an independent role in his thought. It remains utterly subordinated to the will of God as revealed to the prophets. Heschel devotes less than a dozen pages to peoplehood in his major books. He almost certainly adopted this stance to counteract the stress on Jewish ethnicity of his faculty colleague, Mordecai Kaplan, which appealed to many American Jews. For Kaplan, Judaism is the folk culture of the Jews of which religion is but one part, if the most significant. Heschel quietly polemicized against ethnic humanism by reducing to a minimum the Jewish people's role in creating Judaism. God's will, not folk creativity, determines what the Jewish people ought to be and do. His early books say little about the ethnic themes so critical to Kaplan— land, language, the arts and community organization.

Heschel's unconcern with ethnicity was probably more likely due to his desire to be faithful to Jewish tradition. A comparison with Rosenzweig is instructive. Both men believed, against the rationalists, that revelation was the necessary foundation for an authentic Judaism. Heschel's conception of prophecy is more traditional than Rosenzweig's because Heschel defended the content of the prophetic message. As in Rosenzweig's case, the focus on revelation produced an unusual attitude to time and history. Rosenzweig had argued that the Jews transcended these normal attributes of existence. By virtue of following God's commands, the people of Israel was, so to speak, already living in God's kingdom and thus on the plane of eternity. Heschel analogously argued that Judaism is primarily a religion of sacred time—as per the commandments—but not concerned with space. The Jewish tradition did not disparage spatiality for it was an attribute of the creation God had called "good." Contemporary civilization, however, has invested itself most heavily in the spatial aspects of existence, thereby robbing humankind of its special quality, the immediacy and will connected with time. The commandments do the opposite. By making the Sabbath a pivot of daily life, Judaism placed a premium on time, specifically by asking people to sanctify it by holy deeds. The secular existentialist lament, that mortal existence is given only for our destruction, is transformed from a source of despair to a motive for acting as God's partner in completing creation.

Rosenzweig did not hesitate to accept the non-Zionist consequences of centering Judaism on revelation. When the core of Jewishness is sanctifying time through commandments, space becomes almost irrelevant. One can be observant anywhere. In that respect, Heschel's philosophy, like that of Rosenzweig, provides a firm foundation to Jewish life in the Diaspora. It also produced an intellectual challenge for him when Jerusalem came into Jewish hands in 1967, and subsequent interreligious discussions raised the issue of its return or internationalization.

The difficulty is elegantly simple. Jerusalem is fixed in space. The New City, which had always been under Israeli control, though only some yards from the Old City, is simply not to be equated with it. If

Judaism is essentially a religion of the sanctification of time, why should world Jewry insist on continued control over an undivided Jerusalem, particularly when it remains so contested a bit of space? Heschel might have answered that, for all its emphasis on time, God's revelation also deals with space, focusing specifically on the city of Jerusalem. To such a Jewish dogmatic claim others would respond with their own religious counter-claims, thus negating the effect of the argument. Heschel proceeded phenomenologically, explicating what Jerusalem had meant to the Jews throughout their history and the spiritual effect it has on Jews today. No other religion has anything like this unique attachment to the city, therefore implying that Jews have a special right to sovereignty over it. His images are moving and his language, as always, evocative, but no case emerges from them. Phenomenology may disclose one's inner reality but that may not persuade the reader. Heschel has no universal basis for special claims of space. Lacking an effective theory of Jewish ethnicity, he cannot insist upon the central role of the land of Israel or the city of Jerusalem in Jewish duty.

Speaking From Faith to Those With Many Doubts

The mutually reinforcing movements from nature to revelation to deed give Heschel so great a sense of certainty that he regularly speaks with an assurance that can easily disturb inquiring readers. Worse, he often insists that the only choice open to us is one between his view and an absurdity (e.g., either the prophets are accurate or they are mad). He continually dismisses the validity of questions posed from a liberal perspective. Again and again he begins an insightful discussion of a modern problem, shows its implications, and, just as one expects that he will respond to them, he says instead that from the standpoint of faith that is not the real question at all.

When one is fresh to this technique or when the insight is quite striking—religion is not man seeking God but God in search of man; the Bible is not human theology but God's anthropology—the effect can be quite telling. As with a Zen koan or a Hasidic master's epigram, enlightenment may strike through the dramatic reversal of perspective. Repeated use of this device, particularly in works that call themselves "philosophy," makes many readers uncomfortable. Thoughtful people tire of having their questions dismissed as meaningless if not foolish, especially when they do not arise from individual whim but from the major intellects of our era. Unease speedily rises to irritation when positions other than the author's are dismissed as "arrogant," "absurd," "insane," "incredible." Heschel is so certain of his faith that alternatives are simply untenable. Yet not infrequently in the modern world, the product of thoughtful skepticism—e.g., the universality of genuine ethics—has turned out to have more religious significance than the inherited pieties of a given tradition—e.g., the autocracy of religious leadership. Heschel often makes no contact with people who do not have as firm a belief in God's revelation as he has. Accepting religious experience only as fulfilled in biblical revelation takes away much common ground he might have had with the serious modern inquirer. His faith may demand it, but it sets a major obstacle in the way of his addressing people raised in a secular ethos.

Problems With the Reliability of the Bible

When Jews raise objections to Heschel's manner of argument, their negativity might be dismissed as the result of self-hate or some other form of venality. The critics press on to reject the Heschelian interpretation of revelation on the substance of the case. Rationalistic antagonists will marshall the data of biblical literary criticism to argue for the human origins of the prophetic texts. A more telling case can be made from inside Heschel's system. By Heschel's own standards some of the most compelling prophetic passages challenge the Godly authenticity of others. Granting that God has pathos, what shall we say about the accuracy of the prophetic descriptions of God's hot anger? Heschel answers that God's wrath, unlike ours, is never out of moral control. God keeps it under ethical constraint. The Divine indignation is only another form of God's justice, now passionately applied because people have done awful deeds.

Most readers, even traditional ones, have read the texts differently. The prophets seem rather plainly to say that God, having rightfully made demands and quietly waited for people to fulfill them, has finally lost patience with us. God therefore proposes to visit the people of Israel with an awesome destructiveness that far exceeds compensatory punishment. Indeed, the prophet may hope that the threat of God's overwhelming displeasure will cause Israel to repent. Read this way, the prophetic pronouncements about God's wrath are a moral embarrassment. An angry judge is a contradiction in terms because genuine anger always results in injustice. It contaminates the deserved with the undeserved, adulterating this moment's deserts with recompense for past events, confusing this person's guilt with the evils inflicted by others, real or imagined. If one did not need to defend the accuracy of the prophets, one could see the morality behind the prophet's dismay at the people's continued obstinacy. Heschel must defend God's anger to preserve the reliability of prophetic sympathy and thus the doctrine of revelation on which his system rests. If his explanation of God's anger is unconvincing, his entire intellectual structure falls.

The liberals may have made too little of God and too much of humankind. In all integrity, they could not accept biblical text and the rabbinic tradition as God-given or God-empowered. Slavery might be condoned by people in a given historical situation; it was not God's word. Women might be treated as legally separate and hence unequal until recent times; any suggestion that this is God's permanent command must be repudiated. When such troublesome laws are integrated into what we have learned about the growth of all human practices, they become more understandable if less authoritative than of old. Now radical amazement strikes us because the Hebrews, though so much a part of Near Eastern civilization, managed to be so incredibly different spiritually. Again, though the Jews have been intimately affected by every society they were dispersed to,

NEO-TRADITIONALISM: ABRAHAM HESCHEL   183

they remained true to their Covenant with God. The humaneness of the religion itself becomes an invitation to awe.

Heschel's moving validation of a neo-traditional Judaism is unparalleled in twentieth-century Jewish thought. No other thinker has yet presented a systematic defense of Judaism based on God's revelation of the written and oral Torah. Against those who have felt that modernity necessarily implied some version of liberal belief, Heschel carried through the central project of modern Jewish thought by providing a theology of classic Judaism. Even those who cannot accept his system have learned much from him about the spirit which should inform contemporary piety and observance.

Heschel challenges Jews moving from liberalism to greater traditionalism to decide whether personal autonomy should usurp the place of God's revelation. Does an authentic Judaism require the acceptance of God's law as revealed to the prophets and interpreted by the Rabbis, or may it derive from our present-day human understanding of what God demands of us as members of the Covenant people? Heschel grandly made the case for traditional Jewish faith. No one who seeks to reestablish liberalism or to validate classic Judaism in another way can ignore his passionate case for seeking God's perspective. And everyone can benefit from the example he set of the pious Jew as an involved human being. No Jewish community figure of recent years better demonstrated how a believing Jew ought to respond to the crises of our time. His integration of Judaism and modernity in his life was itself a monumental accomplishment.

PART IV

The
Contemporary
Agenda

9

Confronting
the
Holocaust

SINCE Abraham Heschel, no Jewish theologian has presented a full-scale, distinctive exposition of Judaism.* The work of Jewish thought has continued, if anything, in a more varied, vigorous and sophisticated form than previously, but it has been scattered and thematic rather than concentrated and systematic. No topic has drawn more attention and been discussed in greater depth than the theological implications of the Holocaust. Tracking this debate is more than technically difficult; it is humanly daunting. Most of the thinkers involved admit that the Holocaust overwhelms them. They also consider it their Jewish duty to try to come to terms with it, even tentatively. These factors make summarizing this discussion particularly difficult. Nevertheless, a number of basic intellectual positions, often identified with certain protagonists, have emerged over the years. Let us track these points of view and the debates to which they have given rise.

---

*The work of Louis Jacobs, a possible exception to this rule, is discussed in Chapter 11.

The Two-Decade Silence

We begin with a historical puzzle. What caused the hiatus in time between the end of the Holocaust and the beginning of the discussion? Not until the mid-1960's, twenty years after World War II, did the Holocaust become a central topic in Jewish religious thought. Elie Wiesel's *Night* appeared in 1960 to little notice and the articles which Richard Rubenstein wrote then (later gathered with others into *After Auschwitz*), awakened little debate. Why?

Most observers have given a psychological answer, one not without moral overtones. The Holocaust had so traumatized us that we repressed it as too painful to bear. As it receded in time and our anguish lessened, we could open up to the terrible hurt and let it into our consciousness. Surely this is true of the survivors. Only in recent years have they found the inner strength to speak out. With the exception of Elie Wiesel, none of the thinkers presented in this chapter was in the death camps though several fled Europe before the mass murder began.

For most American Jews, the silence resulted as much from guilt at their inaction as from their identification with those who suffered and died. American Jewry had all too readily followed the advice of their leaders who, despite evidence of unprecedented mass extermination, acquiesced to the government's demands for silence and concentration on the war effort. For two decades guilt grew as they realized how great an evil they had abetted. The therapy for that festering wound was exposure—and the new Jewish devotion manifest through the 1970's.

The Cultural Context of the Change

The psychological analysis is persuasive but I believe it improperly isolates Jewish experience from its American context. Though I agree with Irving Greenberg's plea that the Holocaust should lead Jews to break their fawning dependence on modernity, I do not see our change, as he apparently does, as an internal Jewish community affair. I believe our Jewish turn inward substantially arose as part of a shift in the American ethos which made it socially acceptable for Jews to face up to the Holocaust and its implications. Against Greenberg, I view our very discussion of the Holocaust not as a withdrawal from modernity but as another sign of our continuing involvement in it.

As a result of the civil rights movement, the United States entered a period of ethnic reassertion in the early 1960's. Black civil disobedience shattered the notion that minorities had to be well behaved. Etiquette was revealed to be a means of keeping the underprivileged powerless. Polite silence at one's continuing disabilities was no longer considered a reasonable price to pay for having been granted some rights. Blacks, Indians, Poles and other groups became conscious of their guilt and anger at the servility they had gratefully undertaken. Public complaint and hostility to leaders became common; attacks on supposed friends who deserted others in a time of need were heard; and comparisons with Nazis and the Holocaust were a steady theme of minority invective.

American Jews had arrived at the mid-1960's with a new self-confidence. They were unexpectedly influential in the society and probably its single most affluent religio-ethnic community. Once that status would have enjoined a more neurotic conformity. Now it meant being secure enough to speak out.

In my opinion, the old Jewish inhibitions were finally dissolved by the popular acceptance of the Protestant death-of-God movement. Most Americans—and Jews—considered the American Jewish community a religious group. With Judaism one of the country's three great religions, the Jews, despite small numbers and endemic unbelief, had extraordinary social position. Consciously and unconsciously, they tended to emulate the dominant, Protestant mood. In the leading liberal churches this now shifted from a pronounced theocentrism to a death-of-God theology that was quite different from the atheism of another time. Its adherents proposed to stay in the church and rebuild it, in Dietrich Bonhoeffer's words, "as if there were no God." Once religion without God became acceptable in the paradigmatic group, the Jewish release was complete. Jews were bold enough ethnically to attack all anti-semitism and religiously free to do so in terms of giving up belief in God. Richard Rubenstein writes that he was surprised when William Hamilton, the organizer of the death-of-God movement, identified him as the Jewish counterpart to the Protestant thinkers but soon recognized, within limits, what he shared with them. Once again, particular Jewish experience participated in, yet extended, what was happening in the civilization generally.

The Influence of Elie Wiesel

The pivotal figure in the resulting intellectual work is Elie Wiesel, though his works on the Holocaust are mainly fiction. They are not entertainments but learned and reflective narrative explorations of the range of responses one might make to the Holocaust. Wiesel has often characterized his role as that of a witness. His effort to give truthful testimony has been agonizing. How can an author avoid reducing the terror in order to have its horrifying message widely heard? Wiesel's painful effort not to bear false witness is the standard by which the integrity of all who discuss this topic is measured.

In only one of his books has Wiesel permitted himself to describe the suffering during the Holocaust. *Night* is autobiographical and depicts the reactions of a pious teen-ager as he goes from his sheltered village existence to Auschwitz and thence, astonishingly, to liberation. I will not say more for I do not want to give anyone an excuse for not reading the book nor contribute to lessening its impact. A number of its passages have already been cited so frequently they have become our Holocaust clichés, thus emptying them of meaning—exactly the problem of authenticity that so agitates Wiesel.

In *Night* Wiesel enunciated many of the themes around which his writing centers. The death camp experience was unutterably evil. No previous human experience or imagination of suffering explains such horror. Auschwitz, the symbolic name for all the ghettoes and camps, was a unique event in history. More, it was revelatory. Now everything in human life must be seen through its lens. That is not meant as hyperbole but as fact. Auschwitz is the new Jewish Sinai; it must set the context and content of contemporary Jewish views of God, humankind, religion and Judaism. By that standard we can no longer be satisfied with the old Jewish apologies for God's bungling of reward and punishment: Life after death, suffering out of love or for the sake of others, redemption by the Messiah, and the like. They are not utterly false, yet after the Holocaust they are empty. Nothing makes sense any more—even the very act of trying to make sense of things. In the face of such evil, one may well wonder why one should bother with the world of history. But despair too is wrong. It makes the Holocaust more reasonable than existence. We must live—but what can it mean not to despair after the Holocaust? The question haunts Wiesel's work and life.

Wiesel believes there are no "answers" to the Holocaust. He is not even certain we have the right questions. He restlessly moves from one aspect of it to another, afraid to come to rest at any intellectual point and by such relaxation betray the fathomless terror Jews knew. Again and again he suggests that a species of intelligent madness is the most appropriate response to the Holocaust. Were we capable of becoming appropriately deranged we might see in what now appears to us as blackest night. Philosophers who seek to "explain" the Holocaust are engaged in a self-contradictory project. Madmen are more truthful witnesses to the insanity we lived through.

The final word cannot be insanity, else how would we write fiction or try to face life? A cruel duty is laid upon the survivor, not to forget, and not to let the world forget, as it would dearly like to do.

Continuing Work of the Survivor-Witness

Night is the first book of a trilogy whose second volume is *Dawn* and whose final part, "Day" in French, is entitled *The Accident* in English. The increasing light is intentional. *Dawn* treats the partial answer to suffering of a people's national revival in its own home-land—an "explanation" made almost as irrational as the Holocaust by the violence it precipitates. In *Day*, the protagonist confronts the redemptive kindness of a doctor who fights death with all his might and thereby shows the goodness yet to be found in life. *The Town Beyond the Wall* contrasts helping a human being with the iniquity of spectatorship. In acknowledging the power of personal responsibility, Wiesel finds himself open to a positive relation with the God with whom he remains in conflict. By the end of *The Gates in the Forest*, the survivor, racked by the ambiguities of life and the guilts he bears, becomes sufficiently positive in his ambivalent relationship to God to recite the *kaddish*, that extravagant praise of God Jewish mourners offer. And having faced the dead and the God who brings death, he is able to take up marriage and procreation, the primal burdens of life.

Each novel discloses a partial truth and leaves one recognizing how fragmentary our understanding must remain. The ultimate irrationality of existence was given unusual expression in *A Beggar in Jerusalem*. This novel interprets one of the most joyous events in Jewish history, the return of the Old City of Jerusalem to Jewish sovereignty in 1967. It is the only one of Wiesel's novels not written in a realistic style. The swirling, uncertain, dreamlike narration communicates the madness which alone can cope with the paradox: The generation of ultimate suffering has been granted unexpected happiness.

In the late 1960's Wiesel began publishing in other forms. His addresses and articles on the Holocaust, his response to contemporary Jewish issues, most notably a powerful book on the resurgence of Jewish life in the Soviet Union, and his retelling of biblical, talmudic, and Hasidic tales now were increasingly brought to the public. This continuing Jewish devotion puts into relief the one question which never occurs in his work: Should the Jewish people and tradition continue? Wiesel's categorically positive stance toward Jews and Judaism is no narrow self-assertion of ethnicity. His quest is thoroughly universal. He wonders how anyone can affirm life after the Holocaust. He takes it for granted that if there is any proper human response to Auschwitz, it will also be true for Jews. At the same time, since no one knows human suffering better than the Jews, their wisdom is humankind's best source of insight into the mystery called existence. To Wiesel, every Jew and the Jewish people itself, is holy. Promoting Jewish survival is an unshakable dogma after the Holocaust.

Issues Posed by Richard Rubenstein

For all the influence of Wiesel's work, the theological discussion of the Holocaust has not centered about it because its format is intentionally ambiguous. Instead, Richard Rubenstein's book, *After Auschwitz*, focussed the significant controversies of the late 1960's and shaped the form in which they developed. That volume collects articles written over the six years when Rubenstein was evolving his radical Jewish theology. Readers today sometimes find it difficult to determine the position at which he ultimately arrived, though his later writings partially clarify this. Rubenstein agrees with Wiesel that Auschwitz is our Sinai. The refusal of contemporary Jewish theologians to listen to its voice is a damning indictment of anything they might now be shocked into saying about it. Rubenstein proposes instead to make its revelation about the human situation the basis of his illusionless Judaism.

The evil the Nazis perpetrated upon the Jews requires, at the very least, that Jews give up any claim to be chosen. In the western mind, as in much Jewish teaching, chosenness means suffering for God's sake. Persecutors may then have an easy conscience because suffering is the divinely appointed Jewish role. After Auschwitz such attitudes are intolerably offensive. Rather than give any comfort to the oppressor and validate indifference to the victims, Jews should renounce the notion of their appointment as God's suffering servant.

Rubenstein's opposition to chosenness did not arouse much conflict. It had long been reinterpreted, as in Mordecai Kaplan's case, to the point of repudiation. Such connection as it had retained with suffering had largely been severed by the events of the Holocaust. Some traditionalists, such as Harold Fisch, Eliezer Berkovits and Irving Greenberg, have tried to recast the doctrine of necessary Jewish suffering without legitimizing persecution, but none of these views has been widely discussed or accepted.

A major controversy broke out over Rubenstein's rethinking of belief in God. He argued that the Holocaust invalidated all the classic Jewish positions regarding God and evil and requires us to reject classic Jewish faith in God. Rubenstein remained a religious thinker, albeit one whose idea of the Holy Nothing was disturbing to the average Jew, though his reworked understanding of the Jewish people and of Jewish practice was far more recognizable.

The First, Negative Assertions

Rubenstein denies that any of the old Jewish theodicies, the defenses of God despite evil, are tenable after Auschwitz. On occasion he remarks that the death of one innocent child should have been enough to refute them. (Such comments imply, against his normal stand, that *all* evil refutes theism; the Holocaust is not unique but merely gross.) That the Nazis' bestiality was just compensation for Jewish sins; that God must allow such evils so as to preserve human freedom; that it taught a valuable lesson to the world; that God tests our faith; that God has compensated the Jews for their suffering by giving them the State of Israel; or that the Holocaust brutality can be expunged by the bliss of the world-to-come, are all morally unbearable notions. No God who did such things would be worth worshipping. Further, to take refuge in traditional humility and say that God's ways are infinitely beyond us, is an utter abdication of our human judgment and of the victims' human dignity.

Rubenstein calls on us to reject the God of traditional Jewish theology. He makes two quite different statements of his position, one doctrinal, the other a social observation. The former was most concisely put this way:

> Traditional Jewish theology maintains that God is the ultimate, omnipotent actor in the historical drama. It has interpreted every major catastrophe in Jewish history as God's punishment of a sinful Israel. I fail to see how this position can be maintained without regarding Hitler and the SS as instruments of God's will. The agony of European Jewry cannot be likened to the testing of Job. . . . The idea is simply too obscene for me to accept.

In a number of other places Rubenstein similarly objects to what he understands to be the normative Jewish teaching about God's control of history.

Rubenstein does not equate giving up an old doctrine of God with denying God's reality. Atheism involves a metaphysical certainty, a negative one, which is incompatible with Rubenstein's existentialist, person-based thought. Instead, he makes a temporal, immediate judgment concerning our post-Holocaust period. He continues, "No man can really say that God is dead. How can we know that? Nevertheless, I am compelled to say that we live in the time of the 'death of God.' This is more a statement about man and his culture than about God. The death of God is a cultural fact." This too became a steady theme in his thought. Most Jewish thinkers considered these two assertions faulty but I think it will clarify Rubenstein's total position better if we immediately consider his positive teachings.

Recreating Judaism Around the Holy Nothingness

Auschwitz should lead us to agree with the French existentialists

Sartre and Camus that "We stand in a cold, silent, unfeeling cosmos, unaided by any purposeful power beyond our own resources." But Rubenstein is not an atheist. There is, after all, not *nothing* but *some*thing. The source of that being is the focus of Rubenstein's religiosity. He is wary of applying positive terminology to it lest he mask the negativity revealed by Auschwitz and the death that awaits all created things. Borrowing a theme from Jewish and general mysticism, he terms the object of his reverence the Holy Nothingness. "In the final analysis, omnipotent Nothingness is Lord of all creation."

An inverted messianism results from this. In discussing Christian death-of-God theories, he wrote, "There is only one Messiah who redeems us from the irony, the travail, and the limitations of human existence . . . the Angel of Death. Death is the true Messiah and the land of the dead the place of God's true Kingdom. . . . We enter God's Kingdom only when we enter His Holy Nothingness." Rubenstein does not seek that Kingdom "because I prefer the problematics of finitude to their dissolution in the nothingness of eternity."

Though no supernatural basis for Jewish continuity exists, the Jews, compelled by history to be Jews, should now affirm their Jewishness to attain self-protection and mutual caring. The State of Israel models a transformed Jewish identity because it reasserts the naturalness of being a Jew and gives proper attention to one's body and a connection to the soil. With chosenness abandoned, the State need reflect no special standard of quality. It rightly does whatever it must to ensure its survival in an amoral universe.

The Jewish religion should continue as a means of helping individual Jews meet life's inevitable traumas. In so unfeeling a cosmos, people need to share with one another to gain the human strength required to face the existential challenges of life. Human beings, having great emotional depths, will benefit from a religious life rich in ritual and myth, particularly those which do not neglect their primitive impulses. If Jewish theology and practice can be transformed, Judaism has much to offer Jews.

Why These Were Not the Relevant Issues

Rubenstein has often expressed surprise that, as the Jewish death-of-God discussion developed, he became increasingly marginal to it. At first, many Jews responded positively to the morality of his attack on the silence of other thinkers and the inadequacies of the traditional theodicies. Ever since modernization had taken hold, Jews had cared far more about ethics than about God. But the death-of-God discussion soon moved off in other directions.

Rubenstein's first argument, the rejection of a rigidly controlling God, was never disputed because modern Jews had not espoused it. Some sages of the *"yeshivah* world" and some Hasidic leaders, such as the Lubavitcher Rebbe or the Satmarer Rebbe, have declared that the Holocaust was God's punishment of the Jews for their non-observance. Almost all modern Jews agree with Rubenstein that such a view of God and the Holocaust is utterly unacceptable.

This judgment is not a new one. Modern Jewish thinkers had been revising their concepts of God through much of the twentieth century to avoid any mechanical connection between God and human suffering. The God of Cohen, Baeck, Kaplan, Rosenzweig, Buber and other such thinkers was not the "ultimate, omnipotent actor of history." No one who accepted their ideas had a God-concept which required Rubinstein's radical revision after the Holocaust. Except at some atavistic level, even the masses of modernized Jews no longer had believed in a God who operated every historical occurrence. The major response of modernized Jews to the Kishinev pogrom of 1903—the "holocaust" of its day—was a call for Jewish action, not cries of self-incrimination or arguments justifying God.

By 1966, when Rubenstein's book appeared, most American Jews were so thoroughly secularized that, in my opinion, their "faith" was usually some variety of agnosticism. The announcement of God's death only added a historical-moral proof to those other arguments which modernization had long since convinced them were cogent.

To that extent, Rubenstein's second statement of his case, that we live in a time of the death-of-God, confirmed their experience. Since then, another cultural change has taken place. For much of the 1970's, not the absence of God but God's immediate, felt presence in charismatic movements, cults and mysticism has characterized American religious life. "The time of the death-of-God" passed rather quickly. Most Jews consider the lessons to be derived from Auschwitz less ephemeral than that and so their search moved elsewhere.

The Failure to Provide an Adequate Ground of Value

I have argued that the most significant Jewish religious phenomenon of the 1970's was the erosion of Jewish agnosticism. Intellectually, I ascribe it to the confrontation with nihilism which Rubenstein's thought generated. In the heady days of confidence in human rationality, we were comfortable being unbelievers for we could count on the eternal validity of ethics. But Rubenstein's cosmos was utterly devoid of moral standards or values. In that respect he accurately reflected post-World War II secularity. Unlike Hermann Cohen's era, human rationality no longer implied ethical commitment. Reason meant logic and tight thinking, not moral law. As Sartre taught, values were now only what a person chose wholeheartedly to do. By that standard, one had every right to be a Nazi, an outcome utterly unacceptable to those morally outraged at Auschwitz. Any theory of ethics that reduces the distinction between the murdered and the murderers to a social or historical accident is contemptible. The difference between a Nazi and a Jew testifies not merely to our upbringing but to something in the ultimate nature of reality itself. Against the drift of much of modern life and thought, many Jews found themselves believing in the claims of a realm of human value that no longer had a rational foundation. Confronted with Rubenstein's claim that the Holy Nothingness is indifferent to good and evil, a good portion of our community had to acknowledge it believed in a trans-rational, commanding absolute good. For us, that meant a belief in something very much like what previous Jewish generations called God. Astonishingly, the very discussion that sought to lead Jews away from God, led them, like many others in the 1970's, back to God.

Rubenstein sought to meet this problem of the loss of moral standards by arguing that a commanding ethics may be derived from the human body and the self. Had that project succeeded, he would have solved one of the most pressing intellectual problems of western civilization, namely, providing a secular justification for stringent obedience to moral imperatives. Rubenstein's book on this topic, *Morality and Eros*, convinced few thinkers. With the ethical consequences of his thought nullifying the very moral outrage it had raised against Auschwitz, Rubenstein's ideas increasingly lost their appeal in the Jewish community.

The social factor in this change of perspective must not be overlooked. Gross immorality invaded much of American life in the 1970's, manifesting itself most dramatically in sexual license, drug abuse, and wanton violence. Few people could avoid the problem of a compelling ground of moral values. An amoral universe validates doing anything one can get away with, even holocausts. Many Americans knew they must reject any view of reality which taught no serious set of limits and had few standards of quality. With rationalism and other forms of secularism unable to deal persuasively with this intuition, a turn to religion began and grew during the 1970's. We shall return to this topic at the end of this chapter and in Chapter 10.

Fackenheim and the Modern Loss of Revelation

Emil Fackenheim's essays soon became a source of the most significant themes of the continuing Jewish discussion of the Holocaust. Ever since the late 1940's, he had been a leader of the existentialist revolt against the rationalist establishment of liberal Jewish theology. Fackenheim, who teaches modern philosophy at the University of Toronto, utilized his considerable technical expertise to criticize the generally accepted axiom that a modern Judaism had to be a religion of reason. He argued that all authentic religion, certainly Judaism, is based on revelation. Religious rationalism, by basing itself on human reason, had grossly overestimated our human powers and paid too little attention to God's reality. Until the mid-1960's Fackenheim's most influential work focused on restoring God to an appropriately prominent place in the liberal Jewish religious consciousness.

Fackenheim largely accepted Martin Buber's theory of revelation for he particularly admired the way the I-Eternal Thou encounter preserved individual autonomy while yet making God an active, independent partner in the process. Buber had suggested that God gave presence, not words; people provided the language and content. Because God was available, the Divine-human relationship could arise and engender a compelling but non-Orthodox variety of revelation. The reality and immediate presence of God was therefore a critical element of Fackenheim's two-decade battle with the theological rationalists.

Confronted by the issues raised by Wiesel and Rubenstein, Fackenheim felt he must substantially rethink his position. The biographical background is pertinent: a German, one of the last men ordained a liberal rabbi in Berlin and briefly confined in Sachsenhausen after the November 1938 Nazi outbreak, the *Kristalnacht*, he barely escaped to Canada before the war broke out. Opening himself up now to the Holocaust, Fackenheim conceded that Wiesel and Rubenstein were right: God was not present in the Holocaust. What, then, was one to make of this event or of the understanding of Judaism?

In our bewilderment, tradition offers little help. After previous catastrophes, great Jewish spirits have written of God's presence in judgment or in consolation. We cannot do that, not because of some lack of spiritual capacity on our part, but because the Holocaust was a unique act of evil. Here too Wiesel and Rubenstein were right; Auschwitz exposes us to a qualitatively new and unprecedented dimension of suffering. Fackenheim is therefore intellectually outraged by the liberal sentimentality which brackets the Holocaust with any human disaster we seek to condemn. For all their moral odiousness, calling either Hiroshima or *apartheid* another Holocaust, betrays an effort to avoid the uniqueness of the Nazi barbarity.

Arguments for a New Level of Evil

No other Jewish thinker has explored as has Fackenheim what we might mean by saying the Holocaust is without parallel and what follows from that assertion. Obviously, we are not referring merely to numbers or its unexpectedness or its methodical execution. All such matters amplify common cruelty; they do not specify what constitutes the Holocaust as a unique evil. Fackenheim identifies two factors in the Holocaust which newly transform the old problem of suffering. The one stems from the charge leveled against the Jews. Their alleged guilt was independent of their conduct or beliefs. In previous persecutions—say, in the Middle Ages—Jews could often save their lives by conversion. The Nazis condemned the Jews because of their biology. Having one Jewish grandparent became a sentence of death. Being itself was made a capital crime and there was nothing one could do about it. That, Fackenheim argues, was a uniquely evil act.

His other line of argument points to the will of the persecutors. The Nazis knew the evil they were doing. They were educated people whose moral consciousness was shaped by a Christian culture, yet they calmly, routinely proceeded to process the mass murder of Jews. They even did so after continuing the extermination made no sense. During the last stages of the war, when trains were desperately needed for immediate military purposes, the Nazis refused to divert them from transporting Jews to the death camps. The hatred of Jews transcended the drive to self-preservation. They must have kept killing from a demonic desire to do evil for evil's sake, to commit the ultimate sin, a thoroughly evil act done for a thoroughly evil purpose. Nothing like that had ever happened in human history.

With God withdrawn and inaccessible—no small part of the agony—and in the face of this incomparable evil, one might have expected the Jews to despair. But the events of Jewish history, as theologians read them, are often more numinous than Jewish thoughts. Though the Holocaust itself discloses no transcendent meaning, Fackenheim detects a new "revelation" at the base of the Jewish people's response to it. By what logic can one explain why the Jews did not turn their backs on life after the Holocaust? Why, despite all that they had seen and suffered, did the survivors insist on resuming Jewish existence? And, most surprisingly, why did they choose to be Jews in a more self-conscious, manifest way than they had before? On some unconscious, spiritual level, they *had to do* what they did. For them to allow the Jewish people to die would have been, themselves, to complete the Holocaust. That was inconceivable. Individual Jews might be so traumatized they could not care any more about being Jewish. The people itself somehow summoned—or was given—the strength to deny Hitler the ultimate triumph. Absolute evil had aroused absolute commitment.

The Nature of post–Holocaust Judaism

Fackenheim provides an explanation of this incredible act of self-transcendence. Though God was utterly silent, the Jews heard an absolute command come forth from Auschwitz. To emphasize its Torah-like status, Fackenheim has termed it the 614th commandment (though he seems to consider it the most fundamental of all the commandments today). He hears it as having four components. Jews are forbidden "to hand Hitler posthumous victories." Rather, they must survive as Jews. They must remember the victims. They must not despair of God "lest Judaism perish." In this formulation Fackenheim explained to the Jewish community the impetus which motivated its extraordinary postwar return to Jewishness and which continues to energize the best of Jewish life today.

Fackenheim drew three consequences from his reoriented belief and these remain basic to his community leadership and intellectual work. First, he no longer finds it useful to distinguish between religious and secular Jews. Earlier, when arguing for the centrality of revelation in Judaism, he had demeaned Jewish secularism. Seeking to come to terms with the Holocaust, his criterion of Jewish loyalty had changed. Though God is no longer present to reveal, Jews respond to the "commanding voice" of Auschwitz. Any Jew, regardless of label, who helps preserve and maintain or, better, enriches the life of the Jewish people, fulfills the supreme Jewish responsibility of our time.

The second consequence he derives from emphasizing peoplehood is a new regard for the State of Israel. It is the ultimate fulfillment of the 614th commandment. Nothing else Jews have done so fully sums up, expresses and symbolically projects the Jewish people's rejection of death, its return to life, its willingness to face the ambiguities of history and its insistence on remaining visibly, demonstrably, proudly Jewish. The State of Israel is the incomparable answer Jews have given to the incomparable evil of the Holocaust. Fackenheim therefore considers the State of Israel incomparably sacred and demands that every threat to its existence be fought with the utmost Jewish dedication.

This faith is easily misinterpreted. Fackenheim is *not* suggesting that the founding of the State of Israel was God's way of compensating the Jewish people for its suffering. He spurns any such suggestion as morally repugnant, as does Wiesel. He considers such compensation theodicies another effort to compromise the radically unique evil of the Holocaust. The two events have a bearing on one another but each must be understood in its own distinct terms.

Third, Fackenheim concludes that the test of good faith of gentiles who enter discussions on Jewish matters is their willingness to face up to the Holocaust. When people admit that they were, or are, prejudiced against Jews, one knows with whom one is dealing. Far more pernicious is the attitude of those who are so proud of their decency and good will that they are blind to their complicity in Jew-hate. We must never forget how the liberal democracies impeded the entry of refugees to their countries and later would not bomb death camps. Non-Jews must make plain their attitudes toward the Holocaust and the State of Israel if they would truly talk to Jews.

Christianity must stand under special scrutiny in this regard. The Nazis were not Christians in any normal sense but had it not been for centuries of Christian anti-Jewish teaching, the Holocaust could not have happened. Worse, the church as an institution did not oppose the Nazi degradation of Jews or later, when it became known, their extermination. Occasionally Christian behaved nobly, sometimes even giving their lives to help Jews or call attention to their plight. Most Christians quietly accepted what happened, thereby condoning and abetting absolute evil. Until Christians are willing to come to terms with the anti-semitism implicit in much of the church's teaching and confess the guilt the church bears for its sinfulness during the Holocaust, Jews cannot give any spiritual credence to Christianity or its leaders.

The Debate Over Fackenheim's Position

Much of the thinking which arose in response to Fackenheim's point of view has sought a way to restore the dead or absent God to post-Holocaust Judaism. Michael Wyschogrod's trenchant criticism of Fackenheim's arguments is an important case in point. Wyschogrod, himself a professor of philosophy at Baruch College, New York, points out the logical difficulty involved in inferring a positive command from a negative experience. Boldly paraphrasing the Jewish experience, he asks if stamp collectors were subject to a Holocaust, would the remaining stamp-collectors be required not to hand the tyrant posthumous victories? Would they be under a command to carry the special burdens which come from competent stamp-collecting?

Wyschogrod wants to focus our attention on the way a happening might become a commandment of overriding power and authority. In the Jewish case, he does not see why we must say that Jewish secularists heard a "commanding voice" from Auschwitz. Yiddishists, Hebraists, Zionists may now want to go on being Jewish for many of the same reasons as before the Holocaust. Only people who believe in a Transcendent Commander will divine in the decision to-be-a-Jew-despite-everything a response to an absolute, categorical command. The Torah-like imperative is a result of one's prior perspective. It does not stem from the historical experience of Auschwitz or the response to it. In themselves, they remain as ambiguous as all events. The notion that Jews are hearkening to an absolute command makes sense only when one begins with belief in a commanding God. We may not understand God's relation to evil but we nonetheless know what we must do in response to it—a human situation with many precedents in Jewish history.

Wyschogrod also rejects the notion that the Holocaust is a qualitatively unique event of evil. He can understand why Fackenheim is particularly concerned with the Holocaust and why, as against the many monstrous occurrences in recent history, a Jew would want to assert the special quality of Jewish fate. From an ethical point of view, that is, from the standpoint of universal human suffering, Wyschogrod does not see how Fackenheim can substantiate the moral individuality of the Holocaust.

I believe the argument can be carried a step further. Fackenheim's two efforts to validate the singularity of the Holocaust seem faulty to me. That no other people has been singled out for destruction, simply for existing rather than for what they did, seems incorrect. In the history of tribal and national antagonism, one people not infrequently proscribes the members of another people merely for not belonging to its kin.

Less easy to decide is the proper interpretation of the will of the Nazis who carried out the Holocaust. I do not mean to detract from either the perversity of the crime or from its unique significance for the Jewish people when I say that I do not find the charge of an unprecedented Nazi will to do evil convincing. The Germans often made what I consider irrational, because self-damaging, decisions in order to continue the Holocaust. I do not see that they did so to do evil as such. Rather, they obsessively pursued their murderous project because they believed their propaganda that the destruction of the Jews was more important than the possible defeat of the Reich. They persisted in their paranoid devotion to ridding the world of its major enemy. Their words and acts fully accord with this interpretation. Like others who have administered terror, they acted in dedicated pursuit of what they, with demonic misjudgment, saw as the greatest good. I despise what they did but my revulsion is insufficient reason to transform their acts into a uniquely qualitative evil which might in consequence thereby attain uniquely commanding power.

Greenberg's Radically Reinterpreted Orthodoxy

Irving Greenberg has approached the issue of the uniqueness of the Holocaust only indirectly. He insists that Auschwitz is the transforming religious experience of our time but he does not give it precedence over Sinai, as do Wiesel, Rubenstein and Fackenheim. He retains the major categories of classic Jewish faith but subjects them to radical reworking in terms of the Holocaust. His thinking is therefore dialectical, balancing the claims of Orthodoxy and Auschwitz one against the other.

Though Rubenstein asserts that traditional Judaism is no longer believable after Auschwitz, Greenberg finds no reason to explain why the Holocaust does not shatter rather than reshape his Orthodoxy. He only suggests that the contemporary traditional Jew believes in a modern fashion, on the basis of "moment faiths." Explicitly crediting Buber, Greenberg says there remain times when God is known and present, though there are others when one finds oneself in the cruel world of the Holocaust. In Greenberg's case, the occasions of validation still supply the context for coming to terms with the times of doubt and disbelief.

Additional ground for the assertion of a dynamic traditional Jewish faith may be found in Greenberg's vigorous, continually reiterated polemic against modernity. The first lesson which he would have Jews—and all others—learn from the Holocaust is that our wholehearted embrace of modernity was a major blunder. Western secular civilization has shown itself to be deeply demonic and capable of the most monstrous inhumanity. The form and operation of the Holocaust are the consummation of centuries of western religion, intellectuality, science and technology (a theme also dear to Rubenstein). For Jews to have given up their tradition for such spiritual trash, seems to Greenberg unutterably tragic and in need of thoroughgoing reversal. Somewhat like Fackenheim's argument that utter tragedy can be converted into energetic devotion, Greenberg hopes that convincing Jews to give up their dependency on western culture will lead them back to traditional observance. The logic of his case is even less compelling than Fackenheim's. Many Jews, like many other Americans, merely withdraw from all groups to concentrate on the one thing they know they are genuinely committed to, self-gratification.

Aspects of the New Belief and Duty

Greenberg agrees that we are in a post-secular time and that compelling moral affirmation can only be based on a relationship to God. He goes further, arguing that the establishment of the State of Israel validates continued faith in God. As Jewish tradition should have led us to expect, a redeeming act has "matched" the catastrophe. Almost all Jews consider the State of Israel central to their Jewishness and most believe it to be a balance for the horror of the Holocaust. These sentiments do not lead to belief in God by any large number of Jews, particularly the Israelis who remain resolutely secular. Were Greenberg's argument more than a statement of his personal faith, Fackenheim would not need to inveigh so against continuing the distinction between secular and religious Jews.

To revise his traditional faith in God, Greenberg utilizes models derived from Job and Lamentations. These justify, in ways quite familiar from liberal theologies, the *search* for faith against confidence in established doctrine and find argument with God a legitimate Jewish way of maintaining a relationship. Despite Rubenstein's strictures, Greenberg offers a defense of the Jewish people as God's suffering servant. Anti-semitism's eerie quality derives from its satanic theological basis. Because the Jews are a witness to God and testify that the world remains unredeemed, the nations hate them. On a practical level as well, the Jews are a likely target for whatever demonic impulses inhere in a culture. Jewish suffering is not therefore senseless but an active part of the Jewish people's service of God. A limit to such suffering must be invoked, for, as the Holocaust showed, "when the suffering is overwhelming, then the servant must be driven to yield to evil. . . . The redemptive nature of suffering must be in absolute tension with the dialectical reality that it must be fought, cut down, eliminated."

Positively, Greenberg maintains that after Auschwitz our central religious affirmation is the creation of life. By having and properly rearing a child, one shows a primal hopefulness and decisively rejects all that the death camps stood for. For Jews, whose numbers have been radically depleted, propagation is a primary obligation. Simultaneously, any cultural or religious activity which devalues the worth of human beings or any group among them, must be adjudged anathema. From there it is a simple step to the elimination of the secular-religious dichotomy. Anyone who desists from murder or exploitation or, better, who is dedicated to the care of people, must now be regarded as a God-fearer. With humanism now an acceptable piety, Greenberg can identify the State of Israel, despite its committed secularity, as a religious institution. Like Fackenheim, he sees it as the Jewish people's supreme, life-generating response to the Holocaust. He goes beyond Fackenheim by suggesting that in itself—the Holocaust aside—the founding and continuation of a Jewish state on the sacred land is numinous. It must become a generative premise for the construction of an adequate modern Jewish theology.

Berkovits' Argument for a Holocaust Theology of Faith

Eliezer Berkovits, also an Orthodox rabbi, has sought to do more than revise traditional faith as a result of the Holocaust. His new philosophy of rabbinic Judaism is still in process and I must therefore limit this presentation to his special contribution of the discussion of the Holocaust.

Berkovits cannot understand why so many thinkers insist that God was not to be found in the death camps. Many people who were there had the opposite experience. To be sure, a good number did lose their old beliefs and values but numerous others did not; some few even found faith there or later. For them, God was available and this knowledge enabled them to bear their suffering, often with nobility. If anything, the records indicate that in these dire circumstances traditional belief stood up better than modernist and liberal world views, which rather easily collapsed. The Jewish death-of-God theologians have simply ignored this data. Berkovits lays down the principle that those who were not there, but passed the murder era miles away in safety, should be most restrained in making dramatic, negative claims about its lessons.

Berkovits contends that our Holocaust theology has begun with the wrong premise. It has extrapolated from the experience of the disillusioned to create a vision of the cosmos which necessarily then had no God. Surely there is nothing new and certainly not revelatory in evil's producing a loss of faith. Disbelief is the common situation of secular humankind; under the blows of the Holocaust modernized unbelievers would naturally lose whatever faith lurked in their psyches. What naivete about the human condition has led our thinkers to suggest that negation ought to awaken our awe?

Should we not, however, be astonished by the many people who maintained their faith despite everything the Nazis did to them? Their spiritual accomplishment in our time, in their situation, is breathtaking. In this argument Berkovits does not indulge in pathos. He does not try to wring from sentimentality what intelligence and conscience deny. Rather, he reverently calls our attention to the common saints and everyday heroes of the ghettoes and death camps. Their unwavering devotion is awesome by any standards. And Berkovits demands to know why they should not be the foundation of our religious reconstruction after Auschwitz. If the commanding voice of Auschwitz calls us to maintain faith with the victims, they above all should be our models. We should remember them in the most significant possible way, by trying to emulate their faith. Should we find belief difficult—Berkovits admits understanding is utterly beyond us—we ought to give their affirmations more credence than our doubts and honor their memories by patiently awaiting the return of faith.

The full force of Berkovits' negative feelings as a result of the Holocaust is directed against Christianity. Fackenheim and Greenberg have felt a positive obligation to challenge Christians (who would speak to Jews) to acknowledge the depth of Christian religious anti-semitism and its role in making the Holocaust possible. They have made the repudiation of any vestige of Christian anti-Jewishness, the acknowledgment of Christian guilt for the Holocaust and an appreciation of the State of Israel to post-Auschwitz Jews, the conditions of contemporary Christian-Jewish dialogue. Berkovits denies that Jews and Christians can have any significant interchange whatsoever in our generation. The obloquy and persecution of pre-Hitler years should themselves be sufficient to prevent any self-respecting Jew from taking seriously present-day Christian declarations of a change of heart. After Auschwitz and the Christian silence during it and the subsequent threats to the State of Israel, how can any rational person take Christian declarations of good will as anything more than desperate efforts to bolster what is left of their decaying self-image? That some Christians still seek to convert Jews to their faith rouses him to fury. His cry, "All we want of Christians is that they keep their hands off us and our children!", must rank as one of the strongest rejections of interchange with Christians to appear before the English-reading public.

A *Limited God, the One Rational Religious Answer*

Rationalistically-minded Jews have not been impressed by any of these arguments for continued belief in God today. They do not see how thinking people can be asked to believe what they cannot understand. For them, reestablishing faith depends on finding a new conception of God, one which establishes value while making intelligible the occurrence of evils such as the Holocaust. (Rationalists cannot, in principle, accept the notion of the Holocaust as a radically unique act of evil since terming it unique excludes it from universal categories of explanation.)

The alternatives for a rational theodicy are limited. Thinkers after the Holocaust can hardly say that evil is unreal, and claim to be realistic. They might follow Rubenstein and deny that God is good, but that destroys the ultimate qualitative distinction between Nazis and Jews—an unacceptable position for those morally indignant at the Holocaust. That leaves only the possibility that God does not have sufficient power to stop all evil. Instead of being thought of as omnipotent, God should be conceived of as finite or limited. God cannot "do all things" as Job thought, and thus great evil sometimes occurs. With God's power limited, human moral action becomes all the more important if the world is to be redeemed.

Belief in a limited God is not without warrant in the Jewish tradition. The Bible unequivocally states that God granted the very first human beings the power to do or not do God's commands to them. The biblical authors thereby implied that they believed there were limits as to what God could, perhaps would, do. Various rabbinic statements and some of the ideas of Jewish philosophers and mystics similarly restrict the Divine power. None of the modern thinkers we have previously discussed, except Heschel, makes an unequivocal claim for God's omnipotence. Mordecai Kaplan, at the other extreme specifically, identifies God as referring only to the helping powers in nature, thus resolving by definition the classic problem of evil. A number of other pre-Holocaust thinkers taught that God was finite. Henry Slonimsky had elegantly described God as growing in history through human moral acts.

Hans Jonas' Construction of a Limited God

One intriguing outline of a finite God is that of Hans Jonas, who taught philosophy at the New School for Social Research with a particular concern for the philosophy of science. In his Ingersoll Lecture, "Immortality and the Modern Temper," Jonas describes a God in keeping with the naturalistic view that all causes must be internal to the world. Unlike Kaplan's God, who is entirely immanent in natural processes, Jonas suggests that God created the world but, once having ordered it and its values, God allowed it full independence. After creation, God is never a natural cause. But unlike the Deists' God who no longer is involved with the creation, this God, because of values, remains "concerned" with what happens. God's own future, so to speak, has become conditional upon what transpires in creation, particularly once human beings evolve who are free to determine its outcome by their action. Jonas' God may be said to be dependent on creation, as against biblical faith in which all created things depend on God. Jonas can also say that God "cares" what takes place in history for the future of values depends on it. In this context, metaphorical by contrast to Heschel's literalism, God suffers with every ethical defeat in human history.

When, then, the Nazis abuse the freedom natural evolution gave them, we cannot hold God responsible. That God did not act to stop the Holocaust, or did not take away the Nazi's freedom to do evil, or did not miraculously save the Jews, or did not manifest the Divine presence in some spectacular way in the death camps, is not irrational. A God who violates or vitiates human freedom is not the sort of God morally dedicated people would want the world to have. We are overwhelmed by what our people suffered but can take some consolation from knowing that God's own future was damaged by the

Nazi bestiality. We can also understand why Jews and others ought to respond to the Holocaust by fighting every vestige of Nazism or sign of its reappearance. Jonas' lecture does not develop the particular Jewish consequences of his idea of God but it could easily ground a defense of the State of Israel as a major agent of God's work in history.

For all their intellectual appeal, finite doctrines of God have been difficult to accept. In Jonas' case, the rationalistic appeal of limiting God is compromised by the inexplicable reversal of God's energy after creation. By having the creator God suddenly withdraw from nature, Jonas saves God from utter immanence while giving the cosmos independence and people freedom, yet establishing the transcendent authority of immanent values. Jonas himself is forced to admit that the expansion-contraction description of creation involves a mythic, not a rationalistic model of creation, specifically the Jewish notion of *tzimtzum*, God's self-concentration.

Substantively, too, finite theories of God undermine Jewish messianism. Can we still believe that the ideal will one day be made reality if we must depend on humankind to achieve it? After all, the Holocaust has taught us about the limited moral steadfastness of even good people: Should not those whose God has limited power to overcome evil join Rubenstein and despair of human history? Classic Judaism had faith in people because they were in covenant with God. What their righteousness could not accomplish, God's power would ultimately complete. Can any doctrine of hope today dispense with God's help even though we cannot explain just how God acts or why God's saving influence is seen only sporadically and after long delay?

Was It God We Had Lost Faith In?

Let me add a few further observations of my own on the death-of-God controversy. In retrospect, the decade-plus discussion taught us little about God we did not already know. For nearly a century Jewish modernists have given up their traditional beliefs out of respect for science and in response to Nietzsche's cultural arguments for atheism. Then, as our confidence in human capability became less absolute, our atheism dwindled to the agnosticism which, for some time, has been the nearly universal attitude of sophisticated Jews to God. Long before mid-century, there was little of God left to bury.

For modernized believers, as we have seen, modern Jewish thinkers had long since removed God far enough from the world to allow for the human ethical independence they all so highly prized. Even the notion of a finite God was widespread. From the early 1930's on, Mordecai Kaplan and Henry Slominsky had expounded it to their Conservative and Reform rabbinical school students. In my opinion, the Holocaust discussion has yielded only some variations of the well known modern arguments about God.

If so, why did our theological discussion of the Holocaust so agitate us?

I suggest that the Holocaust did undermine our true faith but the term *God* did not indicate what we believed in, only how important our underlying belief was. We can uncover our true concern by applying Ludwig Feuerbach's rule about theology, though in a way he never imagined. In the nineteenth century Feuerbach said that all our assertions about God are really about ourselves; they speak of our vision of humankind. He hoped then to convert supernatural religion, which no modern could accept, into a humanism that would then be believable. Since then, Feuerbach's insight has seemed the definitive refutation of religion, for what we claim to be saying about the reality called God can be called only a projection of human ideals.

But what if the central religious assertion of the mid-1960's was that God-is-dead? What if the religious implication of the Holocaust is that no good God rules the universe? Translated by Feuerbach's rule, these are statements about humankind. And that, I take it, was the utterly unsettling truth buried under the Holocaust talk about God: after Auschwitz we could no longer maintain our modernist faith in humankind.

For *that* was the operative religion of American Jews. We believed in the goodness of people and trusted that education and culture would guide them properly, while psychotherapy remedied their flaws. We counted on politics to bring the Messiah, with an assist from social science. We followed the commandments of self-realization and looked forward to perfecting humankind. Sitting in our homes, walking on the way, lying down and rising up, we spoke of human progress and put our faith in new projects. For us, humanity sat on God's old throne. The debate over Auschwitz gradually has made us acknowledge our covert religion and confess its untenability. And with that recognition death-of-God theology lost the vitality it had once displayed.

More Realism About People Leads to New Openness to God

We have not, of course, stopped talking about the religious implications of the Holocaust. Only for some years now the once fashionably radical calls for non-belief and the once shocking rabbinic admissions of atheism or agnosticism seem old-fashioned and irrelevant. It seems a triumph of illusion today to suggest we should still place our ultimate faith in humankind. The death of our faith in human omni-competence has been shatteringly confirmed by the continuing disillusionments of the past decade and a half. The 1970's made plain to our mounting disgust that nothing human beings have long been involved with remains untainted by moral failure. Our government is suspect, our economy exploitative, our ecology destructive, our families troubled and we ourselves conflicted to the point where avoiding depression is a major species of fulfillment. Humanity is no longer the answer but the problem.

Ironically, as we have become strong enough to face the loss of our old covert faith in ourselves, we have discovered that, despite everything, we probably are far less agnostic than we thought we were. When, in moral revulsion against the vulgarity of our society or in rejection of its temptations to paganize, we insist on living on another level of quality, we can be led to ask: Whence this stubborn devotion to high human value? For us, being Jewish is the likely source of our ethical stubbornness and our most likely resource for its perpetuation in a society indifferent or antithetical to moral excellence. When we insist that our values, for all that they are difficult to define or apply, are not arbitrary acts of our will or the accidents of our upbringing, but fundamental to the universe itself, we base our lives on a transcendent claim of quality laid on human beings, one that our society largely dismisses and to which contemporary rationality gives little credence. If we are determined not to lose our intuition of proper human dignity but to pursue it despite the burdens that quest will impose upon us, we are ready to join those other Jews who now searchingly inquire what being a Jew can mean to them (even as Christians are finding a way back to heartfelt Christian faith). Most Jews moving in this direction are satisfied by a return to the Jewish community, some institutional involvement of *havurah* face-to-face exploration, some study, some folk culture, some ritual, perhaps even some prayer. All these well-documented paths of activity comprise the new search for Jewish identity which has been the surprise and promise of the 1970's.

But if I am right that the central human experience of our generation has been the collapse of our humanistic faith and the loss of our old ground of values, then a choice confronts us. We may say with Rubenstein that the universe is, at best, neutral and order our lives accordingly. Or we may stubbornly insist that righteousness, not nothingness, is ultimately real and therefore properly worthy of our lives' devotion. Taking that latter stance, we are likely at some quiet or critical moment to ask about the root of this crucial belief. What is it, then, that we are trusting in? And more than likely we shall find ourselves realizing that we, in our modern way, are responding to the same commanding presence in the universe to which previous generations of Jews hearkened. In recovering our Jewish identity in depth, we find ourselves on new terms with what our tradition called God. The almost unbelievable, dialectical outcome of our attention to the Holocaust has been that a sizable minority in the Jewish community is now involved in exploring the dimensions of their personal relationship with God. Through mysticism or the study of texts, in liturgy or Jewish activism, some Jews are seeking to draw closer to what they dimly sense is the still living God of the universe. They do not claim to understand God or to explain God's erratic way in history. The Holocaust remains as disturbing as ever—if anything, more so, for the God on whom they base their lives is also the God of the six million. They only know that God is real and the Covenant continues, and they propose to build their lives on these commitments. Theirs is a fragmentary faith but in this empty era even a partial belief is a lot to have gained.

Can one believe when one does not understand? How can God now be present, and then, and often, terrifyingly absent? How could God, the God who grounds all values, not have done something, anything to stop the Holocaust, the antithesis of all value?

Why do the good suffer?

10

A Theology of
Modern Orthodoxy: Rabbi
Joseph B. Soloveitchik

UNTIL RECENTLY, modernity appeared to mandate the abandonment of traditional Jewish belief and practice. Jewish observance
conflicted with the rhythm and style of general society. Remaining
distinctive seemed foolish when non-Jews turned out to be humane
and western culture understood the universe far more comprehen-
sively and demonstrably than did Jewish faith. Modern Jewish
thought largely came from liberal Jews trying to give intellectual
expression to the balance of modernity and Jewishness most Jews
unself-consciously began to live.

The sociology of adaptation seemed so inexorable, some writers
speculated about the length of time it would take for Orthodox
Judaism to be reduced to a few European-oriented enclaves. In a
stunning reversal of all such predictions, the 1970's saw a revival of
American Orthodoxy that has made it a vigorous, powerful part
of our community life.

One reason for that change, not often remarked upon, was the
post-World War II immigration of Holocaust survivors to the United
States. Sizable numbers were observant Jews who spurned the notion
that they should compromise their Judaism to be more acceptable to

a gentile world. Their presence in the community encouraged those who all along had been fighting the creeping accommodation in American Orthodoxy, whose major symbolic battleground was the mixed seating of men and women at synagogue services.

Americanization of the Early Orthodox Immigrants

Sociological observers have repeatedly called attention to the unexpected phenomenon that revitalized Orthodoxy: not immigration but a new mood among native Americans. In their case, a thoroughgoing acculturation has not meant liberalizing belief and practice. Rather, their Orthodoxy stems from deliberate choice, the selection of a life style they believe will be best for them and their children.

One powerful motive for opting for Orthodoxy is the revulsion these American Jews have felt at western civilization. Where previous generations of modern Jews were eager to be fully accepted, many Jews today are repelled by its general amorality and want to be somewhat withdrawn from it. At its most intense, this leads some to immigrate to the State of Israel; at a somewhat lesser level, some few adopt a Hasidic or other European-oriented lifestyle in the United States.

Being a fully observant Jew commends itself as a good way of participating in general society yet remaining sufficiently different from it so as to maintain one's high sense of human values. At one time Conservative Judaism seemed to have worked out the proper balance between Jewish tradition and American adjustment; for many American Jews it still fulfills that role. But surprisingly, in recent years a good number of Jews have come to feel that it makes insufficient demands for Jewish discipline; that, despite its intentions, it has assimilated too much. Many who now propose to undertake living as Jews wish to do so in as authentic a fashion as they can, which to them means becoming Orthodox.

Authentic Living Seeks an Authentic Theory

Two other factors have influenced this develoment. One is the growing number of graduates of Jewish all-day schools. They have the
learning and skills without which traditional Jewish living might
seem burdensome and impractical. Already as children they were
often exposed to Jewish role models whose life style they can now
adapt to their own temperaments.

The other factor affecting the new traditionalism is the flowering
of what has been termed "modern Orthodoxy," the fusion of classic
halachic Judaism and American culture exemplified best by the
graduates and program of Yeshiva University in New York. Its steadfast commitment to Torah does not equate authenticity with a return
to the ghetto and a disdain for western civilization's possible enrich-
ment of Judaism. The modern Orthodoxy which came to maturity in
the 1960's established a pattern of American Jewish living which did
not compromise with central Jewish disciplines (e.g., *mikvah*, the
ritual bath required of women) yet allowed for appropriate modern
activities (e.g., *yeshivah* sports activities).

Today Orthodoxy is an appealing option for Jews seeking to base
their lives on Judaism. That provides the communal base for the
search for a theology of Jewish Orthodoxy. The structure of recent
Jewish thought, mediation between Judaism and modernity, thus
remains unaltered in modern Orthodoxy. Its resulting Jewish theology would be of more than sectarian Jewish interest for it speaks to
the problem of all inquiring Jews.

An Orthodox Jewish theology would likely have one uncommon
characteristic. Most Jewish thinkers have been distinguished by their
competence in contemporary philosophy or theology. Their understanding of Judaism has been based largely on *aggadah*, the nonlegal
rabbinic material, or on medieval Jewish philosophy. Yet. as Franz
Rosenzweig argued in his memorable essay on the proper methodology of Jewish theology, "Apologetic Thinking," all such speculation
has little Jewish validity. Insofar as there was authority in the Jewish
religion over the centuries, it was provided by the *halachah*, the law

which regulated the conduct of the autonomous Jewish community. To come as close as possible to what Jews "had to believe," one ought to explicate the theology implicit in the *halachah*. Rosenzweig and later thinkers left this goal unattained and thus, seemingly unattainable. Philosophers who could make their way through the swirling currents of the law seemed unable to chart its movements in terms of comprehensive religious concepts, while those who could devise an acceptable structure of modern religious thought generally did not know "the small letters" in which the development of Jewish legal thinking must be traced.

The Rav of the Modern Orthodox Rabbinate

All this has made the thought of Rabbi Joseph B. Soloveitchik of unusual interest. As the leading spirit of the Rabbi Isaac Elchanan Theological Seminary of Yeshiva University and as Chairman of the Halachah Commission of the Rabbinical Council of America (Orthodox), his competence to describe Judaism out of its legal tradition is beyond question. His broad-ranging cultural concerns are amply attested in his lectures over the years, as is his mastery of ancient and modern philosophy. (He won a doctorate in philosophy in 1931 at the University of Berlin with a dissertation on Hermann Cohen's theory of knowledge.)

What has thus far appeared of Rabbi Soloveitchik's theology is not easily characterized as a theology of the *halachah*. Some of his writings are directly based on legal materials, notably the accounts of his several annual *shiurim*, his public legal lectures, which focus on specific texts in the Talmud and Maimonides' code, the Mishneh Torah. He gives these an existentialist interpretation. In his general essays, the development of the theme may suddenly include an illustration drawn from the *halachah*. Such mediation of the western and Jewish traditions is unprecedented. Philosophical readers find concepts illuminated in an unexpected way by examples from a most uncommon source, while the *halachicly* sophisticated reader is exposed to a series of *hidushim*, novel interpretations, based on an existentialistic hermeneutic without parallel in Jewish legal literature.

Despite this interplay of illustration, the relation of the *halachah* to the structure and content of Rabbi Soloveitchik's philosophy is not clear. Occasionally he will use such language as, "the Halacha thinks" or "the Halachic idea of." Then the reader, conscious of the author's stature, may perceive a claim that the thought presented is indeed a central element of "the" theology of the *halachah*. The rest of Rabbi Soloveitchik's method throws this supposition in doubt. He never seeks to establish his generalizations by presenting many citations, or by tracing the motif through the ramified Jewish legal literature, or by considering and refuting apparently contrary legal materials. He does not seek to make his case with critical readers but, as one of the master teachers of the generation, he tellingly explicates it. He elaborates a philosophic anthropology (which inevitably involves God) and uses the *halachah* to clarify and amplify it—or vice versa—but does not show us how necessary or sufficient is the connection of the one body of thought with the other.

Putting Fragments Into a Whole

This brief introduction has already plunged us into the thicket of problems involved in presenting Rabbi Soloveitchik's thinking. Analyzing these difficulties will itself help us understand his unique position among modern Jewish thinkers.

Only recently have a substantial number of papers by Rabbi Soloveitchik been published. I have been present when he has lectured by utilizing a portion of a sizable manuscript, but no book by him has appeared. We must make our judgment of his ideas based on a series of disparate writings whose relationship to one another is not clear. The overview of his thinking presented here is, therefore, necessarily provisional.

The problem of the paucity and diversity of sources highlights the dramatic shift in emphasis, if not in thought, from his earliest major publication and the next substantial essays. For nearly twenty-five years those who were not Rabbi Soloveitchik's students knew of his extraordinary intellect through one long paper, *"Ish Hahalachah"* (Halachic Man), published in 1944. In phenomenological fashion, the essay exposed the inner life of the person whose religiosity was channeled and exalted through Jewish law. The author continually contrasted this to the spirituality of those whose lives were centered on religious experience in the subjective, affective sense of the term. The difference between them was far more basic than a simple distinction between intellect and emotion. Thus, he carefully describes how the intellectuality of the *halachic* personality has a passional side, enabling it to rise to the level of ecstasy. Both types are, of course, authentically present in Judaism, but Rabbi Soloveitchik extols the virtues of the *halachic* soul and derogates the spiritual personality.

Most readers thought that Rabbi Soloveitchik had restated the *mitnagdic*, anti-Hasidic, tradition of Eastern Europe and wanted intellect, as utilized in *halachic* reasoning and living, to be the central feature of modern Jewish life. When his later papers appeared, most significantly the lengthy analysis entitled, "The Lonely Man of Faith," it became clear that the early impression was wrong. While an overarching intellectuality is manifest in these later publications, they are concerned with facing the conflicted human situation depicted by modern existentialism, not arguing for a latter-day rationalism. For some years now this pattern has continued and the most recent essays have been the most subjective and personalistic he has given us. We cannot now know if there have been major shifts in his thought over these four decades or whether the progress of his thought has come about by slow evolution.

Problems of Scope and Style

Even Rabbi Soloveitchik's short papers are not easy to contain in a conceptual scheme. He seems to approach each particular topic from an all-embracing conceptuality but this is only hinted at, not yet publicly elucidated. With its full context unknown, any given paper, for all that it communicates, is not fully understandable. Moreover, a relatively brief paper will have a disconcertingly long reach. Rabbi Soloveitchik will examine various of the conflicts of the soul or of the Jewish people, explicating the dialectic which keeps us in tension and probing how *halachah* helps us live with them. His writing is therefore highly subtle and abstract. An unwary reader may easily lose the path of a careful argument in the course of one of his speculative flights. His breadth of allusion is also extraordinarily broad, including, for example, early Greek philosophers, Church fathers, marginal German philosophers and modern playwrights. (Though his references are apt he rarely cites or treats these people in any detail.) His utilization of all the genres of Jewish literature is masterful and his sensitivity to biblical texts is utterly uncommon for one whose reputation rests on his interpretations of Jewish law.

These diverse intellectual concerns are expressed in a style which is as distinct as the thought it seeks to convey and enhance. With cognition subordinated to the human being as an emotional, conflicted, aspiring creature, Rabbi Soloveitchik's writing is charged with sensibility, not infrequently becoming passionate. These feeling tones are central to the message he wishes to impart. They never lead him to the stylistic extravagances of Abraham Heschel, who made artful wordplay a major instrument of his effort to bring the reader to an insight that language cannot convey. Soloveitchik agrees that much of our faith and our selfhood is ineffable, but who we are and what we believe can substantially be comprehended by intellect and expressed in words. He does not write in oracular, epigrammatic fashion as did Buber in *I and Thou*. He has greater confidence in human reason than Buber does and the substantial length of some of his papers indicates his hope that additional description or allusion may communicate the elusive personal point he is trying to make.

A Theology of Alienated Jewish Existence

Rabbi Soloveitchik's published papers center on the human condition. They explore what it means to be a person in relation to God (less so to the people of Israel) as Jewish tradition understands it. Their overriding concern is to delineate and accept the contradictions involved in being human and illustrate how the *halachah* understands and responds to our humanity. In specific theme—loneliness, anxiety, conflict—as in general outline, this is philosophic existentialism. With all due regard for the radical religious differences between them, Rabbi Soloveitchik's philosophical content and method is more like Sören Kierkegaard than Hermann Cohen.

One way of comprehending Rabbi Soloveitchik's distance from rationalism is to observe how, consciously or unconsciously, he utilizes and transforms the method of "correlation" which the Marburg Neo-Kantian had developed. Cohen argued that all statements about God should simultaneously be statements about humankind and vice versa, because we know God only through human reason and rational human beings require an idea of God to attain an integrated world view. Paul Tillich, the great modern Protestant theologian, applied Cohen's method but revised it for use in an existentialist framework. Tillich called for rationality, that is, technical existentialist philosophy, to elucidate the important questions raised by human existence. But reason, which has a limited understanding of existence, was incompetent to answer them properly. Instead, the theologian would draw on revelation to respond to them. For Tillich, theology meant correlating Christian revelation's answers to the questions intellect asked about existence.

Emil Fackenheim, before his work became Holocaust-oriented,

declared that this was the most appropriate framework for creating a modern Jewish theology. He proposed to carry out this program by drawing on the liberal Jewish understanding of revelation. Rabbi Soloveitchik retains more respect for human reason than does the usual philosophic existentialist. He accepts science to the point of labeling as allegory the references in the blessing over the new moon to the ultimate perfection of its "blemish" (the Midrash says it was nized as the only legitimate source of answers. Indeed, exposing another "face" of the Torah is traditionally a meritorious achievement. The existentialist questions only provide Rabbi Soloveitchik with a new hermeneutic level on which to demonstrate the Torah's infinite validity.

Major Currents in Soloveitchik's Thinking

Three major intellectual approaches characterize the available papers. The first of these is the acceptance of Kant's dichotomy between the mathematical-scientific world, characterized by causality, and the ethical experience of freedom and self-consciousness. Rabbi Soloveitchik retains more respect for human reason than does the usual philosophic existentialist. He accepts science to the point of labeling as allegory the references in the blessing over the new moon to the ultimate perfection of its "blemish" (the midrash says it was originally the same size as the sun). He does not believe that people whose lives are dominated by a rationalisitc mentality are thereby unable to find God—another difference from Martin Buber who felt God could not be met in I-It relations to the world. Rabbi Soloveitchik understands the Jewish teaching that the creation is good to mean that nature as such is not Godless and necessarily profane.

As a consequence of his strong sense of the distinction between the objective-scientific aspect of human existence and its personal experiential side, much of Rabbis Soloveitchik's writing is dialectical. He sees division and tension in every area of human existence. His thought seems unable to find a resting place. He constantly shuttles from one facet of human experience to another, showing the contrast between them and indicating the severe conflicts we feel as a result.

This sensitivity to our dynamic subjectivity separates him from the Jewish Neo-Kantians. Moreover, while he makes some references to the ethical aspect of being a person, that category is not so central to his discussion of the human condition as it is to the Kantians. From the material available, I cannot tell whether he would argue for the reality of an autonomous moral law for all rational beings (Kant and Cohen) as contrasted to a revealed one (Maimonides, in the name of Jewish tradition). Where Kant and his reviewers considered it axiomatic that the universe was rational, Rabbi Soloveitchik does not see the world and our situation in it as fundamentally comprehensible. Precisely because we are thinking ethical beings, alienation is the essential state of personal self-consciousness.

Rabbi Soloveitchik describes many of the dimensions of this alienation and shows how Judaism responds to it without, in this world, ever overcoming it. Thus, he builds his description of human religiosity on the human experience of loneliness. His mentors in this regard, as he notes already in the 1944 essay, were Kierkegaard and Ibsen, but more especially, Scheler and Heidegger. Since almost no one in the Jewish community then was concerned with such thinkers, his thought was little understood and his philosophic disciples were few indeed. Even today, despite a new openness to theology among Jews, one cannot say that there are many cognitively prepared to follow Rabbi Soloveitchik in his enterprise.

Thinking by Means of Essential Types

These two conceptual motifs—dichotomy and dialectic—are shaped and controlled by the notion of typology. Rabbi Soloveitchik's writing deals only with ideal types. He does not treat things as they are nor does he abstract certain norms from things. He deals rather with pure forms of existence. These are never found in the world, for all historic phenomena are necessarily imperfect manifestations of the

ideal patterns. By elucidating these ideal types we can hope to understand the reality in which we are immersed. Rabbi Soloveitchik's
utilization of the typological method is fully self-conscious and he
acknowledges being influenced in this regard by Eduard Spranger,
whose work *Lifeforms*, popularized typology in Germany in the early
1920's.

The typological approach to reality can confuse the unsophisti-
cated reader. Most Jewish thinkers work from historical reality and
seek to demonstrate a truth or persuade the reader of an interpretation concerning it. Thus, religious existentialists have argued from
the emptiness of the human situation to the necessity of a choice for
or against God, insisting that in the ultimate decision we will not opt
for meaninglessness. Because Rabbi Soloveitchik often moves
quickly from his pure, theoretical types to the real situation of
people, he may incorrectly be understood to be engaged in this sort
of argument. In fact, he does not seek to move skeptics to faith or to
give convincing answers to those troubled by doubt. He only explains; he makes no direct effort to convert. He speaks as a man of
faith about his faith, not about the reasons why those who stand at its
periphery should accept it. Typology serves him as a means of inter-
preting the Bible or the *halachah*. Where others see only story,
morals or practice, he detects essential truths about the human condition. He is the great elucidator of traditional Judaism's implicit
teaching about ideal human types. For one who believes that God
has given the Torah and commanded us to search out its meaning,
that would seem an appropriate form for Jewish theological activity
to take.

His method is often also more strictly phenomenological. He describes, in as rational and communicable a fashion as possible, his
experience as a human being and believing Jew. He makes no direct
claim that everyone must see what he sees or that his is the only true
understanding. He only tells us about the religious life, his life—but
surely in the hope that the cogency and insight of the picture he has
drawn will move us to recognize it is true of us as well.

The Basic Split in Human Nature

Rabbi Soloveitchik discerns a fundamental dualism in human nature which he explicates in terms of a typology he detects in the creation stories. The Adam of one of these accounts is man the maker, controller, and user. Blessed by God with intelligence, he strives to conquer the earth and use it for his good. In this labor he achieves the dignity which lifts him above the level of the brute and makes him truly human. He is thus a social being, for community is useful in difficult projects and it provides for the exchange by which he can express his accomplishments. Though he can set moral norms for himself and experience aesthetic creativity, these do not bring him ultimate satisfaction. He knows his limits, so that, even in the modern situation, he comes looking for God. The trouble is that he insists on understanding God in his own manipulative terms. That is a contradiction which cannot be overcome and which sets up his conflict with the Adam of the second account of creation.

This pure type is of another orientation. He is submissive for he knows himself to be the servant of God. He is less concerned with creating his own world than with accepting it as God has made it, for he sees God and hears God's command in every aspect of it. In this intimate relationship with God he comes to know himself as an individual and recognizes his uniqueness. So to speak, this gives him his true being and is therefore the most important reality of his life. Yet it is inexpressible, lying beyond all cognition or verbalization. So too, personal verification is a matter of utter isolation, for he can never fully share his certainty with anyone or communicate it to another. Graciously, God provides a setting, covenant, in which he can ease his loneliness. God, "He," becomes the link through which an "I" and a "Thou" can confront each other. Every genuine community of faith exhibits this tripartite relationship. Only there does the man of faith find companionship and community, though never the overcoming of his ontic singleness.

A contrast with Martin Buber is instructive. Buber had said that while the partners in an encounter maintain their individuality, their isolation is overcome. The one is fully known by the other, which gives the I-Thou relationship its fulfilling quality. Indeed, one does not exist in full selfhood outside such encounters. Rabbi Soloveit-chik apparently takes a more atomistic, individualistic view of the self. Though he learns much from Buber about relatedness, he in-sists that isolation and loneliness are so basic to personhood they cannot be overcome, even momentarily.

Since Adam the first and Adam the second are ideal types, it should not surprise us that Rabbi Soloveitchik believes people actu-ally must live in both realms. Religion suffers today because Adam the first is so dominant culturally that only his manipulative way of thinking is acceptable. We are interested in, even needful of, religion but we then insist that it be limited to cognitive, controllable struc-tures. Anyone in whose soul Adam the second becomes preeminent will feel an extra measure of loneliness in contemporary society. Most people spurn the truth on which Adam the second's faithful existence is grounded. These sensitive spirits are driven back upon themselves socially even as they have always been existentially, and thus must live in two distinct dimensions of alienation.

How Shall We Evaluate Our Situation?

A major difference between Christian and Jewish existentialism emerges at this point. Christian theologians identify contemporary alienation with "the fall" of humankind. People need to be saved from their split and struggling condition. With inner division built into their humanhood, people cannot save themselves. Only God can redeem them—and, Christianity teaches, God has, through the Christ, belief in whom brings people to "new being," that is, a healing of the inner split which prevents them from being fully human.

Judaism apprizes the human situation far more positively. People are an integral element of creation. And the Torah characterizes this creation not as potentially good, but as actually very good. Rabbi Soloveitchik makes a powerful case for alienation being the source of human creativity. "Man is a great and creative being because he is torn by conflict and is always in a state of ontological tenseness and perplexity." Rabbi Soloveitchik maintains that people who refuse to utilize their capacities to relate to the world about them live in existential slavery. As troubled as our situation is, only in accepting it and bringing the resources of our spirit to bear on it do we become true persons. The greatness of the self lies in not denying either the conflicted or the creative aspect of our being but in our ability to integrate ourselves ever more fully as persons. He sees the *halachah* designed to keep the warring parts of our being in proper balance with one another so that we are not defeated in this unrelenting inner struggle.

By contrast to Christianity, Judaism may be called optimistic. It does not denigrate the human situation, despite its realism about our embattled nature. It requires no miraculous act of God to make it possible for us to be the persons we were created to be. Our condition is trying but it can be noble. In addition to the spiritual power God put within each of us, God gave us the Torah. It enables people, through human action, to fulfill the best in them.

This positive view, however, is not so rosy-hued as to assert that a complete resolution of our conflicts can be reached in our lifetime. Our struggle inheres in the human condition and any momentary victory is quickly succeeded by renewed tension. These teachings lay down a personal basis for interpretations of the doctrines of the Messiah, of redemption and of the life of the world to come, but Rabbi Soloveitchik has not yet published on these eschatological matters.

The careful student of modern Jewish thought will see in Rabbi Soloveitchik's positive approach to human alienation an existentialist transformation of Hermann Cohen's ethical rationalism. Both systems praise the creative possibilities life provides to human reason; both see a moral-personal task laid upon us for our human good;

both define accepting that challenge as our unique human duty and glory; both insist it can be accomplished only in part but stretches out infintely before us; and both profess that only in God's End Time will humankind attain true being rather than exist in becoming.

Some Consequences of our Conflicted Selfhood

The divided self provides the context for one of Rabbi Soloveitchik's discussion of the problem of evil. In a not unfamiliar way, he describes people as having two fundamental identities, the one conferred by destiny, the other arising out of relationship. The former type relies on cognitive efforts to comprehend a world it structures by cause and effect. By definition, such a person's search for a theodicy must end in despair, since only a fully rational solution would be acceptable. The second type of person breaks through notions of natural order to become a free, creative subject, "a partner of God in the work of creation." Loving God, one does not raise metaphysical questions but accepts what comes as God's beneficently ordained challenge. One only asks of God, "What is required of me?" Of course, real people are necessarily mixtures of both types. In the first mode, we can never be satisfied with theologies of suffering and must continually create better ones. As people of faith, we live content with God and unconcerned about answers. Perhaps this explains why Rabbi Soloveitchik has not written directly about the Holocaust.

He utilizes the same dichotomy in explaining the two varieties of ethics which vie for our allegiance. The one derives from what may be termed our "cosmic consciousness," our sense of the unlimited opportunities before us. On the simplest level, we encounter it in our geographic mobility: we might go and live anywhere. More expansively, our intellectual and emotional potentialities seem to make us creatures of universal proportions. Our "origin-consciousness" is of another sort altogether. We know how limited we are. Born into a given time, rooted deeply in a certain place, habituated to a specific culture, we feel quite insignificant. The great world about us seems more than we can cope with. In the one mood we create philosophic ethics and glory in the challenge of our responsibilities. We seek success in life and mastery over ourselves and our situation. In the other mood, we practice the ethics of withdrawal. Retreat and resignation appear to be the best means of retaining our integrity.

Once again, neither mode is the only proper or true one. Both occur in any authentic human existence. Real people must utilize the ethics of activism and passivity, avoiding an exclusivity which contradicts their divided nature. And again, the *halachah* helps us to achieve a proper balance between them.

The Shifting Typological Structures

Rabbi Soloveitchik sometimes replaces this two-fold understanding of the human being by analyses which utilize three or more aspects of the self. Thus, in arguing against Jewish-Christian theological dialogue, he speaks of three separate, progressive levels of humanhood. As in the typology of the two Adams, he derives these from the biblical account of creation. The earliest stage of humanhood is natural and hedonic, in which creatures are so much at home in the universe that they do not even see it as task or opportunity. In the second phase, they are conscious of nature confronting them, and reach out to tame it with their cognitive and normative talents. Should they grow further, they confront other persons as subjects and not merely as other creatures. Despite the joys of companionship, they discover they cannot overcome the barrier that separates one true self from another. In this three-stage typology, a new level, the hedonic, has been introduced into the anthropology. Since the author connects it with much modern conduct, it would be of great interest to know its relation to the scheme of the two Adams. Then too, the third type differs somewhat from the description of Adam the second, further complicating our difficulties in integrating Rabbi Soloveitchik's views.

A somewhat similar tripartite pattern appears when Rabbi Solovei-tchik discusses the levels of human relationship to God. At their most basic, people come to God in an oscillation of trust and dread, passive before nature and resigned to its laws. They relate to God essentially in dependency. Many people rise beyond this to a rela-tionship of love and fear of God. They are conscious of God's law and responsive to it. They serve God not without a certain sense of coercion but mainly out of an awareness that the law is God's good gift whose observance brings one reward. At its best, this religiosity aims at the imitation of God. For on the third level, that of desire and clinging, every element of compulsion disappears. People serve God out of complete freedom, their will fully identified with that of God.

These three phases of piety do not completely correlate with the previous tripartite scheme, even allowing for the fact that any analysis of religiosity must be far more subjective than one made of ethical motives. Whatever the case here, Rabbi Soloveitchik does not make our task of comprehending him very easy, for elsewhere he refers to four aspects of "the total existential experience—the aesthetic-hedonic, the emotional, the intellectual, the moral-religious . . .". Our desire to have a coherent understanding of Rabbi Soloveitchik's anthropology must therefore await his further elucidation.

Human Beings Are Also Social Beings

Though Rabbi Soloveitchik gives to the individual a central place in his thought, he rejects radical individualism and strongly affirms social existence. Though he has only marginally aluded to his social theory, some of its principles can be set forth. These derive consis-tently from his interpretation of the two Adams. One form of social organization reflects the human needs to organize and use. We organize ourselves in terms of ethical norms and human responsibility. Another form results from the more directly personal aspect of our humanhood. We create covenantal association when we reach out to other people in freedom, accept them as persons, and recognize God as the third partner in our fellowship.

One cannot identify one or another historic religious community with the ideal, covenantal community of faith. All religions necessarily mix the two ideal modes of human existence, the natural and the covenantal. Only unreflective souls can expect that participating in a given religious institution will assure one of the covenantal experience which assuages existential loneliness. Again, Rabbi Soloveitchik insists on a sharp, conceptual distinction between pure types and historical reality.

He also uses this bipolar analysis to describe the people of Israel. He declares that God made two distinct covenants with Israel, one in Egypt and another at Mt. Sinai. He terms them, respectively, a covenant of destiny and a covenant of relationship. The former describes Jewishness as the situation into which one is born, thus linking one with others in a common past, common suffering, and a common responsibility. The latter covenant predicates Jewish identity as a matter of choice; the community may ignore or freely fulfill the Torah.

For Rabbi Soloveitchik, being a Jew is not merely a matter of fate, a less than human situation, but neither is it only a matter of choice, for that might permit one faithless generation to end four thousand years of steadfast service. Since no person is complete in solitariness, a Jew must move beyond individuality to participate in the Jewish community. Human existence has ineluctable structure. "The individual is bound to his nation by the bonds of fate and the ties of its unique national designation." He can ascribe metaphysical reality to *Knesset Yisreal*—the Jewish people as ideal—predicating its existence as independent of the aggregation of the wills of individual Jews. Speaking of the Land of Israel, he says it was "given to the community as an independent entity, as a distinct juridic metaphysical person."

Contrast between Halachic and Experiential Piety

True communities of faith may best be distinguished from one another (though, theoretically, not evaluated) in terms of the sort of character they seek to include in their participants. Rabbi Soloveitchik carefully distinguishes the *halachic* response to the sacred from the type of piety found in more subjective forms of religiosity. In personalistic religiosity, faithfulness can be fulfilled in withdrawal from life. Its devotees see piety as a sanctuary from the difficulties of existence.

Rabbi Soloveitchik, refusing to deny the existential torment of the two Adams, cannot accept peace of mind as the goal of genuine religion. Observing the *halachah* can bring us much personal certainty and assurance but the law provides neither a magical resolution of our ontological problems nor an escape from them. Rather, the *halachah* gives proper balance to the inner tension of the two Adams. Its specification requires that Adam the second express his intimately felt relationship with God in deeds done in the objective order of existence. It also frustrates the designs of Adam the first, who is delighted with an objective religious realm he can use to aggrandize his self-image. The *halachah* continually reminds him that he is serving the One God of all creation. All his religious accomplishments are as nothing, for what does the creature not owe its Creator?

One cannot help but see Rabbi Soloveitchik taking great pains here to dissociate his thought from the common Protestant existentialism. Much of his attack on piety as an inner experience seems an implicit polemic against Christianity, if, as is easy, one takes the "religious" personality as the Christian *par excellence* and the *halachic* figure as the Jew. Yet that easy identification will not do. Rabbi Soloveitchik specifically indicates that he is speaking of pure types and that there are other types of Jews than "*halachic* man." Rabbi Soloveitchik also speaks quite favorably about the mystic personality and uses many citations from the literature of Chabad Hasidism to illustrate the nature and virtue of that type. At the same time he

obviously believes *"halachic* man" is the superior type of Jew. Indeed, the essay *"Ish Hahalachah"* may be read as an anti-Hasidic
tract which seeks to show, by a phenomenology of *mitnagdic* intellectuality, that legalistic rationality contains all the spiritual and
emotional power of Hasidism but manages to correct its subjective
excesses.

Toward a Rational Ground for Jewish Law

There are some hints in Rabbi Soloveitchik's writing of what may,
with some liberties, be called his philosophic validation of the
halachah. By that I do not mean an effort to argue for its divine
origins or establish its worth in general human terms. Such apologetics are foreign to his purpose. To borrow and reapply Heschel's
happy phrase, Rabbi Soloveitchik believes in God's gift of the Torah
to the people of Israel as an "ontological presupposition." One does
not argue one's ultimate premises.

But Rabbi Soloveitchik does make an implicit response to those
existentialists who insist that we are not truly human unless we can
exercise personal autonomy. We can best appreciate his response to
such a liberalistic view of the self by considering the strategy the
Protestant theologian Paul Tillich created to meet this problem. To
people who value *auto*nomy, God's law appears to be imposed on
the free self and hence morally unacceptable—what Kant called
*hetero*nomy. For God's law to be acceptable to one whose dignity is
tied to personal decision, it must be shown to be the fulfillment of
the self and its freedom. This is possible, Tillich opined, precisely
because God is the source of our being. God's law cannot be alien to
us but is, in fact, our completion—*theo*nomy fulfills *auto*nomy.

In a number of places Rabbi Soloveitchik identifies the *halachah*
as God's theonomic completion of our personal freedom. In commenting on the rabbinic comment that an embryo knows the entire
Torah, he says: "by learning Torah man returns to his own self, man

finds himself, and advances to a charted, illuminated and speaking I-existence. Once he finds himself, he finds redemption." He explicitly offers this sort of argument in clarifying what he considers the highest form of relationship to God. Then, "One lives according to the Torah and commandments with great joy. One desires to do the will of God as if the will of the Infinite One (*En Sof*) was also the will of the finite person. The wonder of the identification of wills, we see in the third stage." Obviously, the communion of purpose is possible for an authentic human being because one's personal will is perfected in the Divine will.

Then why does *halachah* occasionally demand acts we do not understand and which, on our own, we would not legislate? Rabbi Soloveitchik answers by reference to the dialectic of the self. One aspect of human existence, we must remember, seeks acceptance and surrender. "Precisely because of the supremacy of the intellect in human life, the Torah requires, at times, the suspension of the authority logos. Man defeats himself by accepting norms that the intellect cannot assimilate into its normative system. The Judaic concept of *hok* [the inexplicable precept] represents human surrender and human defeat."

Problems of Typological Thinking

Rabbi Soloveitchik's unique contribution to the field of modern Jewish thought is not without its critics.

Regardless of one's position on Orthodox Judaism, the substance of his thought, the use of typology as a conceptual tool always raises difficulties for thoughtful readers. Typologies may illuminate, but it is never clear whence the types arise; why these and not others are selected; how the types used for various situations relate to one another; and what gives the total universe of types its integrity. A Christian might well ask, if the *ish hahalachah* is a pure type, must one be a Jew to be an *ish hahalachah*? If so, why do Jews have a separate ideal type? Moreover, not only are types usually universal, many of the characteristics of *halachic* man could easily be applied to personality types in other religions. In Roman Catholicism, one may point to the Jesuits, whose emphasis on intellectuality and observance is akin to *halachic* piety. If acceptable, this interpretation would change the way most Jews read Rabbi Soloveitchik's most famous essay—though he is not to blame for their conversion of typologies into value judgments or authorizations for Jewish practice.

The problem of applying a typology to reality is particularly difficult. Rabbi Soloveitchik used a tripartite analysis of the human situation to argue that Jews might join with Christians in working for common social welfare concerns. Level two, the cognitive-normative level, where these are worked out, is one where all mature people can meet. But the progress to level three, that of true faith, reduces us to utter individuality. Though we may then join in covenantal association with others of similar faith, our basic sense of certainty and the content of our belief remains ultimately incommunicable. Therefore, Rabbi Soloveitchik argues, Jews and Christians should not, because they cannot, discuss theology. But when is direct extrapolation from the realm of ideal types to the real mixed human situation proper and when is it not? To be sure, people have incredible difficulty in communicating with one another about their deepest beliefs, yet Rabbi Soloveitchik's own success in clarifying the nature of the life of faith belies the absolute futility of such efforts by others. Moreover, applied rigidly, this position would prevent our accepting converts to Judaism, an uncommon position in the *halachah*, since conversion involves our deepest beliefs.

The Virtues of Typology for Orthodoxy

If existentialist Jewish theologies suffer from their inability to mandate structured Jewish action, typological theology will not remedy the fault. The movement from pure types to our mixed reality is always open to ambiguity. Knowing that the ideal pattern of human existence must include appropriate authority does not logically lead to the content of that authority, to what a real person must do. Why should one be accepting rather than creative in the face of a *hok*, an inexplicable precept? Rabbi Soloveitchik is content with a typological framework for his thought because he does not require theology to authorize action. That matter is already settled in his faith. He can know—though this is neither as simple nor as free of anxiety as it often seems to the non-Orthodox—what God wants him to do. His theology follows upon that reality. It does not presume to substantiate it. In the writings to date, Rabbi Soloveitchik seeks only to illumine the meaning of believing Jewish existence by exposing its universal human aspects.

Still, typology has a great virtue. It enables a believer to bring a cognitive pattern to bear on what one knows but simultaneously confesses cannot properly be expressed. Where Heschel uses style, shock, and the inversion of questions to awaken and evoke, Rabbi Soloveitchik utilizes typology and phenomenology to expose something of the depth of his faith. He is therefore in closer communication with the thoughtful, but uncommitted inquirer than is Heschel. Though his types hover in some abstract realm transcending reality, they provide cognitive structures for understanding the amorphous arena of faith. Occasionally, too, they are quite compelling when they cast new light on the concrete situations in which people find themselves. For a moment the life of faith as seen by faith stands open.

Typological theology can be particularly persuasive today. Modern intellectuality no longer receives automatic credence when it disagrees with Jewish tradition. Participation in modernity no longer implies the rejection of Orthodoxy. The quality of life engendered by contemporary society seems inferior to that nurtured by traditional Judaism, as influenced by the Emancipation. Many modern Jews consider that a sufficient reason for a return to a more thoroughgoing commitment to Orthodox Judaism. The theological awareness underlying that socially determined attitude is then easy to state and accept. A good God would not leave humankind bereft and unguided. Jewish life and history confirm what Jewish faith has proclaimed: God gave Israel the Torah and those who live by its laws are sanctified and sanctify their people. To those who by life and faith know the truth of traditional Judaism, Rabbi Soloveitchik's thought provides an invaluable interpretation of their most fundamental, if ineffable, intuition.

The Need for a Second Type of Jewish Theology

What remains missing in Rabbi Soloveitchik's thinking is the way by which searching, critical moderns might come to such faith. The traditional Jewish doctrine of revelation—that God revealed the oral as well as the written Torah, including the methods and therefore the conclusions reached by the sages of our time—may be axiomatic to Heschel and Rabbi Soloveitchik, but it powerfully troubles many modern Jews. Their most basic understanding of human dignity and the most important lessons of contemporary intellect, especially history, will not let them accept the notion that any person, code or institution should have sway over their conscience. The traditionalist theologian needs either to establish the Torah's authority for them or help them find a way to believe in it. Heschel speaks to that subject in his particular way. Thus far, Rabbi Soloveitchik does not. From what he has already published, we may reasonably conclude that he will not. His typological method certainly is incapable of that task. Moreover, his effectiveness is limited by his heavy reliance on existentialist categories which he employs to argue that faith is ineffable. One cannot then argue over an orthodoxy. This protects his premises but also limits the usefulness of his philosophy. Most Jews do not begin with his faith but might be open to argument seeking to demonstrate its reasonableness. If, inquiring about a belief they might like to hold but find they cannot, they are told it is beyond any sort of exploration, then this theology cannot speak to their questions.

An unexpected issue now provides the crux of the dispute between revelation and modernity, namely, the question of the equality of women in Judaism. Being *obligated* to do the *halachah* has been seen as the hallmark of Jewish responsibility. If so, the substantial difference Jewish law assigns to the duties of women and men seems to make women not only separate but also a religiously unequal group. Is God the ultimate source of these distinctions or are they essentially human enactments? For all its problems, western civilization has claimed ethical attention by universalizing the biblical doctrine of the equality of all people—a matter of no small importance to a clan as despised and segregated as the Jews once were. Against apparently ethical social pressures, shall faithful Jews not stand firm behind the present interpreters of the unbroken chain of Sinaitic tradition and affirm that Jewish women, as such, must have a different standard of religious obligation? Or is the Torah, for all its sublimity, an expression of the human spirit responding to God, whose sanctifying teachings of one age may need to be rethought in radically changed social circumstances?

Questions such as these necessarily divide those who accept the classic understanding of the Sinaitic revelation from those who do not. Hence there must be two basic types of Jewish theology today, the Orthodox and the liberal, a situation not uncommon in most faiths. If the overwhelming number of Jews accept the liberal option, their reasons are hardly theological. They almost certainly do so for their personal and social convenience. It is also true that, for all the faults Jews have found with modernity, they are not ready to surrender as un-Jewish its most central teaching: that mature people ought ultimately decide for themselves what they ought to do. Many people who wish to live as Jews and to believe as Jews cannot accept Orthodoxy even though they no longer unquestioningly adopt the values of western culture. They seek a postmodern but non-Orthodox Judaism. Their restatement of the old question of emancipated Jewry, how to be modern and Jewish, sets the immediate problem confronting liberal Jewish thinkers.

11

The Crux of
Liberal Jewish Thought:
Personal Autonomy

THOUGH Orthodoxy has clearly established its status as a religious option for Jews committed to modernity, most Jews remain non-Orthodox. Among them, one group manifests a familiar non-observance and unconcern which derives from their continuing satisfaction with the old accommodationist strategy of post-emancipation Jewry. They have not felt the pain of the postmodern situation and prefer to live in the illusion that western civilization provides a proper surrogate for Torah.

A second group of liberal Jews—the mass of our community, I think—flits uneasily between slow assimilation and ethnic affirmation. The emergency needs of Israel and Soviet Jewry galvanized them into Jewish action during much of the 1970's. If the future does not hold some such external motivation, their long-range involvement in Jewish life is problematic.

A third group has embarked on a search for a positive Jewish identity, one more intensive than modernist liberalism created yet one which cannot accept Orthodoxy. The classic expression of their neo-liberal Judaism is the several-volume work, *The Jewish Catalog*. Though a comprehensive, detailed effort to reclaim Jewish law and custom, it had an utterly unprecedented reception, selling several hundred thousand copies. (Its companion phenomenon was the spontaneous rise of the *havurah* movement, the small, face-to-face Jewish identity exploration groups.) *The Jewish Catalog* epitomizes the major American Jewish cultural developments of the past decade.

By its content, the *Catalog* appears to be a work of traditional Judaism. It revels in justifying Jewish practices such as *mikvah*, the ritual bath, that the liberals had dismissed as outmoded. But in form—though unconsciously, and therefore tellingly so—it is radically un-Orthodox. Its authors expect it to be used as a catalog. They knew their postmodern public insists on choosing what it will do. It would not accept a current exposition of a required law, a *Schulchan Aruch*, a "Set Table." A catalog presents resources one can draw on to meet one's personal needs. A good catalog is heavy with suggestions, expanding the reader's horizons. But it only offers; it never presumes to tell its readers what they *must* choose. It never commands. For all its rich Jewishness, then, *The Jewish Catalog* rejects Orthodoxy. Thus, the movement to make Judaism a major part of one's life, though it respects the need for some Jewish discipline, remains true to the basic axiom of modernity: autonomy. People should have the right to choose for themselves how they will live. If this situation may be taken as paradigmatic, the fundamental question of the second, the liberal variety of contemporary Jewish thought, may be framed this way: How can we best understand and mediate the claims made upon us by Judaism and self-determination?

Why Some Jews Must Dissent From Their Tradition

Rabbinic Judaism gives substantial scope to human autonomy. Much of its wisdom comes in the realm of *aggadic*, non-legal teaching. The *aggadah* is highly commended but not mandatory. Thus, in many ethical and personal situations, traditional Judaism expected Jews to utilize their own judgment in determining what they ought to do. Even in the realm of *halachah*, the law, the rights of a rabbi deciding an issue can be extraordinarily wide. Some talmudic legends insist that God too must follow certain rabbinic decisions! Nonetheless, rabbinic Judaism does not allow individual Jewish conscience to determine which provisions of the law remain binding and which may be set aside. In Orthodoxy, the *halachah* sets the limits of personal autonomy. In liberal Judaism, personal autonomy, though set in a frame of Jewish commitment, determines the effective bounds of Jewish "law."

If the liberal affirmation of autonomy is so fundamental a break with rabbinic belief, why do Jews determined to reclaim the Jewish ground of their existence insist upon it? Three general responses to that question have been propounded in the century and a half or so of liberal Jewish thought. First, the evident value of changing Jewish practice, despite traditional prohibitions, implies the legitimacy of an enlarged Jewish role for personal decision. Second, autonomy is validated by the new, academic way of understanding the development of Jewish tradition and by facing up to the internal contradictions this reveals. Both of these approaches seem far more compelling to the modern mind than the dogmatic assertion which creates two radically disparate realms of human knowledge by insisting that Torah is a qualitatively unique instance of Divine revelation. Third, western civilization seems correct in asserting that being self-legislating, rather than other-determined, constitutes a major sign of proper human dignity.

Let us consider each of these arguments in their early versions and in their present restatement.

The first liberal Jews had little difficulty validating to themselves their break with tradition. They had high confidence in the western democracy which, after centuries of segregation, was emancipating them. It seemed self-evident that Judaism could adopt the aesthetic forms of general culture without damage to its essential teachings. The rulings of the rabbinate and the weight of inherited custom must be wrong if they prohibited the changes in style which would allow Jews to take advantage of their new, long-sought opportunities. Having accepted the thesis that their generation had the right to westernize the service, they utilized their new-found autonomy to make changes in Jewish belief and ritual law as well.

The German liberals did not speak of autonomy in the individualistic sense in which the post-Kantians around them used the term. They were more communally and historically oriented. Their radicalism consisted of asserting the legitimacy of each generation of Jews determining for themselves what God still demanded of them. They maintained that rightful Jewish change necessarily had a social aspect, and hoped that corporate action would help their generation avoid anarchy and rootlessness.

The pioneer liberals had a good reason for their innovations. They wanted to reshape Jewish practice to effectively show those who left the ghetto that Judaism still fulfilled the aspirations of autonomous beings. They translated prayers and composed new ones that spoke to modern sensibilities; they gave sermons in the vernacular to congregations that now welcomed women; and they restructured Jewish education so that girls as well as boys might understand Judaism in modern terms. They believed that only if Judaism were made radically accessible and acceptable would it survive the community's social dislocation. They transformed Judaism into a modern way of life in the hope that emancipated Jews would consciously will to follow it.

Understanding Torah as Essentially a Human Creation

They supported this pragmatic intuition by a new theory of the Jewish heritage, one which captured their imagination by its integration with all else that they were learning about the evolution of humankind. For Rabbinic Judaism, the Torah is an exception to all integrated schemes of the development of human ideas or spirituality. Moses Mendelssohn, the first great exemplar of the Jew as a modern, was explicit about this dualism in traditional Judaism. He distinguished sharply between universally available spiritual truth and, in his case, Jewish law. They existed in two utterly different realms: the former was rational, public and dynamic; the latter, the result of an incomparable historic act of God. Mendelssohn apparently had no difficulty in maintaining these two diverse beliefs as the fundamental axioms whence his life's standards derived. Most modernizing Jews since then have found such duality of thought unacceptable. In their personal search for truth they strive to integrate that which they believe and that which they know. As their God is one, so they want their apprehension of religion to reach toward ever greater unity.

The nineteenth-century liberal mind was overwhelmed by the convincing way modern history explained Judaism as part of universal human experience. Hebrew was one of many Semitic languages. The Jewish creation and flood stories were paralleled in the ancient Near East and in many other folk cultures. Jewish religious law and institutions reflected the typical concerns of many faiths the world over. What had heretofore been claimed as utterly incomparable seemed rather another instance—if a qualitatively extraordinary one—of the common human search for God.

This disclosure of the humanness of Judaism also commended itself on another count. It provided the least forced explanation of the anomalies found in a Torah that claimed to be God's own word: the duplication of stories; the lies or deceits of the patriarchal exemplars; the misspelled or miscopied words; the hanging letters in the text; the miracles; the factual errors; the primitive science; the fictions accepted as fact; and commands that seemed unethical—for example, that Abraham sacrifice Isaac, or that the Israelites kill every man, woman and child of the seven nations occupying the promised land. The rabbis had employed casuistry to explain away our instinctive reaction that these matters are unworthy of God who "can do all things." But if the Bible is essentially a human document—though composed in response to God—then we no longer need exercise extraordinary ingenuity to defend God's honor and the Torah's reliability. We would naturally expect such problems with ancient human writings and we need not be defensive about them. If anything, seeing the biblical books as the product of their historical situation makes all the more impressive the astonishing way in which they transcend their provenance and disclose a lasting truth.

Modern Jews found the humanity of the Bible validated by contemporary scholarship. The Graf-Wellhausen hypothesis, utilizing the best historical-philological thinking of the day, neatly explained the stages by which the Torah text had come into being. A "J" (Jahvist) document of the tenth century B.C.E. was fleshed out with an "E" (Elohist) document of the ninth century B.C.E. These combined southern and northern Hebrew traditions were eventually supplemented by a "D" (Deuteronomist) strand related to the religious reform of King Josiah of Judah in 621 B.C.E. This proto-Torah was supplemented after the sixth-century Babylonian exile by the "P" (Priestly) traditions. A final redaction ("R") about 400 B.C.E. produced the Torah books largely as we know them today. The theological implication of this "scientific" study of the Bible appeared irrefutable: Judaism is a continuing human encounter with God and each generation has the same right its predecessors had to reformulate its perception of God and God's proper service.

The third line of liberal reasoning did not require much elaboration because moderns considered it self-evident: being fully human depends largely on being free to choose one's values and a life style which embodies them. To live only by inherited rule, or according to the authority of church or class or tribe, betrayed one's reason and conscience, the distinguishing faculties of human beings. Heteronomous existence also denied the basic premise of democracy, that all citizens could discern what was best for them and should share in determining community policy.

For Jews, the argument for autonomy had immediate personal significance. Their emergence from the ghetto was premised on the right of one generation of gentiles to reverse their tradition, the oppression of Jews. To deny conscience the human power to alter social arrangements was equivalent to asking to return to the ghetto. For most Jews the decision to modernize involved a commitment to some measure of autonomy.

Restating the Liberal Arguments

As long as confidence in humankind and in western civilization remained high, devout Orthodoxy seemed out of the question. Entering the 1980's, that optimism has been shattered. For the Jewish community, shaken by its confrontation with the Holocaust, and for America generally, reeling from a decade or more of deepening disillusion, autonomy no longer possesses an unassailable, paramount value. One consequence, as noted, has been Orthodoxy's emergence as a living option for modern Jews. But while liberalism no longer seems self-evidently necessary, the preponderant number of serious-minded Jews still consider it the most compelling form of Judaism. Let us consider the way they would now restate the three older arguments for their position: the need to change the law, to integrate the human mind, and to affirm personal autonomy.

The growth of a modern Orthodoxy seems to liberals a tacit admission that they were correct in their aesthetic proposals of a century or so ago. Today the ground of the argument for needed change has shifted to the internal problems of the law.

Liberals charge that the Torah contains precepts which are unethical and hence are better understood as a product of early human spirituality rather than as God's perfect, eternal commands. A case which caused a stir in the State of Israel a few years ago exemplifies the problem.

As the story went, a gentile had been involved in an accident on the Sabbath. A Jew, coming to his aid, was denied the use of a telephone in an observant Jewish home because of *Shabbat* and was thus unable to call an ambulance to get the gentile to a hospital.

Traditional Jewish law is relatively straightforward in such cases. Sabbath observance has unique importance in Jewish law. No other "ritual" act is mandated by the Ten Commandments; elsewhere, the Torah text describes it as the sign of the Covenant between God and Israel. Those who desecrate it are subject to capital punishment. However, if a life is at stake, all Jews who might be of help are commanded to break whatever Sabbath laws they need to in the hope of saving it—but only on the explicit condition that the endangered person is a Jew. As rabbinic law puts it, if someone is buried under a ruin on *Shabbat*, all Jews must work to remove the heap and save the person's life. Should they discover that the person is dead or is not a Jew, the usual Sabbath law instantly comes back into effect. They leave the corpse or the gentile under the ruin until the Sabbath is over.

The Israeli case turned out to be a hoax, but the prankster had made a point by arousing public indignation. God's law should not be discriminatory and unethical. Though the law was not actually applied in this instance, there are observant Jews who would follow it should the case actually confront them. A factual instance of a somewhat similar ethical dilemma arose some time later concerning a ruling that two Israeli young adults carried the status of *mamzerut*, Jewish illegitimacy.

The Langer children were the offspring of an Israeli marriage contracted by a woman whose husband had apparently died at the hands of the Nazis. Decades later the first husband and the wife chanced to meet, precipitating the problem. Since her first marriage had not been legally dissolved, her second marriage, despite all good intentions, was invalid. Her relations with her second husband now became adultery and their offspring were *mamzerim*, Jews who were forbidden ever to marry a proper Jew and permitted only to marry other *mamzerim*. When the Langer children applied to the rabbinate to be married, they were refused.

A storm broke out over the Langer case. Many observant Jews felt embarrassed and called on the rabbinate to utilize its legitimate powers of interpretation to find a way out of the difficulty (a procedure with much distinguished precedent). The Chief Ashkenazi Rabbi, Shlomo Goren, did come up with such a decision—invalidating the first marriage on technical grounds, thus making the second one legal—and he personally conducted the weddings of the Langer children. His ruling was treated disdainfully by the Israeli right-wing traditionalists and their American counterparts. They

publicly and rather insultingly repudiated Rabbi Goren as a competent Jewish legal authority. They charged him with compromising
Jewish marriage law, one of the strictest categories of *halachic* regulation, as a result of pressure from the unbelieving and unobservant.
As they saw it, the Torah's law was clear. Regardless of the mother's
good will and the children's outstanding citizenship, the young
adults were *mamzerim*, and their offspring in turn would forever be
mamzerim. If Israeli newpaper accounts are reliable, Rabbi Goren's
office still maintains a list of several hundred Israeli *mamzerim* who
can be married only to other *mamzerim*.

To liberal Jewish eyes, all such provisions of the *halachah* are
not God's revelation but faulty human creations. As Ezekiel said and
morality affirms, children should not be punished for the sins of their
parents. Once we no longer need to save God's honor by ingeniously
proving such laws are not unethical but can face them as they are,
they should be abrogated unequivocally. The need to resort to elaborate casuistry to do what is obviously right seems less a proof of the
system's God-given flexibility than the categorically imperative call
of conscience. In demanding such changes in Jewish law, liberals
continue to assert the primacy of autonomy over tradition.

Seeing the Law as Human

Most modern Jews also remain convinced that envisaging the Torah
as largely a human creation best integrates with all our other knowledge about human development. The Graf-Welhausen theory of the
origins of the Torah text has come under substantial academic
attack in recent years. Despite this, it remains fundamental to most
modern studies of the Torah books and, in some measure, still lends
humanistic support to the liberal position. More impressive is the
continuing study of biblical language and ideas in the light of ar-
chaeological finds in the Near East. Liberals see archaeology as con-

firming their view of the Bible as the product of its culture rather than God's utterly unparalleled gift to the Hebrews. Yet what the Hebrews made of that culture was utterly unique.

In our present situation, the internal problems generated by the administration or development of Jewish law make its human basis seem more evident. The classic case of *halachic* procedure contradicting other Jewish values is the *agunah*, the woman who cannot remarry. Generally the circumstances are that her husband will not give her a divorce or the court does not have proper evidence to declare her husband dead. The *halachic* stipulation that women can only receive but not give divorces, seems to liberals less God's will than an instance of ancient Semitic sexism. To be sure, many great Jewish legal authorities prided themselves on being able to find ingenious ways of liberating the *agunah* from her status. To liberals this procedure is exactly what results when human institutions age and become ponderous with precedents and self-importance. Relying on the compassion of *halachic* decisors hardly seems a way of meeting this ethical challenge; some women remain *agunot* and some authorities are not lenient. Particularly in a day when every Jewish marriage is a precious addition to our diminished folk, Jewish laws that inhibit remarriage for procedural reasons seem utterly untenable.

Another, less well known case in point is the current struggle among American Orthodox authorities as to whether a legitimate Sabbath *eruv* has been instituted in our major cities. This legal fiction, often employed in Europe, makes it possible to carry things on the Sabbath. Without an *eruv*, carrying on the Sabbath in a public domain would be prohibited. The *eruv* is a cordon that marks out a specified area within which carrying is permitted. The modern Orthodox, while remaining scrupulously observant, are also eager to utlize the law's inherent possibilities for easing the burdens of Sabbath observance. In this, instance, they want to make it possible for mothers to wheel their toddlers to the synagogue on the Sabbath. The rabbinate of the *"yeshivah* world" has protested the *halachic* legitimacy of the *eruv* in most cities and publicly insisted they are not *kosher*.

The principle involved in the argument over restrictive regulation becomes clearer when the instance is extended somewhat further. Were the *eruv* to be declared valid, Orthodox Jews would still have to walk to their synagogue in the rain without umbrellas. While carrying one would then be legitimate, opening an umbrella is forbidden work under the proscribed category of making a tent, even as throwing an electric switch is prohibited under the category of making a fire. One may, before the Sabbath, set an electric timer to turn on a lamp during the Sabbath, but if one has forgotten to do so or if it malfunctions, one must do without that light. To liberals, this seems another example of bureaucracy triumphing over human and Jewish values, not God's own instruction as to how alone Torah can be elaborated. They maintain that we are more likely to have a proper Jewish Sabbath by utilizing rather than prohibiting the use of many modern conveniences.

Observing the way change finally takes place in contemporary Orthodox practice gives liberals further reason to see Jewish law more as a human than a divine system. At the turn of the century, contraception was almost universally forbidden by traditional Jewish authorities as one of its distinctive stands. The Orthodox right wing continues this prohibition. The masses of Jews, as they modernized, broke with this traditional ruling. They knew intuitively that their Jewish goals for themselves and their children would best be fulfilled by careful family planning. According to social historians, they almost universally began to practice contraception—with such proficiency that for some decades American Jewry has barely reproduced itself. Many modern Orthodox rabbis are troubled by this contradiction between the law and their congregants' practice. Judging by the size of their own families, they and their wives apparently also utilize contraceptive devices. The change has been accepted *de facto*, but only rarely have I heard a modern Orthodox rabbi state that contraception for purposes of planning, not health, has Jewish legitimacy. At best, their cautious attitude stems from their respect for the orderly processes of the law God gave. To liberals it seems easier to understand as institutional inertia, here intensified by the difficulty of admitting that what previous generations presented as God's unchangeable legislation now has reversed its stand.

We can no longer avoid the issue of the status of women in Jewish law. I have refrained from discussing this at length thus far because it arouses such passion that disputants often forget it is only one instance of the many ethical problems moderns find with the *halachah*, though an important one. Let me only add a procedural note to all that has been written on the topic.

How did it happen that women gained certain rights in modern Orthodoxy, most notably that of receiving a full-scale Jewish education? Almost certainly, the change from the mid-nineteenth to the mid-twentieth century was an unacknowledged response to the liberals' previous insistence on breaking with traditional Jewish practice in this regard. As so often in human history, what an orthodoxy first proclaims as alien and heretical is later cautiously accepted and finally claimed to be what the institution had really stood for all along. One can see developments similar to the education of women already at work in a number of other cases in Orthodox Judaism. It has drawn a line at counting women in the *minyan*, or giving them an *aliyah*—calling them to say the blessings before the reading of the Torah—or ordaining them as rabbis. Nonetheless, Orthodoxy's image of the proper Jewish woman has subtly shifted from one whose life is exclusively fulfilled in providing the context for her husband to fulfill the commandments. In the slow if grudging acknowledgment that a Jewish woman is entitled to be a person in her own right, liberals see another vindication of their view that conscientious response to God today, not a previous generation's law or custom, should set the standards for authentic Jewish living.

The Orthodox do not deny that the law is substantially human and that some of its difficulties are common to all religio-legal institutions. For their part, many liberals will agree that Jewish law is not merely human convention but reflects the inspired sense of what our people has come to know God wants of it. The positions do not pit against one another an exclusively Divine and exclusively human origin of the Torah. They debate the balance between the two partners involved in determining what constitutes Jewish law. For all its humanity, Orthodoxy teaches that God established the law in its details and in its method of modification: for it, the human role is substantially subordinate to the Divine. Liberals, for all that they see in Jewish law a response to God, essentially consider it an expression of human spiritual creativity. They believe the social sciences adequately explain the operation of Jewish law, including much of the theological claim made for it. Knowing the *halachah's* human origins, liberal Jews can accept its faults, compensate for them and glory in the Jewish people's continuing human accomplishment in seeking to remain faithful to God's commanding presence.

Autonomy Remains the Hallmark of Human Dignity

Recent history and experience have intensified the third liberal stand against Orthodoxy, that without the exercise of autonomy, people are not yet fully human. We feel the loss of personhood permeating our culture and respond in alarm. The government and corporations order our lives; the mass media shape our opinions; and mass marketing gives us our taste. We work at jobs structured by the needs of others and spend the rest of our time playing roles society has ordered for its convenience. If we are to be human, we must struggle to be more than ingeniously conditioned animals. We may be reduced to gestures of wearing our hair in unconventional fashion or espousing esoteric varieties of vegetarianism, but if we stop fighting for self-determination we have as good as given up our humanity.

Jews have special reason to proclaim the primacy of human autonomy. Our outrage at the Holocaust demonstrates our faith that people can know the right despite their society and ought to have acted on it despite their totalitarian government. The trials of the

Nazi warlords at Nuremberg dealt with justice, not the victors' vengeance. The Nazi leaders remained human beings who knew right from wrong. They should not have committed their war crimes. Even lesser figures, when given an inhuman order or struck by an impulse to commit a barbarity, should have recognized evil and found the moral courage to refuse to do it. One expects that of autonomous human beings. And for the same reason many Americans were deeply troubled by the Vietnam War.

Thank God, few people have the power to do terrible evil in their daily lives. Considering carefully what we do with such power as we do have regularly makes us aware of our human frailty and helps us realize how often we suppress our conscience and collaborate in our society's evil-doing. We need not be saints to be human and happily most of us avoid being scoundrels. But post-Holocaust Jews ought to be particularly devoted to the primacy of moral responsibility. In that spirit postmodern liberal Jews will dissent from their tradition where its precepts or teachings conflict with the mature exercise of their ethical-spiritual autonomy.

The Central Affirmation of Liberal Judaism

In my own liberal Jewish philosophy, personal autonomy has emerged as the most fundamental intellectual theme. Other thinkers believe that accommodating Judaism to science or the Holocaust or the State of Israel ought to be our major conceptual focus. For all their importance, I would argue that none of these issues deserves priority over the need to clarify the meaning and practice of personal self-determination within the people of Israel's continuing Covenant relationship with God.

The least compelling case can be made these days for the scientific challenge. The objectivity and value-free stance which has given science so much of its power, has, through the mass application of technology, given rise to the specter of an inhuman society peopled by programmed beings. I consider it almost self-evident that believing Jews would clearly prefer a Judaism concerned with the survival of humankind's humanity rather than one whose dominant interest is intellectual rapport with the scientific world view.

Assigning a secondary if formative place in a Jewish theology to the Holocaust or the State of Israel cannot be an untroubled decision. No Jewish thinkers I know would rest easy if they believed their thought had given the impression that they deprecated the Jewish tragedy of the former or the Jewish triumph of the latter. To be precise, the distinction required is not one between essential and dispensable topics. We want to decide, rather, which aspect of Jewish modernity ultimately sets the frame for the rest of what we have undergone, no matter how significant these other experiences remain.

The Holocaust critically affects my judgment of human nature, of western civilization and of Jewish vulnerability. These insights transform the optimistic liberal Jewish response to modernity and have major implications for our understanding of God, the Jewish people and Jewish duty. Note, please, the difference between *entirely changing* and *substantially influencing* our theology. Perhaps this emerges most clearly by focussing on the relation of the Holocaust to the issue of how we should conduct our everyday Jewish lives. For all the threats about us and the anxieties within us, our daily existence is not a continuation of the Holocaust or of events which are like it, if such a comparison is permitted. Not the least absurdity of the post-Holocaust situation is that life can once again be quite ordinary. Some few political and social-ethical decisions excluded, the overwhelming majority of our hours revolve about the little evils and small pieties that make most lives commonplace. The Holocaust may prod us to be alert to human sinfulness and cognizant of what we can, realistically, expect ethically of ourselves and others. But hour by hour, day by day, how we should live as Jews cannot reasonably be faced in terms of the death of the six million, but in relation to what we still affirm about God, the Jewish people, and Torah.

The State of Israel, for all its importance to Diaspora Jews, has even less impact on our daily lives than does the Holocaust. Israeli life is not a model for authentic Jewish existence elsewhere, particularly when that is understood to be primarily religious. Corporately, the State of Israel exemplifies healthy Jewish self-respect and vigorous self-expression. Its support must command our concern and energy, especially in perilous times. But this concern, and the Israeli songs, dances, artifacts or phrases we have brought back from our visits are not very much with which to construct a Diaspora Jewish way of life. Only those contemplating and preparing for *aliyah* can make the State of Israel the axis around which their Diaspora Jewish lives revolve.

Besides, the establishment of the State of Israel itself constitutes the most radical exercise of autonomy in Jewish history. Against religious tradition and the inhibited style of emancipated Jewry, the Zionists dared to call the Jews a nation, to organize them politically and to establish Jewish political sovereignty in the homeland. If modern Jews had not asserted their autonomy, Zionism could not have existed. In my opinion, autonomy, not science or the Holocaust or the State of Israel, must have priority in the construction of a system of modern Jewish thought.

Redefining Authentic Judaism

The affirmation of human autonomy does not introduce a totally new, western concept into Jewish thought, thereby adulterating it. The liberal rethinking of Judaism, as noted above, involves a shift, a not unimportant one, in the traditional roles of God and the Jewish people in the Covenant. The book of Exodus describes the giving of the Torah as an agreement based on the people's assent, the famous *naaseh venishma*, "we will do and we will hearken." For all Biblical Judaism's stress on God's power as the role Sovereign of the universe, God was also understood to have granted human beings genuine autonomy; and in the act of commanding free creatures, as well as in covenant making, God shows respect for this unique human quality. Liberal Judaism, swayed by the experience of people taking action for their own purposes, gave much greater scope to human choice than traditional Judaism did. Liberalism goes so far as to reinterpret God's "giving" Torah, as human discovery or intuition. Radical consequences ensue. The absolute authority of traditional Jewish law and teaching can no longer claim Divine sanction. Perceived as substantially human, they are subject to the criticism and renovation of all other human creations.

Liberals accept the responsibility for this break with tradition for, among other reasons, they believe it to be mandated by the modern conception of human history. Whenever one studies Jewish records by accepted academic methods, one sees adjustment and adaptation, mostly unconscious, at the heart of Jewish life as of all other social experience. Jews survived because Judaism changed. That thesis has become so uncontrovertible that, reversing the fervent opposition of a century or so ago, modern Orthodox leaders acknowledge the dynamism of Jewish history. They only insist that human creativity not obscure the Divine origins of the written and the oral Torah and that innovation be restricted to the forms which carry God's authorization.

Liberals cannot accept the division of the human spirit into two disparate categories of explanation—the one generally human, the other uniquely Jewish. They strive for coherence and envisage the Torah text and its amplifications as part of the one human-Jewish process of seeking God's will. This leads them to a daring assertion: if human responsiveness to God has been the secret of Jewish survival over the millenia, then liberal Judaism, which self-consciously emphasizes it to enhance life under the Covenant, is the most authentic Judaism today. Liberal Jews strongly deny that their lives are "less Jewish" than those of Orthodox Jews, for they do not measure Jewish authenticity in terms of traditional observance. Rather, if a dynamic response to God's will must characterize Covenant loyalty, they feel confident that their creative reshaping of Jewish discipline for our day only continues what the Jewish sages all along were, in fact, doing.

Can Liberalism Overcome its Drive to Anarchy?

If personal autonomy is axial to liberal Judaism, how can the Jewish people long hope to stay together, especially in the Diaspora? If Jews are free to choose Jewish obligations for themselves, what will guarantee the historic continuity of the Jewish tradition? Does not autonomy breed anarchy and unravel what remains of the Jewish heritage? How do liberal Jewish thinkers limit Jewish self-determination so as to promote the perpetuation of Judaism while authorizing effective personal autonomy?

The nineteenth-century philosophers felt confident about their solution to this problem. With the Kantians, they considered it obvious that human autonomy was fulfilled in rationality. In mature people, personal freedom would thus be contained within the ethical bounds provided by reason. Their social order reinforced the constraints set by their philosophic optimism. Their culture gave most people little latitude. Instead, a heavy weight of social convention severely restricted most efforts at self-determination. Jewishly, knowledge and custom were effective checks on individual liberty; while externally, the limits society set to Jewish integration, including anti-semitism, kept Jews united. If to present-day eyes they seem disturbingly unconcerned about the dangers ahead for Jewish particularity, we must remember that, being so freshly out of the ghetto, their overriding concern was adjustment to their new freedom.

We have come so far from their enchantment with rationality and western civilization that we can think of ourselves as postmoderns. Instead of pursuing culture we seek to strengthen our Jewish roots in hope of counteracting its deleterious effects upon us. We cannot count on Jewish knowledge, experience or family precedent to sustain in this quest. The threat of anti-semitism and the troubles of Israeli, Soviet and other Jewries do unite us as a people but only spasmodically and then largely for fund raising and political action.

Our corporate existence has suffered even more from the collapse of almost all the old rationalistic and social controls on our autonomy. We have little confidence in human reason; cults promising

salvation burgeon and experiential groups offering fulfillment multiply. Rationality tends to be reduced to being logical rather than
mandating a qualitative ethics. Being true to oneself can now be
taken literally; self-serving and narcissism become forms of "ethics."
The autonomy which once was fulfilled in conscience and social
responsibility now is directed to getting in touch with oneself, that
is, one's body, one's sensations, one's feelings, and one's inner
satisfactions.

The dramatic selfishness of such people has brought personal autonomy to an ethical individualism unimaginable to the early liberals. It has infected our society with callousness and moral rot. If our
civilization suffers so grievously from the assertion of inviolable personal autonomy, will not corporate Jewish existence be even more
endangered by it? Should not devoted Jews reject a doctrine which
intensifies the seductiveness of assimilation by giving Jewish validity
to self-determination no matter where it leads?

Containing Anarchy by Institutional Means

Several responses to these questions have been offered, none of
which seem convincing to me. One calls for the reinstitution of
community standards for Jewish behavior. Some advocates suggest
we set minimums for Jewish practice while others believe only a
return to some form of Jewish law can save American Jewish liberals
from anarchy. They propose that Jewish discipline, rather than self-
legislation, become the sign of a serious commitment to Judaism.

I find this "law and order" approach theoretically indefensible and
practically unfeasible. On what theological basis could a required
law of even minimum standards be instituted? We have no modern
theory of revelation which can place God's authority behind specific
statements of belief or rules of practice. If only human authority is
invoked, why should we surrender our rights of conscience to anyone
else? We may be willing to be persuaded that certain communal

practices will benefit Jewish life or that we ought to go along with certain rules even though we don't like them. But we will not have law or required practice as long as our compliance is based on personal decisions as to each enactment's worthwhileness. Practically speaking, ours is a time of deep-seated skepticsim of all institutions and their leaders. Can we expect that an abstract call for Jewish unity will bring many people to give up the right that they now exercise to choose for themselves their Jewish obligations?

The American Jewish community is founded on voluntarism. Unlike its European predecessors, it has no connection with the government. It can only persuade; it cannot coerce its members. For some time most American Jews have taken advantage of the fact that they may be as free in their religious lives as they wish to be—and they have done so even if they prefer to be affiliated with Orthodox synagogues. Identifying personal Jewish self-determination as a threat to Jewish survival will not bring many American Jews to surrender their freedom. I see no theoretical or practical way around the issue of autonomy. Except for the true Orthodox, it remains the primary shaping concept of modern Judaism.

A more promising approach has been suggested by the ideologists of Conservative Judaism. They have argued that Judaism, even in its pattern of change, proceeded on the basis of law; hence, any authentic Judaism must have a *halachic* character. They agree with the Reform Jews that the radically changed social and intellectual situation of modern Jews validates substantial change in traditional Jewish practice. Against the Reformers they believe that any innovations ought to be made by *halachic* methods, with great respect for legal precedent, by masters of the *halachic* tradition. They disagree with the Orthodox about the extent of the changes needed—mixed seating at services—and the leeway the *halachic* process still possesses to institute changes. Conservative thinkers believe that positive Jews, recognizing the importance of law to Judaism, will voluntarily subordinate their personal freedom to communal standards which are *halachicly* authentic and socially progressive. Concretely, the Conservative movement has established a Commission on Law and

Standards whose decisions are binding on Conservative Jews—with some conditions—due to the erudition of its members and the flexibility of its interpretation of the law. Thus, the Commission recently ruled that congregations which wished to do so might validly include women in the *minyan*, the quorum for public services.

This institutional resolution of the problem hopes to avoid the theological issue of revelation. It appeals to a historical judgment about Judaism's necessary legal nature to which it now gives new communal expression. The solution must therefore be judged in terms of its practical results.

Evaluating their movement on the occasion of its ninetieth anniversary, the spokesmen of Conservative Judaism found many of their accomplishments praiseworthy. They were pleased with their group's Hebraism, its scholarship, its ethnic loyalty and its Jewish warmth. However, on the major point of their ideology, they sadly acknowledged that they had failed to win any significant number of Jews to accept and live by the discipline of Conservative Jewish law. Like other non-Orthodox Jews, most Conservative Jews will listen to what their movement says they ought to do, but insist on determining for themselves what they will do. Against the position which their leaders say distinguishes them from other groups, they are determined to live on the basis of personal autonomy.

Already in the 1940's Mordecai Kaplan had argued that this reliance on flexible experts would not work. Despite its Jewish precedents, it lodged power in a learned elite, yet hoped to win the allegiance of a constituency trained to democracy. Kaplan proposed instead that the Jewish community establish an assembly representing all who were interested in the survival of the Jewish people. This body would then legislate for our community. Since all loyal Jews would be represented in its decisions, we could expect many Jews to accept them as binding even as they do American law.

Much of the Conservative leadership was fearful of Kaplan's suggestion. It contained no guarantee other than mass representation, that the assembly might not dispense with major provisions of traditional Jewish law. Theoretically, they read Kaplan correctly. He believed in the right of the Jewish people to determine its own norms today as in the past. Should the survival of the folk today make it necessary to break with the *halachah* then they might legitimately do so. So to speak, Kaplan's Jewish assembly was too autonomous for the Conservative leadership. In due course Kaplan became sufficiently marginal to the Conservative movement that, against his original intentions for Reconstructionism, he and his disciples established a separate congregational group, rabbinical school and rabbinical association. They have not been able to create a community-wide legislative body. Many of the Reconstructionist movement's own decisions regarding practice seem considerable departures from traditionl Jewish law. As yet, its thinkers have not gone beyond the individual cases to resolve the theoretical problem of Jewish autonomy. Practically, most Reconstructionist Jews seem to live on the basis of a personal freedom they enrich by participating in the Jewish civilization.

Another Unsatisfactory Alternative: Radicalizing Autonomy

Some Reform extremists, notably Alvin Reines and Sherwin Wine, have suggested that Judaism finally carry through an uncompromising identification of modernity with autonomy. If human dignity is realized in the exercise of freedom, nothing should be allowed to stand in its way, not even Jewish tradition or Jewish folk responsibility. Until now, Jewish modernists have refused to embrace wholeheartedly the cardinal rule of the Enlightenment, that neither the past nor society should be allowed to override thoughtful self-determination. These Reformers consider it an illusion to hope that autonomy can be co-opted without revolutionizing Judaism. Literally, autonomy means that the self and only the self should legitimately legislate for one. No one determined to have a fully authentic human existence should compromise that principle.

This radicalism need not entail a complete rejection of the Jewish tradition. People who have personal ties to Judaism can find it a valuable resource for the pursuit of true selfhood. Abraham, the first Jew, broke sharply with his culture in pursuit of a truth no one around him knew and which, once he found it, no one could comprehend. The prophets preserved a similar individualism, proclaiming against their society that God's service was found less in maintaining inherited institutions than in the pursuit of truth and justice. The Jewish people, which has produced such figures as Marx, Freud and Einstein, should not be content with a tradition whose world view is prescientific, whose imagery is mythological and many of whose practices reflect magical notions. In its place autonomous moderns ought to seek out the most appealing truth they can rationally discover in contemporary culture. One left-wing liberal group finds this in secular humanism which it enriches by Jewish ethnicity. Another party affirms a Sartrean radical freedom relieved by a quest for God as the infinte possibility of being (a notion resembling Tillich's conception of God as the ground or power of being).

I disagree with the radical assertion of autonomy for it remains confidently modernist. It maintains the old Jewish liberal faith that contemporary culture knows far more about reality than does Judaism and it therefore rigorously subordinates everything Jewish to that universal truth. I deny that premise. The postmodern Jewish spiritual swing arose because many of us lost our old, ultimate faith in western civilization and acknowledged how wise Judaism remained. After what we have seen happen to the quality of life in our time, Jews such as I can no longer give our primary loyalty to western culture generally or contemporary philosophy in particular. For us, a sensitivity to human values alone would require that Jews move from servile dependency on our society to a maturely independent engagement with it. Indeed, we feel we need to be more Jewish in order to stay fully human in this culture. To our ears, the call to reduce Judaism only to what a radical pursuit of autonomy warrants, appears little more than an effort to reincarnate a long since outmoded strategy of Jewish modernity.

Affirmation of Autonomy is Itself an Act of Faith

Reflection, not mere experience, challenges the new radicalism. On what basis should people invest so much faith in personal autonomy that they make it the fundamental affirmation of their religion? One might do so if one had the sort of God the Bible directs us to or if one could still share the blissful rationalism of Kant and the Enlighteners. But on the basis of what we have learned in recent years about human nature, why should we give such absolute worth to our apparent freedom to be self-legislating? Indeed, we must now dare to ask about that which liberals simply took for granted: Why should people affirm themselves? Illusion aside, most of us discover ourselves to be deeply unworthy of absolute acceptance. We may be reasonably decent or have worthwhile traits, but such limited value does not confer inalienable dignity upon us.

I am not appealing here to our neurotic self-deprecation. Even after we have completed our therapy we must still face the question of our ultimate human worth. Psychological maturity does not resolve our existential predicament. The emotionally healthy also continually fail to live up to their ideals or the reasonable demands of those they love. We have made self-acceptance a psychic imperative precisely because our hard-won realism about ourselves gives us such good reason for denying it. The atheistic French existentialist, Albert Camus, said that the central problem of contemporary philosophy was why one should not commit suicide. It was a question with which he struggled nobly and to which, having only a secular world view to base himself on, he could give no satisfactory answer. The new fascination with suicide as the ultimate act of self-assertion testifies to the inner contradiction of the self seeking to be the ground of its ultimate worth.

The command to live autonomously finds as little ground in most religions as it does in our culture which regularly tramples on it. Confucius wanted us to accept the discipline of the old social values. Lao-tzu summoned us to empty ourselves of self-assertion so that the way of nature might become our way. Hinduism proposed to dissolve the individual existence in the Absolute One and Buddhism rejects the self as a reality to be enhanced and strengthened. But in Judaism, and its daughter religions, a strong sense of autonomy becomes possible, perhaps even necessary.

Without a faith like that of traditional Judaism, in which a transcendent God bestows inestimable worth on us by covenanting with us yet leaving us a measure of genuine self-rule, why should people regard themselves or their autonomy as having absolute value?

I do not find these alleged radicals radical enough. They need to reexamine their own basic premise with the critical vigor they normally reserve for exposing the obsolescence of the Jewish heritage. I agree that a return to Judaism without an affirmation of personal autonomy would take us back to premodern times. Nonetheless, asserting the commanding value of autonomy as if it were self-evident or self-validating seems only the dogmatic convulsion of an outdated liberalism.

In my view, postmodern liberal Jewish thought needs to be fully dialectical. It should not make Judaism subservient to a truth derived from the culture, as the old liberals did, yet it should not require the sacrifice of personal autonomy to the Torah, as Orthodoxy still demands. Instead, it must live in a dynamic balance of tradition and autonomy. I see the central intellectual task of liberal Jewish thinkers today to be the creation of such a dialectical Jewish theology. Let me sketch in some of its possible features.

Revising the Covenant Model of Relationship

We may begin by seeing the traditional Jewish understanding of covenant prefiguring the relationship we now dimly intuit. The Bible describes human beings as the only creatures formed in God's image and therefore capable of serving as God's partners. Though God's sovereign rule of the universe is utterly unimpeachable, people under the covenant need not surrender their selfhood to God. If anything, to participate properly in the alliance they must affirm their freedom for they are called to acceptance and resolve, not servility. They are given commandments, not mere instinct, and are capable of refusing to do them. Having such negative power, they achieve great merit when they will to observe God's law. And on special occasions, they have the right to stand up to God and question God's failure to carry out the Divine responsibilities under the covenant.

Our present-day commitment to God's Covenant with the people of Israel cannot be a simple reiteration of classic Jewish faith for we cannot deny the spiritual truth we have learned since the Emancipation. Pious Jews had once become so dependent upon God and God's saving power that they seemed to have forgotten how to help themselves. They were abject and passive before social injustice and historical abuse. They could only go to Palestine to die, not to rebuild themselves or the Jewish people. Jewish liberalism came into being to remind human beings that they have greater dignity than that. Its history, as religious reform or Zionist reconstruction, has legitimized the modern Jew's commitment to autonomy. The postmodern reaffirmation of the Covenant must therefore include the right of conscientious dissent from what Jewish tradition once required or strongly urged.

To my mind the issue of the place and form of proper dissent constitutes the critical unresolved issue in the otherwise highly rewarding work of Louis Jacobs. In two separate books, one a discussion of Maimonides' "creed," *Principles of the Jewish Faith*, and the other a historical account of the major Jewish beliefs, *A Jewish Theology*, Jacobs has utilized his extraordinary perceptiveness to Jewish texts, to explicate the nature of Jewish belief today. Compared to Kaufmann Kohler's similar, pioneering venture early in the century, Jacobs' work is far more persuasive. He is uncommonly open to the variety of voices in the Jewish past, the legal as well as the ethical, the mystical as well as the philosophic. But his approach remains historical, which creates the intellectual problem with his theology. History teaches no lessons, only historians do. Until we know the principles by which the student of the past evaluates the multitudinous facts, we do not know why history has been read just this way rather than another; producing this faith and no other. Why should we find this data significant but not other data, pursue this theme rather than another, or, most important of all, predicate one position still tenable while another needs to be replaced by a more modern point of view?

These issues are directly philosophical or theological. As I see it, the contemporary Jew is too skeptical or inquisitive to accept an interpretation of Jewish tradition which does not carefully qualify when and, if possible, why it allows for personal dissent. As a result, the historical exposition of Jewish belief needs to be accompanied by a direct intellectual analysis explaining when acceptance and rejection of the Jewish past is warranted. Making personal autonomy as well as commitment to the Covenant a basis of our Judaism requires some such effort. If Jacobs could direct his theological work in this direction it would be a major contribution to contemporary Jewish thought.

What is the Counter-claim to Autonomy?

Stressing the troublesome, autonomous aspect of the dialectic, as I have just done, might appear to suggest that I think it should be dominant—a view which would lead us back to the problems of early liberalism. Against the power of an unimpeded autonomy, I would vigorously press claims of Jewish affirmation. Autonomy is not self-grounding but derives from being God's Covenant partner. To me that means that, if anything, somewhat greater priority must be given to Judaism in the balance of belief than to personal self-determination. Concisely put, for a believing Jew, the historical reality of the Covenant grounds one's personal existence.

This emphasis on tradition, though with the possibility of dissent, authorizes Judaism to criticize the general culture. The estrangement Jewish piety engenders, which once made Judaism a burden to the newly emancipated, now becomes particularly precious. In spiritually alienating us somewhat from this society, Judaism imparts to us an independent awareness of value that we may then bring to it. As faithful Jews, we not only learn from the society but seek to instruct it.

Our special perspective should help us determine which form of modern thought we should use as the medium of explaining our belief. Before we ally ourselves with any modern intellectual structure, we need to inquire about its congeniality to classic Jewish faith as well as about its cultural acceptance and cognitive persuasiveness.

In terms of my Jewish affirmations and intellectual perceptions, religious existentialism provides the most suitable philosophic idiom available. I seek to remain conscious of its instrumental role in my thought and prevent it from usurping the primary place of Jewish faith in my life. Thus, when religious existentialism contradicts what study shows to have been classic Jewish faith, I do not automatically judge Judaism to require revision. Perhaps I agree with the existentialists and here autonomously dissent from the tradition. I may also autonomously agree with the tradition and thus be led to criticize and correct religious existentialism. Let me give three significant examples of this dialectic as it operates in relation to our views of society, history and law.

With regard to society and history I find the existentialists short-sighted and in need of the interpersonal, time-oriented vision of Judaism. Most existentialists fix on the self so compulsively they must struggle to create a positive doctrine of society. Judaism has long seen the individual as indissoluble from community, nation and humankind. Similarly, existentialistic individualism, though sensitive to the demands of the present moment, has little appreciation for the claims of the past or our responsibility to project our existence through time into the future. Judaism has always been radically historical. It knew that life must be evaluated by more than immediate experience, that only a lifetime of integrity can fulfill our humanity. A Jew aspires to the wisdom of age rather than to the vigor of the perpetually young.

This quick critique of existentialist individualism starts us toward the answer we seek concerning anarchic autonomy. In Jewish belief, the self cannot be the exclusive object of its primary concern. Its meaning is very largely given it by its relations with others. We are true persons, in the Jewish view, only as we fulfill our responsibilities to those with whom we live. Because we are historical creatures, we necessarily are obliged to those who came before us and those who will follow after us. A Jewish existentialist theology would reject a radically individualistic view of human nature and consequently, a libertarian ethics.

Similarly, it would remove the basis for an anarchic Jewish liberalism. The autonomous Jewish self derives its autonomy as part of the people of Israel's Covenant partnership with God. Such a Judaism knows no isolated, atomistic, worthy self. Rather, selfhood itself necessarily involves God, people and history. Every decision of a Covenanted Jewish self intimately depends on transcendent and ethnic as well as personal considerations. Such a Jew is self-legislating but only in terms of what God wants of this individual as part of the people of Israel's historic-messianic service to God. The decision is individual but the content is more than personal. The autonomy is genuine but is exercised in terms of realities as real as one's self.

Despite precluding anarchy, this personalistic Judaism does not yield *halachah*. In the case of religious law I find neither the Jewish nor the existentialist position fully acceptable. I have a Jewish conviction that all authentic existence must be structured, something existentialism denies. I am also moved by the existentialist vision of individual needs to rework Jewish law in personally open terms it could not traditionally tolerate.

My Judaism is more dynamic than static. To stay alive, the self must be open to new ideas and activities; yet to have a firm ground it must again and again win its traditionalism through personal affirmation. It is obviously quite pluralistic. I do not see that the freedom of the self which I believe a modern Judaism demands could survive our religion's again becoming a body of required doctrine or behavior. Both negate our conscientious self-development. The Jewish stability we seek should be worked out on a far more existential level, one we may call personal style. Without sophistication one has be-havior but not style. Without structure one is only erratic. In recog-nizable style, mind and action interpenetrate, integrating in life what it left to mind alone would be paradox. Jewish style emerges from living one's life in devotion to God as part of the people of Israel's Covenant with God. If enough Jews began to live so faithful an existence, I can conceive that what began in an individualistic fash-ion might go on to become community patterns. That would be the autonomous Jewish equivalent of what once was Jewish law.

I do not know that it will be easily possible to win large masses of Jews to so religious a base for modern Jewish life. I believe that Judaism survived over the centuries largely because an elite based their lives on it and by their example and leadership strengthened the masses around them. Far more Jews today are open to the possibility of personal Jewish faith than anyone would have imagined in the heyday of secularism a decade or so ago. Liberal Judaism has some-thing deeply significant to say to them, particularly if they are con-cerned about the quality of our individual and social existence. It knows that when people confront themselves in ultimate seriousness they stand ready to transcend themselves. Knowing we cannot ex-plain our worth, yet intuiting its ultimate significance opens us to a faith that many of us, following the social cues, have long repressed. The question, "Who are we?", if radically pressed, leads to "Who is God?" Anthropology in depth leads on to theology. I believe an increasing number of Jews are reaching for a spirituality which speaks in such human yet traditional fashion.

The existential Jew lives a paradox. Judaism grounds our au-tonomy and that in turn gives us the personal basis for making the Jewish tradition a responsible choice, not an accident of inheritance. Each position reinforces and qualifies the other. Around the two poles of non-Orthodox Jewish faith is generated the ellipse of modern Jewish existence, different in form and content from the Judaisms of other eras yet just as surely their authentic, contemporary expression.

PART V

A
Concluding
Reflection

12

Facing up to the
Options in Modern
Jewish Thought

WITH JEWISH thinkers today differing so widely in their views, how can one hope to get a clear and coherent accout of what one believes as a Jew?

The common strategy, compromise, will not work. We cannot simply collect what we find most appealing in the ideas of each thinker and thereby gain a coherent philosophy of our own. Cohen's God, Baeck's mystery, Kaplan's peoplehood, Buber's Covenant and Heschel's prophetic sympathy, will not mesh together. The premises on which they are founded substantially contradict one another. Indeed, the thinkers consciously created their systems out of a desire to take a different approach to Judaism from that which had existed before and which they considered inadequate. (The thinkers included in this book were chosen because they are the best representatives of the divergent streams of thought in contemporary Judaism.)

At the other extreme, some people find that one of the major Jewish thinkers still speaks for them. They see the competing views as so essentially flawed that they do not constitute a serious challenge to the one they espouse. Such problems as they perceive in their own position merely represent the agenda for their Jewish intellectual growth, not a reason for giving up or radically revising it. Thus one not uncommonly meets disciples of Kaplan, Buber or Heschel in the Jewish community today.

Most thoughtful Jews, I find, can follow no one intellectual line. They remain undecided whether God's revelation, or Divine-human encounter, or human reason or experience ought to be the basis for understanding Judaism. Each standpoint has its appeal but each also has its weaknesses. Optimally, we need a fresh philosophical approach which would reshape our concept of Judaism so that we would retain all the gains of previous systems while circumventing their faults. I would like to encourage as many students of Judaism as I can to undertake that creative task. Through their efforts, Jewish theology will carry on in as lively a way in the future as it has done in recent decades.

I myself do not see that any currently suggested system, or any that I may devise, can hope to convince most thinkers that they should accept its transformation of the system and the problems of Jewish philosophy. The complexities of our time simply exceed our present theoretical capabilities. From within, our diverse understandings of Judaism and our clashing methodologies about how best to study it, preclude any easy agreement as to what constitutes authentic Jewish thought. From without, the fragmented and discordant motifs which sound in our culture and social sciences cannot provide a context for a freshly integrated Judaism. We live in a time of intellectual uncertainty, one far greater than that of previously searching and unsure generations. The fundamental premises of every discipline and of thinking itself are continually being challenged and our civilization's high esteem for doubt makes such skepticism difficult to refute. Moreover, education, the widespread diffusion of new ideas and unceasing proposal of radically diverse views keep us keenly aware of the unprecedented intellectual pluralism amidst which our thinking needs to be done.

I do not see then that we can think about Judaism in quite the same relatively self-assured way that modern Jewish philosophers have customarily followed. Each proclaimed his own theories as if they fully constituted Judaism and referred to divergent views only by inference or in passing. Each was so confident that his system settled all the significant problems of his time that he did not undertake a direct confrontation with the theorists who differed from them. I suggest that our unsettled intellectual situation requires a less self-centered approach. It should proceed in two successive steps.

Clarifying the Options, Explaining One's Choices

We would begin studying a topic by utilizing a comparative approach. That means inquiring about the divergent views of thoughtful interpreters of Judaism writing about this issue. (The fateful problem of the proper utilization of non-Jewish thinkers for elucidating the contemporary content of Jewish faith must be faced by the investigator at this point.) A careful contrast and comparison of their positions should clarify the major issues facing the thoughtful Jew. Since taking one intellectual option over another always involves certain gains and losses, exposing the consequences of a given choice—"If . . . then . . ."—becomes a central task in this method. Furthermore, because we have no agreed standard for evaluating one suggestion over another, knowing the practical consequences of accepting a given position may be decisive for determining which philosophy we can accept. By candidly exposing the various theological alternatives, thinkers can better perceive and clarify their own assumptions while equipping their readers to think for themselves more responsibly. Obviously, my preference for this approach stems from my deep concern for personal autonomy but I believe that less personalistically inclined thinkers should employ it to remain conscious of the variety of questions and proposals facing our community.

On one level, this book is my response to that challenge. But, though it deals with important themes of Jewish faith, one does not need to be a Jew to do this part of the task. Any competent, empathetic student of ideas could produce such an intellectual geography.

Only at a second level does this activity become distinctively Jewish. Thinkers then respond to the intellectual options by indicating what they personally believe. They set forth the reasons—to the extent they are able—for having rejected other positions and accepted just the ones which they affirm. In the process, they ought to demonstrate the interrelationships and internal harmony of their beliefs. They bring their work to a fitting climax by showing the consequence of their ideas for Jewish life and responsibility.

I should therefore like to conclude this book with a small sample of my efforts to make a substantive statement of my Jewish faith. In 1977, the Central Conference of American Rabbis invited me to prepare a paper on God which its members could study in advance of a discussion on this topic at their annual conference. I quickly discovered I could not satisfactorily deal with this central issue unless I also explicated the assumptions on which my treatment was based and the consequences to which it led, at least intellectually. What follows is one of the concluding sections of that lengthy, detailed paper (found in its entirety in their *Yearbook* for 1977) in which I tried to give a brief, positive summary of my views.

My Theology of Judaism: A Provisional Statement

I do not see any way to begin theology afresh, without preconceptions and as if there were no history. The very hope of doing so is itself the result of a Cartesian tradition and marks its proponent as an adherent of the European liberal academic community. The problem of what tradition one finds oneself in, which one proposes to affirm or reject or that one then chooses, is fundamental to the theological or philosophical enterprise and substantially determines the content which will ensue. The modern Jewish theologian faces this problem with special difficulty because of being situated between western culture and Jewish tradition. These partially clash, the former being dominated by Christianity insofar as it is religious and antipathetic to religion insofar as it is secular. As a liberal Jewish theologian I add to this problem my inability to accept the Jewish tradition absolutely and use it as the measure of my involvement with the culture. I necessarily begin from a history of some generations of liberal theology.

In terms of what is perceived as the present agenda, I can try to assess the successes and failures of the old liberalism, and in terms of the contemporary intellectual scene or my creativity, make some determination of where I will take my intellectual stand. Two corrections of classic liberal theology seem to me to be necessary. One, a redirection of its concern with science, might still be accommodated by its usual rationalism. The other, a commitment to substantial particularist consequences, seems incompatible with known rationalisms.

Classic liberal theology was mainly concerned with accommodating religion to science and a culture which largely accepted the naturalistic world view. While affirming the continuing importance of science to our sense of things, I do not see it as the dominant challenge to our human self-understanding. Rather, the accomplishments of science have themselves (by their threats to our personhood) raised to primary concern the problem of being a person (socially as well as individually understood). Unfortunately there seems no satisfactory way to bridge the person-science dichotomy. Despite the problems this causes me, I feel I must stand on the person side of the struggle. The notions of self and the concept of relationship (genuine interpersonal involvement) then become my central hermeneutic for the explication of a contemporary pattern of Jewish belief. (On its admitted inadequacies and some remedies for them see my other writings.)

Liberal Jewish thought might have accepted some sort of existentialist personalism as it once was willing to substitute naturalism for Neo-Kantianism (or stands ready to adopt Whiteheadian or phenomenological theologies), as long as this did not disturb its accustomed universalistic focus. Yet for all that classic liberal Jewish theology performed the valuable and necessary task of making exghetto Jews citizens of the world, it did not motivate them to be particularly learned or observant Jews. This lack of motivation was an explicit problem before the Holocaust, the establishment of the State of Israel and the contemporary spiritual emptiness of Western civilization. Today an inability to speak to the particularistic needs of liberal Judaism would be a major intellectual disaster. I believe that instead of validating itself by its universalism, a contemporary liberal Jewish theology must do so by the power of its particularism. The task is complicated by the proper rejection by most liberal Jews of a purely or largely particularistic theology. The contemporary agenda is set by the need to maintain the gains of universalism (by which Jews have their rights in modern society) while giving equal priority to the people of Israel and its distinctive way of life. Having less confidence in Western culture than in Jewish tradition, though taking neither as an absolute, I give Jewish tradition priority in my thought. Tradition makes authoritative but not irresistible claims upon me and I respond to them out of my Western culture situation in a personal, not systematic way, utilizing the notions of self and relationship to clarify what Jewish belief means to me.

Classic Jewish Faith and the Modern Notion of the Self

A possible incoherence already emerges in the linkage of Jewish tradition and selfhood. The former is more concerned with God's objective will, Torah, than with personal self-determination; and the latter makes autonomy, not law, tradition or community, usually not even God, its foundation. Identifying the two (reason-equals-revelation as in the medieval solution of this problem) not being feasible, in my opinion, only a dialectic between self and tradition can be affirmed. Since this cannot be stilled, it produces a dynamic to this position which keeps it necessarily fluid. However, I believe it can be saved from the charge of destructive contradiction. Realistically exposed, the self is not self-evidently worthy of the dignity we assign to it. It therefore requires some sort of meta-existentialism which Jewish tradition, with its teaching of humankind created in God's image, can provide.

More difficult is the assertion that the tradition, in some way, would, on coming in contact with the modern concept of the self, find it an appropriate and valuable insight to assimilate to its teaching. Historically, Jewish selfhood was exercised only within the rigorous limits imposed by law, tradition and community. Practically, today, the leaders of traditional Judaism seem more concerned with the defense of the law and its structures against the self than with incorporating something of the modern sense of the self into the actual operation of their system of authority. Against this it must be noted that the overwhelming majority of modern Jews consider themselves essentially self-legislating (and this despite party label or institutional affiliation). The unprecedented, full-scale abandonment of the *halachic* system is unlikely to be reversed. Insofar as it has a positive intellectual basis (as against social causation) it stems from the acceptance of the autonomy of the individual. Since there are some intuitions of this in Jewish tradition, since it appeals to the Jewish sense of individuality, since it is hoped that an integration of selfhood and tradition, mutually influencing and transforming, can be carried out so as to yield the mixed particularist-universalist theology sought, the marriage of tradition and the modern sense of self seems a valuable option to pursue.

Where mind is the primary model of theology, one speaks of ideas. In naturalism, one prefers forces or processes. If our concern is persons we speak of relationship, the way the self links itself to the world or anything in it. The fundamental relationship in which the Jew stands is the Covenant. However, it was made and is maintained primarily with the people of Israel and not the individual Jew. To be sure, the people of Israel is not an entity outside of its individual members and no claim is made that it possesses some folk-soul or national-will of its own. Nonetheless the individual Jew's direct, personal relationship with God is not begun by that Jew but by the historic experience of the Jewish people into which the contemporary Jew is born. (There is obviously a major difference here between

Christian notions of "getting faith" and the Jewish sense of entering the Covenant.) Individual Jews then, are immediately involved in a dialectic not only of self and God (thus setting a limit to the anarchy of atheistic existentialism) but of the self and the Jewish people in relation to that God (thus setting a limit to the exercise of an anarchic because individualistic liberal Jewish sense of autonomous selfhood).

Implications of Existence in Covenant

This sets the agenda for contemporary liberal Jewish apologetic theology. As against all secular interpretations of being a Jew, commitment to the Covenant insists that a relationship to God is primary to the life of the Jewish people and the individual Jew. The first concern of our apologetics, then, needs to be the recapture of the living reality of God in individual Jewish lives and thus in the Jewish community. The major target in this regard is the crypto-agnosticism with which most Jews have evaded this issue for a generation or more. In the face of contemporary nihilism, I am convinced, the old hope of serious values without commitment to God is increasingly untenable. The second concern of our apologetics is to help the individual Jew identify personally with the people of Israel. That is somewhat easier in our present time of high regard for ethnic difference and the search for one's own folk roots. Yet the primary model most people use in their thinking remains the Cartesian one of the detached self seeking truth without preconceptions or commitments. This has particular appeal to Jews since it immediately releases them from Jewish attachment in accord with the social pressures on any minority to assimilate to the majority.

Moreover, if there is no universalism then Jews lose whatever right they have to be part of general society. It thus becomes important to argue that all selfhood, though possessing universal dignity, is historically and particularly situated. Because of its uncommon worth, if for no more theological reason, Jews should will to make the fact of their being born into the Covenant the basis of their existence.

This construction of our situation as Jews overcomes what I take to be the fundamental difficulty with previous theories. Those which were God-centered were reductive of our peoplehood. Yet those which made the Jewish people central so reduced the role of God in our folk life that they effectively secularized us. Furthermore, if peoplehood is the primary factor in Jewish existence what remains of the autonomous self? When the Covenant relationship is the basis of our understanding of Judaism, self, God and people are all intimately and immediately bound up with one another. This does not settle how in any instance the self will respond to God or to the Jewish people, relationship being too fluid for that; yet Covenant sets up a constraining dialectic in place of liberal Jewish anarchy, universalism or secularism.

Covenant Theology: God—and Evil

As to God, a new humility emerges. Persons have relationships which are deeply significant for their lives without fully or nearly understanding those with whom they have such relationships. As against rationalist models, *concepts* of God (clear intellectual envisagements of God) are of subsidiary interest—if not positively discouraged. Making concepts primary tends to make thinking a substitute for relating and implies a thinking humanity is God's equal. In a relationship thought is not abandoned but it must not dominate. It serves as a critic of faith and as explicator of its consequent responsibilities. This is the safeguard against superstition and cultism. At the same time there is openness to many forms of envisaging God. That is, any concept of God which makes relationship possible (or is appropriate to living in Covenant) is acceptable here. This seems closer to the traditional model of *aggadic* thinking than liberal theologies have been as a result of their emphasis on an idea-of-God as the essence of Judaism. And it provides for continuing intellectual growth in our understanding of God, a characteristic of all of Jewish history, particularly in our time.

Specifically, I do not see that thinking in terms of Covenant pro-hibits after-the-fact explanations of the God with whom one stands in relation, as an impersonal principle, or a process which has certain person-like characteristics (e.g., the conservation of values.) For my-self, however, the most appropriate model of thinking about the God with whom I stand in relation is a personal one. That is not to make a detached, metaphysical observation concerning the nature of God but only to say that, when I try to think about God, this is the best basis I have found for drawing an analogy to the God with whom I stand in Covenant. Persons being the most complex things in crea-tion, I find this an intellectually reasonable procedure. Further, my experience of being involved with God being a personal one, this envisagement seems appropriate. Some additional explication of what it means to say that God is person-like might, I think, be given.

The notion of relationship provides an approach to living with the problem of evil and, specifically, the Holocaust. Relationships exist not only when there is immediate confirmation of them but also in its absence. To trust means that the relationship is considered still real though no evidence for it is immediately available. One also believes such confirmation will yet be forthcoming. The practice of Judaism, the life of Torah, is an effort to build a strong relationship with God. Within the context of such closeness, Jews have largely been able to live with the evils in the world.

There are special reasons why it has been difficult to continue this approach in modern times, most notably the loss of our belief in personal survival after death. The Holocaust raised our problems in this regard to an unprecedented level of tension, for some to the point of breaking the relationship with God. It remains stupefyingly inexplicable. Yet, perhaps to our surprise, it has not destroyed the Covenant. For most Jews the ties with the people of Israel are far stronger than anything we had anticipated. The absence of God during the Holocaust cannot be absolutized. It should not be used to deny that God has since been present in our lives as individuals and in that of the people of Israel (notably during the victory—rather than the new-Holocaust—of the Six-Day War of 1967).

The perception of a transcendent demand upon us to preserve the people of Israel, the affirmation of a transcendent ground of value in the face of contemporary nihilism, have led some minority of Jews to a restoration of our relationship with the other partner in the Covenant, God. The absence of God and the hurt we have felt are not intellectually explained. Yet it is possible, despite them, to continue the relationship. For the intellectually determined the most satisfactory way of dealing with this issue is to say that God's power is limited. For those to whom this raises more problems than it solves, there is acceptance without understanding. Both positions are compatible with relating to God in Covenant. I find myself constantly tempted to the former though mostly affirming the latter, a dialectic I find appropriate to affirming the Covenant.

Covenant Theology: The People of Israel

As to the people of Israel, a full-scale ethnicity is presumed here, with the understanding that this ethnicity has itself been transformed by the Covenant relationship. In the transition which the Jews have been undergoing since their entrance into modernity, our social situation has tended to lead us into accepting either religious or secular definitions of the Jews. A sense of the Covenant relationship discloses that such interpretations are reductionist of the multiple layers of Jewish existence. With Covenant primarily a social relationship, primary attention must be given to the effort to live it in social form. The people of Israel having its historic-religious roots in the Land of Israel, the creation there of a Jewish society faithful to the Covenant becomes the primary manifestation of fulfilling Jewish existence.

The Jewish society on the Land of Israel, however, is always subject to the special judgment implied in the unique task it has undertaken, building the Covenant-centered society. While it is theoretically conceivable that such a Jewish society might exist without the political apparatus of a state, in our time statehood is the indispensable instrument of social viability in the Land of Israel. The State of Israel, then, as state, is a means to the fulfillment of the Covenant and not its end. Therefore criticism of it from the vantage of the Covenant purposes of the Jewish people may be considered a Jewish duty.

At the same time, since Jews can fulfill the Covenant relationship anywhere, it becomes possible to validate Diaspora existence. Jewish life there, however, will be judged not only in terms of its faithfulness to God but in terms of its creation of the sense of community so fundamental to the Covenant.

Covenant Theology: Torah—Duty as Personal Responsibility

As to Torah, our sense of Jewish duty emerges from standing in relationship to God as part of the people of Israel. Various theories of revelation might be appropriate to accepting relationship as basic to our existence. For me, the personalist teaching of God's presence as commanding permits me to retain my autonomy while setting me in an individual bond with the people of Israel. I find it especially harmonious with Judaism seen as existence in relationship and my experience trying to live it. However, it should be understood, as against strictly antinomian interpretations of such revelation, that I take the Jewish self not to be atomistic, unattached and individual when standing in relationship with God, but as one of the Jewish people. Hence, responding to the Divine presence cannot only be a matter of what is commanded to me personally at this moment (or what was commanded to the people of Israel at some other time) but what is commanded to me as one whose individuality is not to be separated from my being one of the historic Jewish people.

I therefore come to God with a cultivated consciousness of my people's past and its recorded sense of what God demanded of it. But this apperception is not determinative for me. The immediate experience of relationship with God is. I respond to God autonomously. Yet I do so out of a situation, Covenant, in which Jews have been over the ages and which many other Jews now share. While my time and place, while my individuality introduce certain new factors in the determination of what my duties must now be, I am very much like other Jews of the past and today. Hence, what my reactions to God will be are likely to be very much like theirs. Such responses must also include my consciousness of being one of the people of Israel today. Perhaps, in a heuristic spirit, the Kantian corollary may be displaced to give us some guidance: respond to God with such a sense of your duty that you could will that anyone of the Covenant people, being in such a situation, would respond with a similar sense of duty.

This approach does not restore Jewish law to us or the sense of disciplined action connected with law. I do not see how we can do that theoretically or practically. Law and autonomy are incompatible as long as we are not in the Days of the Messiah. We modern Jews therefore stand in a post-*halachic* situation. That is one of the keystones of our liberalism. Yet it is important to overcome the anarchy which autonomous individualism can easily lead to in so pluralistic a time as ours. (Since our Covenant relationship to God is as a people, it implies some common way of Jewish living.)

The older liberal approach of containing autonomy only within the moral law will no longer do. Intellectually it is not clear that every rational person necessarily must be obligated to the sort of ethical responsibility Kant and his followers took for granted. Jewishly it is clear that limiting autonomy by ethics necessarily makes all the rest of Jewish observance instrumental and therefore unessential. Practically this results in an enforcement of the societal pressures to live as universalists and ignore Jewish particularity. If particularity is of greater concern to us today theologically, the old ethics-ritual split must be rejected as conflicting with our intuition of our present Jewish duty. When action is determined by living in the Covenant relationship, no radical distinction can be made between the source of our ethical duties and our more directly "spiritual" ones. They all come from one relationship and therefore cannot be played off hierarchically one against the other. Yet within this I would suggest that something of the old insight of the liberals as to the primary significance of ethics remains. Our sense of how we must respond *to other human beings* comes rather directly from the personal quality of the relationship between us and God, thereby highlighting the personhood of all people and our responsibility to them. Our sense of what we wish to express *to God* directly comes mainly from who we are and what we as a community feel we want to do in response to God's reality. The former is more closely related to our sense of God, the latter to our response to God—though each involves the other aspect. They are not two disparate realms of commandment but points on a spectrum of relational response.

Obligation Without External Discipline—and Hope

I do not see that law can arise from such a sense of commandment. Yet it is quite conceivable that something like Jewish "law" might yet surface in our community. One referent of the decision-making process by the individual is the community. We could reach a time when a sufficient number of Jews trying to live in Covenant would do things in sufficiently similar a way that their custom could become significant for them and for other Jews to take into account in determining their Jewish duty. In some stable American-Jewish situation, one might then create, on a Covenantally autonomous basis, a communally influential pattern of living. This would be less than law but it would be more than folkways for the primary response would be to God. The creation of such patterns would be the modern substitute for *halachah* and it is thus possible to suggest that we live in a pre- *"halachic"* time, in this Covenantal sense of the term.

The goal for the individual Jew and the Jewish community remains what it has always been, to create lives of such everyday sanctity and societies of such holiness that God's kingdom will become fact among us. Restoring personalism to Judaism makes personal piety again possible, even mandatory. Ethics can no longer displace God's presence in our lives. Our recent tradition had so little confidence in human power that it waited with virtual resignation for God to bring the Messiah. The liberals had such unbounded confidence in human power that they as good as dispensed with God in trusting to themselves and in humankind's progressive enlightenment to bring the Messianic Age. A sense of Covenant makes messianism a partnership between God and the people of Israel. It requires patience on our part as well as continued religious action; yet it gives us courage despite our failures and hope despite an infinite task which laughs at our successes, for God too is bringing the Messiah.

A Basic Reading List

This compilation could easily be expanded. It consists of some of the books I and my students have found particularly useful. Since the number is great and retrieval difficult, articles are listed only in exceptional cases. •

Some comprehensive works in this area should be noted, particularly as they often give a point of view different from mine. A simple introduction to some of the personalities and themes is provided by *Great Jewish Thinkers of the Twentieth Century*, edited by Simon Noveck (B'nai B'rith, 1963) and its companion reader, *Contemporary Jewish Thought*. More conceptually oriented but still accessible is Samuel H. Bergman, *Faith and Reason* (Schocken, 1963). Arthur A. Cohen's evaluation of various thinkers is found in the newly reissued and expanded version of *The Natural and the Supernatural Jew* (Behrman House, 1979). Eliezer Berkovits' Orthodoxy is evident in his extended critiques of the liberals in *Major Themes in Modern Philosophies of Judaism* (Ktav, 1974) while William Kaufman's naturalism similarly guides his *Contemporary Jewish Philosophies* (Behrman House, 1976). The last section of Julius Guttmann, *Philosophies of Judaism* (Schocken, 1974) deals with our period as does Natan Rotenstreich, *Jewish Philosophy in Modern Times* (Holt, Rinehart and Winston, 1968), both taking the term philosophy in its academic understanding.

1. The Challenge of Modernity

Howard M. Sachar, *The Course of Modern Jewish History* (Rev. ed., Dell, 1977), gives the data while Jacob Katz, *Tradition and Crisis* (Free Press), shows the religious turmoil the Emancipation started. Michael Meyer, *The Origins of the Modern Jew* (Wayne State, 1967), clarifies the early problems of adjustment. Moses Mendelssohn's *Jerusalem and Other Jewish Writings* has a fresh translation by Alfred Jospe (Schocken, 1969). *The Jew in The Modern World* (Oxford, 1980), edited by Paul R. Mendes-Flohr and Jehuda Reinharz, is a splendid collection of documents relative to this transition period.

2. Neo-Kantianism: Hermann Cohen

The easiest access is through the shorter writings, a selection of which, with valuable introductions, has been made by Eva Jospe, *Reason and Hope* (Norton, 1971). The classic, *Religion of Reason Out of the Sources of Judaism* (Ungar, 1972) is only occasionally easy to read.

3. Religious Consciousness: Leo Baeck

The Essence of Judaism (Schocken, 1948) is the indispensible guide to Baeck's thought. In my opinion, the later *This People Israel* (Holt, Rinehart & Winston, 1965) only continues its line of reasoning. The important essays, "Mystery and Commandment," and "Romantic Religion" are found in the collection, *Judaism and Christianity* (Jewish Publication Society, 1964). A good study of Baeck's thought is Albert Friedlander, *Leo Baeck: Teacher of Theresienstadt* (Holt, Rinehart & Winston, 1968).

4. Nationalism: the Zionist Interpretation of Judaism

Arthur Hertzberg, *The Zionist Idea* (Doubleday and Herzl Press, 1959) has gathered selections from all the major Zionist thinkers and supplied the whole with a searching introduction. Shlomo Avineri treats the Zionist as thinkers in *The Making of Modern Zionism* (Basic, 1981). In English, one may find the *Selected Essays of Ahad Ha-Am* (Jewish Publication Society, 1912) and *Essays, Letters,*

Memoirs (East and West, 1946). For contemporary Zionist thought see Hillel Halkin, *Letters to an American Friend* (Jewish Publication Society, 1977) and Harold Fisch, *The Zionist Revolution* (St. Martin's, 1978), as well as the quarterly journal *Forum* (Organization and Information Department, World Zionist Organization).

5. Naturalism: Mordecai Kaplan

Nothing has taken the place of *Judaism as a Civilization* (Reconstructionist Press, 1957). Kaplan's position on specific issues is often most easily found by consulting *Questions Jews Ask: Reconstructionist Answers* (Reconstructionist Press, 1966). We await a good study and evaluation of Kaplan's thought which is scattered over many books and magazine articles. The Kaplan centennial issue of *Judaism* (No. 117, Vol. 30, No. 1) has the best rounded collection of reflections on Kaplan as community leader and thinker.

6. The Pioneer Existentialist: Franz Rosenzweig

The standard introduction to this difficult thinker remains *Franz Rosenzweig: His Life and Thought* (Schocken, 1973) by Nahum Glatzer. The descriptive material of the first part is nicely balanced by the judicious anthology of Rosenzweig's writings in the second part. For some simple essays and the conflict with Buber on law, see *On Jewish Learning* (Schocken, 1965). *The Star of Redemption* (Holt, Rinehart & Winston, 1971) is for the intellectually intrepid.

7. Religious Existentialism: Martin Buber

The easier introduction remains Malcolm Diamond, *Martin Buber: Jewish Existentialist* (Oxford, 1960) but the more searching, standard work is Maurice Friedman, *Martin Buber: The Life of Dialogue* (University of Chicago Press, 1955). The best way into the rounded Buber seems to me through the essays in *Israel and the World* (Schocken, 1965) though at some point one must read the fundamental work, *I and Thou*, particularly parts one and three. It is available in two translations, one by Walter Kaufmann (Scribners, 1970) and another by Ronald Gregor Smith (Scribners, 1958).

8. Neo-traditionalism: Abraham Heschel

The pivotal work remains *God in Search of Man* (Jewish Publication Society, 1956), which can then be supplemented by any of the numerous books Heschel wrote. Thus, the discussion of evil is found in the collection *The Insecurity of Freedom* (Farrar, Straus & Giroux, 1965), the discussion of time versus place in *The Sabbath* (Farrar, Straus, and Young, 1951), and that of the Land of Israel in *Israel: An Echo of Eternity* (Farrar, Straus & Giroux, 1969).

9. Confronting the Holocaust

To the extensive list of Elie Wiesel's works there should now be added the first theological treatment of them, *The Vision of the Void*, (Wesleyan, 1978), by Michael Berenbaum. Richard L. Rubenstein, *After Auschwitz* (Bobbs Merrill, 1966) should be supplemented by *Eros and Morality* (McGraw Hill, 1970). The change in Emil Fackenheim's thought is seen in the collection *Quest for Past and Future* (Indiana University Press, 1968), given definitive shape in *God's Presence in History* (New York University Press, 1970) and applied in *The Jewish Return into History* (Schocken, 1978). Michael Wyschogrod's striking review of the middle Fackenheim book is found in "Faith and the Holocaust," *Judaism* (Vol. 20, No. 3, Summer 1971). Irving Greenberg's thought is summarized in "Cloud of

Smoke, Pillar of Fire: Judaism, Christianity and Modernity after the
Holocaust," in *Auschwitz: Beginning of a New Era?* (Ktav, 1977), ed.
Eva Fleischner. Eliezer Berkovits' most significant work on this topic
is *Faith after the Holocaust* (Ktav, 1973). Arthur A. Cohen's, *The
Tremendum* (Crossroad) appeared as this book went into publication.

10. A Theology of Modern Orthodoxy: Rabbi Joseph B. Soloveitchik

Two substantial collections of his otherwise scattered occasional papers exist in Hebrew, *Al Hateshuvah* (Department of Torah Education and Culture in the Golah, World Zionist Organization) and
Besod Hayihud Vehayahad (Orot, Jerusalem), both brought together
by Pinchas Pelli with useful introductions by him. The former also
has appeared in an English translation. *Shiurei Harav* (Hamevaser,
Yeshiva Univ.), contains English reworkings of the various annual
lectures and other such compilations now regularly appear. The
more substantive papers may be found in various issues of *Tradition*
magazine; a significant one is to be found in *Hadarom* (Vol. 47,
Tishri, 1979), "Uvikashtem Misham."

11. The Crux of Liberal Jewish Thought: Personal Autonomy

The older Reform Jewish approach to modernity is well captured in
the excellent anthologies by Gunther Plaut, *The Rise of Reform
Judaism* (World Union for Progressive Judaism, 1963) and *The
Growth of Reform Judaism* (World Union for Progressive Judaism,
1965) and Joseph Blau, *Reform Judaism: A Historical Perspective*
(Ktav). For the contemporary situation, see Eugene B. Borowitz,
Reform Judaism Today (Behrman, 1978). The older Conservative
Jewish ideological position is seen in Robert Gordis' *Judaism for the
Modern Age* (Farrar, Straus & Cudahy, 1955) and is brought into the

present situation by his *Understanding Conservative Judaism*. Two useful anthologies also exist here, the older *Tradition and Change*, edited by Mordecai Waxman (Burning Bush Press, 1958) and *Conservative Judaism and Jewish Law* (Rabbinical Assembly, 1977), ed. Seymour Siegel. The ninetieth anniversary of Conservative Judaism was the subject of an issue of *Judaism* (Vol. 26, No. 3, Summer 1977). The position of the radicals in the Reform community may be found in their institutional journals, the non-theistic or atheist *Humanistic Judaism*, and the theism of Alvin Reines in *Polydoxy*, though articles by him have appeared in the *CCAR Journal*. Louis Jacob's major theological works are *Principles of the Jewish Faith* (Basic Books, 1964) and *A Jewish Theology* (Behrman House, 1973).

My attitude toward autonomy was presented in *A New Jewish Theology in the Making* (Westminster Press, 1968), exemplified in *Choosing a Sex Ethic* (Schocken, 1970) and given communal and theological context in *The Mask Jews Wear* (Simon and Schuster, 1973). A volume of my theological essays, tentatively entitled, *Pondering God—the Jewish Way*, is scheduled for publication soon (Jason Aronson).

Index

Aesthetics
  in Cohen's philosophy, 34
  in Kant's philosophy, 32
Aggadah, 4, 220, 244
Agunah, 252
Alienated Jewish life, 225–227, 231
Aliyah, 85, 90, 92, 94, 95, 258
Americanization, 11, 41, 98, 108–109, 219
Anarchy, personal autonomy and, 260–264, 271
Anti-clerical character of Classic Zionism, 83, 85
Anti-semitism, 5, 60, 77, 99, 160
  ending, through Zionism, 79–81
  Greenberg and basis of, 208
  Jewish identity and, 14–16, 52, 92
  need for Christians to come to terms with, 204
  pogroms, 6, 197
  in Soviet Union, 167, 243
  U.S., 16, 94, 109
  See also Holocaust
Assimilation, *see* Americanization; Emancipation; Liberal Judaism
Augustine, 123
Auschwitz, *see* Holocaust
Autonomy, *see* Personal autonomy

Baeck, Leo, 48, 53–74, 136, 275
  appraised, 71–74
  Christianity and, 62, 67–69
  God in philosophy of, 57–62, 66, 67, 71, 166
  Harnack and, 54–56

Heschel compared with, 170
  inadequacy of rationalist explanation and, 56–58
  Jewish law and, 70–71, 74, 165
  Jewish people and, 66–67, 69–70, 72–74
  Kaplan and, 101, 106
  post-Holocaust thought of, 64–66
  two major premises of, 58–60
  theory of evil of, 62–64
Barth, Karl, 64, 123
Ben-Gurion, David, 78
Berdichevski, Micah Joseph, 91
Berkovits, Eliezer, 194, 209–210
Bonhoeffer, Dietrich, 189–190
Brenner, Yoseph Hayyim, 91
Buber, Martin, 91, 129, 104–163, 165, 276
  and Covenant, 157–159, 163–166, 275
  criticality of ideas for, 144–145
  critics of, 159–164
  dualistic approach of, 145–146; *see also* I-It relationship; I-Thou relationship with God
  Fackenheim and, 200
  Greenberg and, 206
  Heschel compared with, 168, 170–172
  and new spirit of liberal piety, 154–155
  origins of thought of, 143–144
  relating religiosity to reality and, 156–157
  Rosenzweig's debate with, 136–138, 161, 162

Buber, Martin (cont.'d)
    Soloveitchik compared with, 224,
        226, 229–230
    theory of evil of, 152–154
Bultmann, Rudolf, 64

Camus, Albert, 196, 266
Chosenness
    Baeck's view of, 66–67
    Kaplan's view of, 113–115, 120,
        194
    Rubenstein's view of, 193, 194,
        196
Christianity, 7–9, 12, 24, 53, 210, 231,
        278
    Baeck and, 62, 67–69
    Buber and, 158
    and Christian existentialism,
        230–232, 236
    Harnack and, 54, 55
    Heschel and, 176–178
    humanity as viewed in, 123
    and need for Christians to come to
        terms with anti-semitism, 204;
        see also Anti-semitism
    Rosenzweig and, 133–136
    Soloveitchik and, 234, 238–239
    teachings and dogmas of, 124
Civilization
    and Jewish state as spiritual center,
        88–89
    Judaism defined as, 103–107
    See also Culture
Cohen, Hermann, 26, 29–52, 106,
        170, 198, 275
    appeal and influence of, 45–47
    Baeck compared with, 53–58, 60,
        61, 72, 74
    ethics of, 34–39, 42, 45, 46,
        48–50, 53, 54, 231
    evaluated, 51–52
    God in philosophy of, 36–37, 43,
        47–49, 58, 59, 166
    Jewish law and, 165
    Jewish observances and, 44–45,
        47–49
    Jewish people and, 49–51
    and religion of reason, 39–44
    Soloveitchik and, 221, 225,
        231–232

Commanding voice from Auschwitz,
        202, 203, 205
Confucius, 266
Conservation Judaism, 17, 98, 115,
        116, 177, 219, 262–264
Contraception issue, 253
Correlation method of Cohen, 38
Covenant, 3–4
    in Buber's philosophy, 157–159,
        163–166, 275
    in Heschel's philosophy, 178
    in liberal Judaism, 258, 259,
        267–269, 271, 272
    Rosenzweig and, 135, 137
    Sabbath observance and, 249
Covenant theology, 281–289
    good and evil in, 283–285
    Jewish life in, 4, 282–283
    people of Israel and, 285–286
    Torah in, 286–288
Creation of life, as religious
        affirmation, 208
Creativity
    alienation and, 231
    and tension between Judaism and
        modernity, 19–20
Cultural Zionism, 87–91
Culture
    challenge of modern, 20–22; see
        also Modernity
    galut, 91
    Holocaust and cultural context of
        change, 188–190
    Zionism turning religion into
        national, 83–84
    See also Civilization

Darwin, Charles, 155
Death of God, 175, 189, 195–198,
        209, 214, 215
Democracy
    challenge of, 20–22
    ethics and, 35–36
    See also Emancipation; Modernity
Descartes, René, 127
Diaspora existence, 4–5, 84, 85
    in Buber's philosophy, 166
    Heschel's philosophy and, 179
    Kaplan's philosophy and, 104, 108
    liberal Judaism and, 260

in Rosenzweig's philosophy, 140
  significance of prayer in, 114
Dilthey, Wilhelm, 55, 64
Dostoevsky, Fiodor, 155
Dubnow, Simon, 77
Durkheim, Emile, 100, 102, 106, 118, 119

Eichmann, Adolf, 14
Einstein, Albert, 265
Elchanan, Isaac, 221
Elitism, Zionism as, 87–88
Emancipation, 5–11, 52, 75, 124, 240, 245
  Brenner and, 91
  effects of, on Jewish thought, 29, 30
  individual rights and, 7–8
  Jewishness and, 9–10
  Jews as nation and, 78–79
  Nationalism and, 99
  Zionist view of, 80
  See also specific philosophers
Eruv, 252–253
Eternal Thou, see I-Thou relationship with God
Ethics
  of Baeck, 55, 56, 58–63, 72–74
  of Cohen, 34–39, 42, 43, 46, 48–50, 53, 54, 231
  of Kant, 30, 31
  of Kaplan, 103, 105
  Reform Judaism and, 81
  of Rubenstein, 198–199
  of Spinoza, 44
  See also Good and evil
Ethnicity
  Kaplan and, 119, 166, 178, 275
  rise of self-conscious, following Six-Day War, 13–14
Evil
  Baeck's theory of, 62–64
  Buber's view of, 152–154
  Fackenheim's arguments against new level of, 201–202
  Heschel's theory of, 175–176
  Kaplan's theory of, 112–113
  See also Anti-semitism; Holocaust; Sin

Exile (galut), 84–86, 91–92, 94–95, 104, 176
Existence
  relationship and givens of, in Rosenzweig's philosophy, 127–128, 130–132
  See also Diaspora existence; Jewish life; Social existence
Existentialism
  basic tenets of, 141
  as most suitable philosophic idiom, 270, 271
  See also specific philosophers

Fackenheim, Emil, 199–208, 210, 225–226
Feuerbach, Ludwig, 119, 214
Fisch, Harold, 96–97, 194
Formstecher, Salomon, 25
Freud, Sigmund, 119, 155, 265
Fundamentalism of Heschel, 173

Galileo, 20
Galut (Exile), 84–86, 91–92, 94–95, 104, 176
Geiger, Abraham, 18
God
  in Baeck's philosophy, 57–62, 66, 67, 71, 166
  in Buber's philosophy, 137, 138, 143, 145, 153, 165; see I-Thou relationship with God
  Cohen's concept of, 36–37, 43, 58, 59, 166
  in Heschel's philosophy, 169–178, 181–183
  in Kantian philosophy, 33, 59
  in Kaplan's philosophy, 100, 102, 109–112, 118–120, 166
  in liberal Judaism, 258–259, 261, 269, 271, 272
  post-Holocaust views on, see Post-Holocaust view of God
  in Rosenzweig's philosophy, 127, 129–134, 136
  in Soloveitchik's philosophy, 222, 225, 226, 228–232, 234–238

Good and evil
  in Covenant theology, 283–285
  See also Evil
Gordon, Aharon David, 90
Goren, Scholomo, 250–251
Greenberg, Irving, 188, 189, 194,
  206–208

Ha-Am, Ahad (Asher Ginzberg) 87–92,
  94, 104, 105
Halachah, 4, 220–221, 244
  liberal Judaism and, 251, 252
  theology of, see Soloveitchik,
    Joseph Baer
Halevi, Yehudah, 25
Halkin, Hillel, 95
Hamilton, William, 190
Harnack, Adolf von, 54–56, 69
Hasidism, 9, 23, 82, 143, 167, 175,
  236
Haskalah, 26, 79, 264
Havurah movement, 17, 244
Hegel, Georg Wilhelm Friedrich, 30,
  32, 33, 126, 129
Heidegger, Martin, 128, 227
Heine, Heinrich, 9
Herzl, Theodor, 77, 80
Heschel, Abraham, 165–183, 187,
  211, 212, 276
  critics of, 180–183
  God in philosophy of, 169–178,
    181–183
  Holocaust and, 175–176
  Jewish people and, 178–180
  movement from universalism to
    particularism in, 170–172
  prophecy and, 172–174, 178
  prophetic sympathy in philosophy
    of, 172–173, 275
  Soloveitchik compared with, 224,
    240, 241
  Ten Commandments in
    philosophy of, 176–179
  unique style of, 166–168
Hirsch, Samson Raphael, 23
History
  Baeck's view of Jewish role in,
    69–70
  challenge of modern, 20–22
  See also Jewish history

Hitler, Adolf, 72, 75, 81
  See also Holocaust
Holocaust, 13, 15, 17, 51, 75, 81, 96,
  280
  Baeck and, 63–66, 71, 72
  Buber and, 152–153
  and Covenant, 284
  Heschel and, 175–176
  Jewish theology based on,
    opposed, 256–258
  Kaplan and, 112, 113
  liberal Judaism and, 249, 255–256
  Soloveitchik and, 232
  two-decade silence following, 188;
    see also Post-Holocaust
    philosophies
Holy Nothingness, 195–196, 198
Human dignity, autonomy as hallmark
  of, 255–256
Humanity and human nature
  Christian view of, 123
  Cohen and, 39
  loss of faith in, and new openness
    to God, 215–217
  modernity and confidence in,
    22–23
  Soloveitchik and, 229–230,
    232–233
  See also Existence; Good and evil
Hume, David, 31–32

Ibsen, Henrik, 155, 227
I-It relationship, 145–147, 154, 160,
  161, 226
Individual rights, 7–8
  See also Liberal Judaism; Personal
    autonomy
Intermarriage, 8
Israel, State of, 109, 196
  aliyah to, 85, 90, 92, 94, 95, 258
  Baeck and, 65
  as compensation for Holocaust,
    194
  daily life in, 95
  expressions of Jewishness in, 158
  Fackenheim and, 203–204
  Fisch and, 96
  founding of, 19, 51, 140, 280
  Greenberg and, 207–208
  Ha-Am and, 90

Jewish theology based on,
    opposed, 256–258
Kaplan and, 107, 108
liberal Judaism and, 243
national loyalty issue of Diaspora
    Jewry and, 93–94
people of, in Covenant theology,
    285–286
questions raised by existence of,
    75–76
relationship of, to world Jewry, 86,
    87, 108
and Six-Day War, 11, 13–15, 284
    See also Zionism
Israeli-Egyptian peace treaty, 15
I-Thou relationship with God, 144,
    147–151, 154–156, 162–165,
    172
critics of, 159–161
Fackenheim and, 200
fulfilling quality of, 230
Jewish law and, 162–164
nature of, 150–151
signs of, 147–150

Jabotinsky, Vladimir, 79
Jacobs, Louis, 268
Jewish history
    dynamics of, 259
    Jewish belief and, 3
    place of rationalism in, 124–125
    pre-modern, 3–5
    *See also specific aspects of Jewish
        history*
Jewish identity and Jewishness
    anti-semitism and, 14–16, 52, 92
    Emancipation and, 9–10
    expressions of, in Israel, 158
    Fackenheim and post-Holocaust,
        202–204
    modernity and, 10–13
    new search for (1970s), 17,
        215–217
Jewish law
    Baeck and; 70–71, 74, 165
    Buber and, 159, 161–165
    Cohen and, 165
    and Covenant theology, 228–289
    Kaplan and, 105, 115–116, 165
    liberal Judaism and, 243, 249–255

Mendelssohn and, 24
Rosenzweig and, 135–140
Rosenzweig-Buber debate and,
    137–138
Soloveitchik and, 237–238
    See also: Halachah; Jewish
        practices and observances;
        Torah
Jewish life
    alienated, 225–227, 231
    in Covenant theology, 4, 282–283
    pre-modern, 3–7
    See also Diaspora existence
Jewish people
    Baeck and, 66–67, 69–70, 72–74
    Buber's concept of, 163, 165
    Cohen and, 49–51
    Heschel and, 178–180
    Kaplan's view of, 105–107
    Rosenzweig's view of, 139–140
    Soloveitchik and, 235
    See also Chosenness
Jewish practices and observances,
    72–73
    Buber and, 166
    Cohen and, 44–45, 47–49
    Heschel and, 178, 179
    and Holocaust as punishment for
        nonobservance, 197
    personal autonomy toward, 261,
        262, 264
    See also Prayer; Sabbath
Jewish state
    determining priorities of, 89–90
    as spiritual center, 88–89
    See also Israel, State of
Jewish tradition and heritage
    notion of self and, 280–282
    personal autonomy and need to
        dissent from, 244–246
    personal autonomy and
        perpetuation of, 260–261
Jonas, Hans, 212–213
Judah the Prince, 20

Kabbalah, 5, 82, 164
Kant, Immanuel, 30, 57, 59, 226, 227,
    237, 266, 287
    See also Cohen, Hermann

Kaplan, Mordecai, 48, 98–120, 211,
212, 214, 276
chosenness and, 113–115, 120,
194
critics of, 118–120
ethnicity and, 119, 166, 178, 275
God in philosophy of, 100, 102,
109–112, 118–120, 166
Heschel compared with, 171, 178
Jewish law and, 105, 115–116,
165
Jewish people and, 105–107
Judaism as civilization and,
103–107
personal autonomy and, 264
prayer as viewed by, 113–115, 120
questions raised by views of,
116–118
response of, to changing social
mood, 107–108
responses to program of, 108–109
social scientific approach of,
100–103, 117, 118
theory of evil of, 112–113
Kierkegaard, Sören, 123, 225, 227
Kishinev pogrom (1903), 197
Klatzkin, Jacob, 92–93
Knowledge
in Cohen's philosophy, 34, 221
in Kant's philosophy, 30–31
Kohler, Kaufmann, 268
Kook, Abraham Isaac, 90
Krochmal, Nachman, 25–26

Langer case, 250–251
Land, nationality, statehood and,
77–78
Lao-tzu, 266
Leibnitz, Gottfried Wilhelm von, 23
Liberal Judaism, 279, 280
anarchic, 260–264, 271
Covenant in, 258, 259, 267–269,
271, 272; see also Covenant
theology
God in, 258–259, 261, 269, 271,
272
Jewish law and, 243, 249–255
and personal autonomy as central
affirmation of, 256–258; see also
Personal autonomy

restating arguments of, 249–251
Torah in, 246–248, 258–259
See also specific liberal philosophers
Life
creation of, as religious
affirmation, 208
See also Existence
Limited God, 211–214
Lubavitcher Rebbe, 197

Maimonides, 221, 227, 268
Mamzerut status, 250–251
Marx, Karl, 265
Mendelssohn, Moses, 23–25, 246–247
Messianism
and belief in limited God, 213
Cohen and, 38, 39, 44
Rosenzweig and, 131–132
Zionism and, 81–83
Mikvah, 220, 244
Mirabeau, Marquis de, 8
Mishneh Torah, 221
Mitzvot, 105, 178
See also Jewish law; Ten
Commandments; Torah
Modern Orthodoxy
liberals and, 249
women status in, 254
See also Soloveitchik, Joseph Baer
Modernity, 3–26
and challenge of history, science,
and democracy, 20–22
confidence in humanity implied
in, 22–23
creative tension between Judaism
and, 19–20
French Revolution marking
beginning of, 5, 6; see also
Emancipation
liberal Judaism and, 23–25; see
also Liberal Judaism
philosophy of Judaism and, 17–18
precursors of contemporary
discussion in, 25–26
redressing balance between
Judaism and, 16–17

Napoleon I (Emperor of the French),
7–8

National culture, Zionism turning
 religion into, 83–84
Nationalism, *see* Zionism
Naturalism, *see* Kaplan, Mordecai
Nationality, 76–79
 concept of, 76–77
 Emancipation and, 78–79
 land, statehood and, 76–78
Neo-Kantianism, *see* Cohen, Hermann
Neo-Traditionalism, *see* Heschel,
 Abraham
Newton, Sir Isaac, 20
Niebuhr, Reinhold, 175
Nietzsche, Friedrich, 33, 91–92, 214

Observances, *see* Jewish practices and
 observances
Original sin
 Baeck and, 62
 Judaic and Christian views of,
 123–124
Orthodoxy, 17, 18, 22–23
 eruv and, 253
 of Fisch, 97
 Greenberg's reinterpretation of,
 206–207
 Heschel and, 177
 liberal Judaism and, 244, 249,
 255, 259, 267
 modern, *see* Soloveitchik, Joseph
 Baer
 Rosenzweig and, 135, 139
 women status in, 254
 Zionism and, 82–83
Otto, Rudolf, 57, 136

Pathos of Heschel's God, 173–176, 181
Personal autonomy
 affirmation of, as act of faith,
 266–267
 counter-claim to, 269–272
 as hallmark of human dignity,
 255–256
 Jewish law vs., 138–140
 and need to dissent from tradition,
 244–246
 radicalizing, 264–265
 redefining Judaism on basis of,
 258–259; *see* Liberal Judaism

Philosophical options, 276–278
 clarifying, and explaining one's
 choice of, 277–278
 need for fresh, 276
Philo, 29, 125
Pinsker, Leo, 80, 83
Plato, 34
Pogroms, 6, 197
Politics
 and Heschel as political activist,
 167, 175
 Zionism and, 81–82
Post-Holocaust philosophies
 of Berkovits, 194, 209–210
 and cultural context of change,
 188–190
 of Fackenheim, 199–207, 210,
 225–226
 of Greenberg, 188, 189, 194,
 206–208
 of Rubenstein, 51, 188, 190,
 193–201, 206–208, 210, 211,
 213, 216
 of Wiesel, 188, 190–193, 200,
 201, 203, 206
Post-Holocaust views of God, 194
 of Berkovits, 209
 and death of God, 175, 189,
 195–198, 209, 214, 215
 of Fackenheim, 200, 202, 204
 Greenberg and, 211–214
 and loss of faith in God
 questioned, 213–215
 and new openness to God,
 215–217
Prayer
 Buber's view on, 113–115, 120
 Kaplan's view on, 113–115, 120
Prophetic sympathy, 172–173, 275

Rashi, 20
Rationalism and reason
 Buber's view of evil and, 160
 models based on, *see* Baeck, Leo;
 Cohen, Hermann; Kaplan,
 Mordecai; Zionism
 place of, in Jewish history,
 124–125
Reality-itself, 32, 33
Reason, *see* Rationalism and reason

Reconstructionism, *see* Kaplan,
    Mordecai
Reform Judaism, 9, 17, 280
    personal autonomy and, 262, 264
    Zionism and, 80–81
Reines, Alvin, 264
Religious consciousness, *see* Baeck, Leo
Repentance (*teshuvah*), 40, 44–45, 63,
    153
Revelation, 18
    Baeck and, 56
    Buber and, 158–159; *see also*
        I-Thou relationship with God
    effects of modernity on confidence
        in, 22–23
    Fackenheim and, 199–201
    Heschel and, 176, 179–181
    Rosenzweig and, 130–132, 134
    See also Torah
Rosenzweig, Franz, 41, 123–129, 168,
    179, 220, 221
    characteristics of new thinking of,
        128–130
    debate of, with Buber, 136–138,
        161, 162
    God in philosophy of, 127,
        129–134, 136
    Jewish law and, 137–140
    relationships and givens of
        existence in philosophy of,
        127–128, 130–132
    star of redemption of, 132–133
    true religions in view of, 133–135
    views of, on death, 126, 127
Rubenstein, Richard, 51, 188, 190,
    193–201, 206–208, 211, 213,
    216

Sabbath
    Cohen and, 45
    liberal Judaism and, 249, 250,
        252–253
Sartre, Jean-Paul, 12, 196, 198
Satmarer Rebbe, 197
Schechter, Solomon, 18
Scheler, 227
Schelling, Friedrich Wilhelm Joseph
    von, 25
Schleiermacher, Friedrich, 57
Scholem, Gershom, 56, 59, 60

Science
    challenge posed by modern,
        20–22
    in Cohen's philosophy, 34, 37–38
    in Kantian philosophy, 30
    Soloveitchik and, 226
    See also Social sciences
Self, the
    tradition and heritage and notion
        of, 280–282
    See also Individual rights; Personal
        autonomy
Self-fulfillment, Kaplan and, 101–102,
    105, 110–113, 117, 118
Shelilat Hagalut, 91, 92
Sin, *see* Original sin
Six-Day War (1967), 11, 13–15, 284
614th commandment of Fackenheim,
    202–203
Slonimsky, Henry, 212, 214
Social existence, Soloveitchik and,
    234–235
Social sciences, 21–22
    Kaplan's use of, 100–103, 117,
        118
Soloveitchik, Joseph Baer, 23, 218–242
    appeal of Orthodoxy and, 220–221
    dualism of human nature and,
        229–230, 232–233
    God in philosophy of, 222, 225,
        226, 228–232, 234–240
    halachah and experiental piety
        and, 236–237
    Jewish law and, 237–238
    Jewish people and, 235
    major currents in thought of,
        226–227
    scope and style of, 224–225
    and social existence, 234–235
    theology of alienated Jewish
        existence of, 225–227, 231
    typology of, 223, 227–228,
        233–234, 238–242
Soviet Jewry, 167, 143
Spinoza, Baruch, 44
Spranger, Eduard, 228
Star of redemption of Rosenzweig,
    132–133
Statehood
    nationality, land, and, 77–78
    See also Israel, State of

Steinheim, Solomon, 25
Sumner, William Graham, 118
Sympathy, act of, prophecy as,
    172–173, 182

Tefutzot, see Diaspora existence
Ten Commandments, 249–250
    Heschel and, 176–178
Teshuvah (repentance), 40, 44–45, 63,
    153
Tillich, Paul, 64, 225, 237, 265
Tonnere, Clermont, 8
Torah, 4, 53
    confidence in humanity exceeding
        confidence in, 22–23
    in Covenant theology, 286–288
    as human creation, 246–248
    and issue of women's equality,
        241–242
    Land of Israel and, 97, 103–104
    liberal Judaism and, 246–248,
        258–259
    Soloveitchik and, 237, 238
    See also Jewish law; Revelation
Typology of Soloveitchik, 223,
    227–228, 233–234, 238–242
Treitschke, Heinrich von, 41
Tzevi, Shabbetai, 82
Tzimtzum, 213

Wiesel, Elie, 188, 190–192, 200, 201,
    203, 206
Wine, Sherwin, 264
Women
    in Conservation Judaism, 263
    liberals and status of, 241–242,
        246, 254

World-itself, 32, 37
World Jewry
    State of Israel and, 87, 88, 108
    Zionism and centers of, 85–86
    See also Diaspora existence; Jewish
        people
Wyschogrod, Michael, 204–205

Yom Kippur, Cohen and, 44–45
Yitzchak, Levi, 176

Zionism, 18–20, 79–92, 120
    Baeck and, 72
    Buber and, 142, 158, 166
    centers of world Jewry and, 85–86
    Cohen and, 49, 50, 72
    and demands made by Jews on
        Jews, 86–87
    as elitism, 87–90
    ending anti-semitism through,
        79–81
    Kaplan and, 104, 107, 108
    of Klatzkin, 92–93
    nationality concept put forth by,
        76–77
    Orthodoxy and, 82–83
    politics and, 81–82
    religious, 96–97
    as reversal of Judaism in Exile,
        91–92
    Rosenzweig and, 135, 139
    term Exile politicized by, 84–86
    turning religion into national
        culture, 83–84
    See also Israel, State of; Jewish
        state; Nationality